How Do Emotions Drive Money Decisions?

EURO

Jorge Rivera, Ph.D.

Hamilton Rand Publishers

London-Madrid-New York-Bellflower, CA 907065901 USA

How Do Emotions Drive Money Decisions?

Available in bookstores, Barnes and Noble and online retailers, electronic formats ePub, Mobi, iPad, iBook, and Kindle from Apple.com; BarnesandNoble.com; and amazon.com

Offered and distributed worldwide to academia and libraries by INGRAM

Also, available in paperback, for a tax-deductible donation;
from: www.americanhopecharities.org

Library of Congress Cataloging-in-Publication Data is on file with Library of Congress

ISBN 978-0-9863478-7-0 (Hardback) Export Edition.
ISBN 978-0-9863478-8-7 (Softcover)
ISBN 978-0-9863478-9-4 (eBook)

Printed in the United States of America

December 2014

First Edition

DEDICATION

LOVE, my family and friends.

Dear Pete

Thank you for your support and friendship. The best compliment you can give me is to share your views and benefits of this book with family and friends.

Rivera

1/21/15

Contents

	Acknowledgments	vii
	Preface	1
1.	Are Europeans in Financial Trouble?	5
2.	Women and Financial Literacy	13
3.	Emotions and Financial Decision-making	21
4.	Financial Literacy and Lifespan Detours	33
5.	Building Lifelong Financial Survival Skills	45
6.	Human Behavior and Financial Personality	63
7.	Money and Stress Silent Killers	73
8.	Emotional Intelligence and Money	81
9.	Personal Banking and Financial Discipline	121
10.	Earning and Saving	161
11.	Investing and Financial Future	183
	Conclusion	243
	Resources	245
	References	253
	About Author	255
	Index	257

Acknowledgments

One of the most pleasant parts of finishing a book is to thank those who contributed, in different ways, to its making.

My humble thanks to My Counselor, the King of Kings. Also to Professor Sean O'Connor, Neurologist and Psychiatrist. Professor David Golden, Psychologist and former Director, Department of Behavioral Sciences, Israel Department of Defense. Albert Jenkins, member of the United States Financial Literacy and Education Commission. David J. Downey, Associate Director, U.S. Department of Education. LTG (Ret.) Carlos Brooks, Former Commander, U.S. Army Special Forces. Robert North (Ren), Special Liaison, Office of Intelligence, Department of Energy. Julee Cain, Crime and Intelligence Analyst, South Gate Police Department. Gilberto De Murgia, Author. Gilbert Claure, Securities Agent. Lucia Castaneda and Marisol Hermosillo, Bankers. Karen Eldridge, Bookseller. Susan Funk and Katja Warmuth. Frankfurter Buchmesse. Claudia Oglialoro, International Multilateral Affairs and Digital Divide. Minister for Innovation and Technologies, Italy. Comenius players: Alexander Austen, Margaret O'Shea, Carlos De Goya and Sofia Pirandello. Erasmus players: Jacques Sartre, Benjamin Buchanan, Catalina Gomes and Albrecht Schopenhauer. Da Vinci players: Nicolaus Luxemburg, Joseph Maeterlinck, Maria Bolivar and Louis Liszt. Grundtvig players: Juliet Haydn, Britani Ullmans, Larry and Laura Von-Schiller. Development Team: Maria Van Auken andMaria Maya-Smith. Editorial: Monique Beeson, Lucille Molina Martinez, and Jonathan Harrington. Book designer, Susan Hashimoto.

"Just as it was not possible to live in an industrialized society without print literacy—the ability to read and write—so it impossible to live in today's world without financial literacy. To fully participate in society today, financial literacy is critical."

—**Annamaria Lussardi,** *Academic Director of the Global Financial Literacy Center; and Denit Trust Distinguished Scholar in Economics and Accountancy at the George Washington University, School of Business.*

Preface

The purpose of this work is to empower secondary school, university and vocational training students, members of the Millennial Generation, and all adults' residents of Europe regardless of age or nationality by assisting them to develop sustainable personal banking and financial literacy skills.

This book asks the reader to consider key points that relate to financial literacy such as the difference between a need and a want; the connection between love and financial security; effects of stress and money on one's intimate life; and how emotions trigger one's behavior and impact financial decision-making. These questions are difficult to answer in part because secondary schools and universities in Europe and other countries pay insufficient attention to the role of money in society and in one's personal life. The costly result is financial illiteracy. To be financially educated, one must possess the practical skills about the economics of emotion and behavioral aspects of financial decision-making. Understanding how money drives emotions and how behavior in turn affects a person financial decision-making can transforms one's life forever.

The author has attained advanced academic qualifications in both disciplines—human behavior and economics. He has devoted his life to investigating, studying, and teaching these disciplines to university students. The vision of this work is to attempt the eradication of personal banking financial illiteracy. He has noticed a gap between what scholars know and what the public understands when it comes to sustainable money management and financial planning. He felt compelled to call attention to this disconnect and do what he can to meet the significant need for viable personal banking and financial literacy of residents of Europe.

The reader will be able to apply these skills to his or her personal financial situation immediately. He or she will have access to a diagnostic structure to determine the behavioral, social, and psychological factors affecting their present level of personal banking and financial literacy. He or she can expect to use this information to help his or her understanding of their habitual financial conduct.

This work is the result of research from primary sources of information. These include the European Commission, Directorate-General for Economic and Financial Affairs; Federal Deposit Insurance Corporation; U.S. Securities Exchange Commission, U.S. Department of Defense; Economist Intelligence Unit; and the United Nations Organization. Other resources include the Organization for Economic Co-operation and Development; World Bank; European Bank for Reconstruction and Development; Eurasian Economic Community; Gulf Cooperation Council (Bahrain, Kuwait, Oman, Qatar, Saudi Arabia, and United Arab Emirates); International Monetary Fund, and; existing data on financial education initiatives worldwide.

The reader that follows the advice in this book will experience a subtle financial transformation as he or she experiences the power of financial competence.

The events in this book take place in Europe, United States, Canada, Israel, and Saudi Arabia. The content is an active dialog between the author, Adjunct Professor of transnational economics, personal banking and finance strategy, U.S. Department of Defense, along with his colleagues Sean O'Connor, Professor of Neurobiology and Psychiatry; and David Golden, Professor of Behavioral Sciences and Psychology.

Together, these subject matter experts will be guiding the reader to initiate a new thinking process to identify key personal banking and financial behaviors that will explain how his or her emotional reactions and financial literacy explains the way they act about money. This systematic work focuses on four areas of personal banking and financial knowledge presented in a series of interdependent modules entitled CashMax^3. Each module incorporates one or more of three core attitudes that all financially well informed people display: financial discipline, earning and saving, and investing.

This work is the result of scholarly research. However, it presents all concepts in an easy to understand format because the author wants the reader to have access to the underlying investigations. It is to inspire readers continuing financial education and personal growth. The research has included at the end of this book a comprehensive bibliography of works. In addition, annotations within the text offer a variety of reference entries presented as footnotes to highlight the methodological aspect of each case.

A unique narrative style of communication leads the transfer of knowledge in this book to the reader. Its purpose is to enrich the reader participation within a "think factory" environment. This effective approach will help the reader define his or her current financial condition and connect with real people, who have experienced similar situations. To share this transfer of knowledge and real-life experiences, the author has invited representative groups of secondary school, university, and vocational students, members of the Millennial Generation and adults that reflect the audience of this book.

The first group consists of the following secondary school students: Alexander Austen, Margaret O'Shea, Carlos De Goya, and Sofia Pirandello. The second group consists of the following University students: Jacques Sartre, Benjamin Buchanan, Catalina Gomes, and Albrecht Schopenhauer; and The third group consists of the following Millennial and vocational students: Nicolaus Luxemburg, Joseph

Maeterlinck, Maria Bolivar, and Louis Liszt. The fourth groups consist of the following adults Juliet Haydn, Britani Ullmans, Larry and Laura Von-Schiller.

To assist the reader with a greater understanding of the dynamic conversations surrounding the teachings in this personal banking and financial literacy reference the work, the author assists the dialog by addressing the effects of emotional intelligence to financial decision-making. In addition, this book guides the reader in implementing the wise use of money to his or her personal situation. A glossary of terms title "Resources" and within the "Answers" to the questions asked is located at the end of this book.

Chapter 1

Are Europeans in Financial Trouble?

Financial difficulty continues to be a critical problem for residents of Europe regardless of age, education, or nationality. This fear is the direct result of personal banking and financial illiteracy.

How important is the intelligent use of money to the reader's peace of mind?

The answer to this question may surprise the reader and help him or her understand their financial conduct. Financial decision-making is a complex process involving human emotions and behavioral psychology that changes across the readers' lifespan. This book will prove that emotions and human behavior in financial decision- making begins with the reader beliefs, values, and is vital to his or her survival. It is critical to the peace of mind and the overall well-being of the reader and family. Financial literacy is essential to the reader credibility, reliability, and sustainability of his or her personal relationships and all others affected by the day-to-day financial conduct. To grasp an understanding of the severity of the financial illiteracy problems that may affect European residents the immediate focus is to examine the roots of the problem.

Income inequality will pose the single greatest challenge for the European Union in the coming decades. The gap between the rich and the poor has widened. Austerity programs enacted by a series of European governments since 2009, with the aim of reducing budget deficits, have had disproportionate effect on those with lower incomes and intensified income differences, fueling expectations that inequality will further increase in years to come. Not only does this represent a reversal of progress for the European Union—income inequality had declined in most member states in recent decades—but it also is at odds with one of the foundational purposes of the Union: inclusive growth.

Income inequality is just one of several dimensions of widening inequality across the European Union. The interaction of all these dimensions—the income gap, skills gap, an age gap, a gender gap, the digital divide, the polarizing effects of new technologies, and the heightened vulnerability of particular household compositions. These issues could feed a vicious cycle for vulnerable groups, including secondary school and university students and adults, pensioners, low-skilled workers, migrants and their children, as well as single parents and their children.

If European societies wish to counter these trends[1], they will need to help citizens equip themselves with the numeracy and financial skills that are in demand in the labor market and will need to protect the most vulnerable against misfortune. The priorities for investment should be early childhood education, secondary school, vocational, lifelong learning and apprenticeships in important and upcoming fields in the near future.

Magnitude of the Problem

To give the reader a vivid picture of the magnitude of the financial illiteracy problem in Europe, the reader should picture reading a world statistical population report; a key graph shows Europe's total population 333 million. He or she spends every day being busy over the issues of life and enjoying the EURO (€) consumer purchasing power benefits. These advantages will spread even more widely as other

---

1 RAND Corporation, Rand Review. Spring, 2014. Vol.38.No 1 pp37-44.

European countries adopt the euro.[2] The intelligent use of money is the measure of consumer power to meet their personal needs and fulfill their wants for products and services.

This single currency, (€), is shared by 18 of the 28 European Union's member countries,[3] which together make up the euro area.

The introduction of the euro in 1999 was a major step in European integration. In addition, it has been one of the Europe's major successes. It became the new official currency of 11 countries, replacing the old national currencies — such as the Deutsch Mark, Italian Lira, and French Franc. At first, the euro was an accounting currency for cash-less payments and accounting purposes, while the old currencies continued to be used for cash payments such day-to-day purchases. Since January 1, 2002, the euro is circulating in its current physical form, as banknotes and coins. The euro is not the currency of all European Union countries. Two countries, Denmark and the United Kingdom, preferred "opt-out" clauses in the Treaty exempting them from participation, while the remainders (several of the more recently acceded European Union members plus Sweden) have yet to meet the conditions for adopting this single currency.

Personal Banking and Financial Illiteracy Reality

Given the great importance of the financial illiteracy problem in Europe, the author and team of subject matter experts, examined three leading studies conducted by the International Network for Financial

2 All member states of the European Union, except Denmark and the United Kingdom, are required to adopt the euro and join the euro area. To do this they must meet certain conditions known as "convergence criteria". All European Union Member states are part of the Economic Monetary Union, which means they coordinate their economic policies.

3 The following countries adopted the euro on these dates: 1999, Belgium, Germany, Ireland, Spain, France, Italy, Luxemburg, the Netherlands, Austria, Portugal and Finland. 2001, Greece. In 2002, the introduction of the euro in its current form, banknotes and coins. 2007, Slovenia. 2008, Cyprus and Malta. 2009 Slovakia. 2011, Estonia. 2014 Latvia.

Education (INFE)[4], and by the authorities of 28 countries of the European Union. Results of these studies and comparisons with data from the Gateway on Financial education[5] indicate that most school students and adults of all ages, residing in Europe are ill equipped to take advantage of new financial opportunities and responsibilities. In addition, reviewed studies commissioned in 2013 by the Organization for Economic Co-operation and Development; the International Network of Financial Education; and the World Bank[6], determined that on average, Europeans and households display some basic financial knowledge. These studies further concluded that an understanding of basic personal banking and financial concepts, such as compound interest, and risk diversification is lacking among sizeable proportions of the European population in every country.

Furthermore, these investigations documented two additional studies conducted nationally (e.g. in the United States, by the Financial Industry Regulatory Authority (FINRA 2009 and 2013).[7] Results also demonstrate that American and European consumers tend to overestimate their financial knowledge, making them unaware of their immediate needs for personal banking and financial literacy education. Additionally, the

4 Given the importance of financial literacy issues for governments worldwide, the Organization for Economic Co-operation and Development OECD and INFE is currently developing Guidelines for the involvement of Private and other non-pubic stakeholders in financial educations, to be finished in (2014). Please see, PISA. Fin. Lit Financial Literacy Option of the OECD Program from Student Assessment (OECD 2013). Also, see OECD/FINE Survey (2013a).

5 For a database of existing financial education initiatives worldwide, please see the International Gateway on Financial Education (www. financial-education.org).

6 The Organization for Economic Co-operation and Development (OECD) created the International Network for Financial Education in 2008. It now gathers 107 countries and over 240 public institutions (such as central banks, ministries of finance and education, financial supervisory authorities). It also bring together into one group international organizations and supranational authorities as Associate Members (Alliance for Financial Inclusion, European Commission, European Insurance and Occupational Pensions Authority, European Securities and Markets Authority, International Labor Organization, International Monetary Fund, Development Bank of Latin America, the World Bank).

7 FINRA (2009), Financial Capability in the United States. Initial Report of Research Findings from the 2009 National Survey. Also, FINRA (2013) Report of Findings from 2012 National Financial Capabilities Study. Please see (www.usfinancialcapability.org).

examination of three studies in emerging economies, showed the level of financial culture and awareness of available existing financial products is at best partial (Atkinson and Messy, 2012;[8] Monticone and Messy, 2012;[9] Garcia, Grifoni, López and Mejía, 2013)[10]. Worldwide, school students, Millennial Generation[11] and adults of all ages; also tend to display limited personal banking and financial skills. While sizeable shares of the population across different countries appear to be relatively good at short-term money management skills, seven personal banking and financial behavioral aspects are more problematic. These include:

(1) Absence of financial discipline;

(2) Lack of checking accounts;

(2) Insufficiency of saving accounts;

(3) Inadequate investments in formal financial products;

(4) Excessive reliance on credit;

(5) Using credit cards to make ends meet,

(6) Difficulties in choosing relevant financial products; and

(7) Population is making inaccurate and poorly informed financial decisions.

Results from these studies also cover wide variations of financial literacy between and within countries of Europe.

---

8 Atkinson, A. and F. Messy. (2012), "Measuring Financial Literacy: Results of the OECD/ International Network on Financial Education (INFE) Pilot Study," OECD Working Papers of Finance, Insurance and Private Pensions, No. 15, OECD Publishing.

9 Messy, F., C. Manicone. (2012), "The Status of Financial Education in Africa," OECD Working Papers on Finance, Insurance and Private Pensions, No. 25, OECD Publishing.

10 Garcia, N., A. Grifone, J. Lopez and D. Mejia (2013), "Financial Education in Latin America and the Caribe Rationale, Overview and Way Forward", OECD Working Papers on Finance, Insurance and Private Pensions.

11 Millennial Generation is a term used to refer to the Generation, born from 1980 onward, brought up using digital technology and mass media; the children of the Baby Boomers; also called Generation Y.

International and European studies revealed that specific groups across socio-demographic characteristics, including gender, find it particularly hard to deal with money matters and display lower levels of financial literacy. These groups can differ depending on national circumstances, but generally include youth, Millennial Generation, and adults — in almost all countries — women in a majority of countries, with a few exceptions, and recently financially included migrants as well as the elderly. Financial literacy education of Europeans' is essential to the success of the "Single Market for 21st Century Europe." This concept brings direct purchasing power benefits to European Union residents, particularly by empowering them to travel freely, work where they wish, and shop around for the best financial services, whether in their own country or across borders. The reader whether he or she is a student, Millennial, or an adult of any nationality residing in the European Union, will be able to take full advantage of these financial opportunities. The first step is for the reader to become aware of his or her real needs for financial literacy and then develop an interest to learn how to take advantage of new financial opportunities. The goal is to have an inner desire to act on the newfound knowledge in this book.

Europeans' Financial Literacy Needs

Review of the 2013 assessments of population needs, conducted by 28 European countries, evidence from the European Union surveys indicate Europeans' low level consumer numeracy and financial literacy. For example, the evidence showed that 45% of Europeans responding to these assessments could not calculate six percent, (6%) of €50.000.[12] In addition, the first comprehensive international survey of adult skills shows that one in five adults in Europe have low financial literacy and numeracy skills, and even a university degree in the same subject is no guarantee of the same level of skills

12 Marco Habschick, Britta Seidi, Dr. Jan Evers. "Survey of Financial Literacy Schemes in the EU27." VT Makt/2006/26H-Final Report.

in different countries.[13] This Survey's key findings:

- 20% of the European Union working population has low financial literacy and numeracy skills;
- 25% of adults lack digital skills to solve problems in technology-rich environments; and
- There are striking differences between countries in skills provided through formal education.

Further, findings in same assessments also showed that consumers perceive financial services as complex and difficult to understand. For example, 50% of respondents would like to see simplification of certain financial products, including pensions and mortgages.

The European Commission on financial education considers the youth residing in Europe its top priority. Population groups with greater level of financial vulnerability, depending on national circumstances include:

(1) Women;

(2) Migrants;

(3) Small entrepreneurs;

(4) Workers;

(5) Low-income citizens; and

(6) Elderly segments of the European population.

The Netherlands and the United Kingdom are also refining their financial literacy education approaches. These approaches are to target audiences through a risk-based method or identification of key life stages and teachable moments in individuals' lives and financial behaviors across domains. These concepts of lifelong learning and financial literacy are essential to Europe's competitiveness in the knowledge-based and digital economy. It applies to all levels of education and training. It concerns all

13 The Commissioner for Education, Culture, and Multilingualism and Secretary General of the Organization of Economic Cooperation and Development "Survey of adult skills highlights need to improve education training" 08.10, 2013.

stages of life, as well as the different forms of apprenticeship.

This book aims to provide the reader and other European residents with practical, easy-to-use, and sustainable personal banking and financial knowledge. In addition, the information he or she needs to understand their emotions and human behavior that drives financial decision-making. Furthermore, the facts the reader needs for personal financial development, social integration and participation in the world knowledge and digital economy.

The European Union has united four key essentials of permanent education across the reader lifespan called *"Lifelong Learning Program,"* These demographic groups are:

- Comenius, for secondary schools, — named after Carlos Amos or Jan Amos Kemensky, (1592-1670), Monrovian educational reformer;
- Erasmus, for higher education, — named for Desiderious Erasmus Roterdamus, (1466?-1536), Dutch humanist, scholar, theologian and writer;
- Da Vinci, for vocational training and education —named after Leonardo Da Vinci, (1452-1519), Italian painter, sculptor, architect, musician, engineer, mathematician and scientist; and
- Grundtvig, for adult education — named after Nikilaj Fredrik Servin Grundtvig, (1783-1872), Danish, pastor, author, poet, philosopher, historian, teacher and politician.

Therefore, accomplishing one of the objectives of this book begins with an understanding of the reader financial literacy. It does not matter whether the reader belongs in Comenius, Erasmus, Da Vinci, or Grundtvig. Reading, studying and experiencing this book in action is the single most important step in understanding emotional reactions, resulting behaviors and solving financial literacy needs for day-to-day sustainable financial decision-making.

Chapter 2

Women and Financial Literacy

Women financial education is essential to live a comfortable life. Happy lives are possible with money, and financial literacy is crucial to the intelligent use of money. It will provide females and youth with the foundation to take advantage of economic opportunities in their own country and within Europe. Women economic and financial opportunities are becoming increasingly relevant at both national and international levels. Addressing the importance of women to improve their financial empowerment, opportunities, and well-being was at the center of the Fifth Anniversary of the G20[14] Leader's Meeting agenda in June 2013. Recognizing the need for women and youth to gain access to financial services and financial education remains critical.

The Organization for Economic Co-operation and Development with the support of the Russia Trust Fund for Financial Literacy and Education, are collaborating with the Global Partnership for Financial Inclusion, the International Network on Financial Education and the World Bank, to identify barriers that women are facing to gain access to financial services and financial education. A number of barriers indicate a relationship to gender differences in financial literacy (Hung et al.,

---

14 The members of the G20 major economies are Argentina, Australia, Brazil, Canada, China, France, Germany, India, Indonesia, Italy, Japan, Republic of Korea, Mexico, Russia, Saudi Arabia, South Africa, Turkey, the United Kingdom, the United States and the European Union.

2012). [15]In many countries of Europe and elsewhere, women display lower levels of financial knowledge than men do and women are less confident in their financial decision-making and money management skills. Both women and men need to be financially competent to participate in all economic activities and make appropriate financial decisions for themselves and their respective families. However, women have less financial knowledge and therefore, lower access to financial services and products than men. As a result, women need to improve their financial knowledge and skills for themselves, and more importantly, for transmitting financial habits and money management skills to their children, and to future generations.

Unfortunately, the reality is that European women have a weaker labor market position than men. As women live, longer than men they have shorter working years, and lower average income from which to save for old age. These issues, lower labor market position, income, and less working years are becoming more important because in many countries public policies — especially pensions and health care — have shifted the burden of long-term financial decision-making onto the reader by placing the responsibility of pre-retirement planning square on the shoulder of the reader. At the same time, the complexity of financial markets is increasing. Therefore, women need to become financially literate, gain risk confidence and the necessary skills to participate in relevant economic activities and financial decision-making within and outside their households.

To validate the gender differences in financial literacy, the Organization for Economic Co-operation and Development and International Network on Financial Education conducted among its members two surveys that identified in (2011 and 2012) case studies of

15 Hung, A., J Yoong and E. Brown (2012), "Empowering Women Trough Financial Awareness and Education" OECD Working Papers on Finance, Insurance and Private Pensions, No. 14.

financial education programs for women [16]

Key Findings

- Women need more skills to effectively participate in economic activities and make effective financial decisions, for themselves, their children and their families.
- Women often lack financial knowledge and confidence in their financial competence and skills.
- Women have less access to financial products and services than their male counterparts have, and display more vulnerabilities in some aspects of financial behavior, such as the need to make ends meet saving and choosing financial products appropriately.
- Barriers to financial empowerment for women include limited access to financial education, employment, entrepreneurship, and formal financial markets for women than for men, as well as social norms and legal treatment towards men and women in many countries.

Women Have Lower Financial Literacy

In Europe and in a large number of other countries, women have lower financial knowledge than men do. These results are consistent with other international evidence on gender differences in financial knowledge and understanding (Hung, A., 2012)[17] about financial decision-making. Gender differences in financial literacy reported in

16 Countries that contributed with case studies and/ or evidence to the 2011 and 2012 questionnaires on gender differences in financial literacy education for women and girls: Australia, Austria, Cambodia, Canada, Colombia, India, Indonesia, Lebanon, Mexico, New Zealand, Philippines, Saudi Arabia, the Solomon Islands, Spain, Sweden, Turkey, the United Kingdom, and Zambia. Belgium, Chile and the Czech Republic, Denmark, Ecuador, Finland, Malaya, the Netherlands, Japan, Paraguay, Poland, Portugal, Serbia, Slovakia, Switzerland. Thailand responded to inform that that they have no programs for women. Additional contributions and evidence provided by Brazil, Egypt and Japan in 2013.

17 Hung, A. "Closing the Gender Gap: Act Now, OECD, Paris., doi: 10.1787/9789264179370-en

Germany, Italy, the Netherlands, Sweden, Japan, New Zealand and the United States. These studies used worldwide cross-country comparable data and methodology (Bucher-Koenen, Tabea and Annamaria Lusardi, et.al, 2012)[18] Lusardi and Mitchell (2011a, 2011 b)[19]. Evidence from these studies indicates that in most countries women have lower levels of financial knowledge than men based on a short test of financial literacy. However, in Russia and East Germany, financial literacy is lower than in many other countries for both men and women, and gender differences are not significant Klapper and Panos 2011)[20].

Average Financial Literacy Score by Gender (young people)

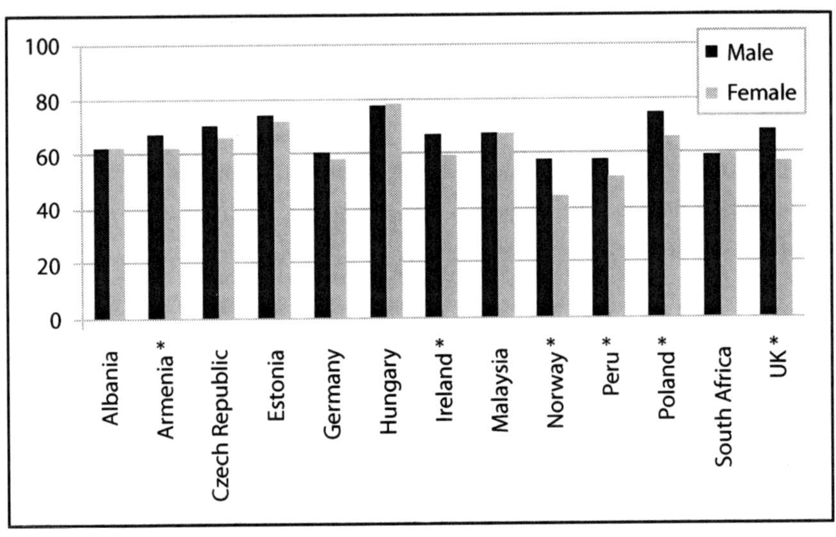

Source: Atkinson, A and Messy, F.A. (2012) "Measuring Financial literacy: Results of the OECD/INFE Pilot Study," OECD Working Papers on Finance, Insurance and Private Pensions, No. 15.

---

18 Bucher-Koenen, Tabea, Annamaria Lussardi, Rob Alessie, and Maarten van Rooij (2012) "How financially literate are women? Some new perspectives on gender gap." Nespar, Panel Paper 31.

19 Lusardi, A., O.S. Mitchell (2011a) "Financial Literacy around the world and overview." Journal of Pension Economics and Finance, 10, pp 497-508. Lusardi, A., O.S. Mitchell (2011b) "Financial Literacy and Retirement Planning in the United States" Journal of Pension Economics and Finance, 10, pp 509-525.

20 Klapper, L., and G.A. Planos (2011) "Financial Literacy and Retirement Planning: the Russian case." Journal of Pension Economics and Finance, 10 (4) pp 599-618, October 2011.

Women and men have different financial opportunities and experiences during their lifespan. These can be the result of gender differences in financial literacy. In addition, demographic, social and other economic factors affect these changes. Men and women age differences, marital status, income, education and social status may reduce but not eliminate the gender differences in financial literacy in the Netherlands. Comparable study on the United States population shows that education, income, and current and past marital status reduce by 25% the observed gap in financial literacy (Fonseca et al., 2010)[21].

Financial literacy levels for both men and women exhibit interesting differences. Focusing on women by investigating which subgroups show the lowest financial knowledge, results of the Organization for Economic Co-operation and Development, and International Network on Financial Education survey shows that there are marked differences amid women according to their education, occupation, household income, while there is little or no difference by marital status or age. In most countries, there is a little difference in women's financial literacy by marital status according to the same survey. This suggests that married women are not learning from their "partners" and single women are not learning "by doing." In addition, widows show lower financial knowledge than married women do even after taking in consideration income. There is a connection between women's financial literacy and occupation, education and household income.

Unemployed women, including retired, students, as well as homemakers have lower financial literacy levels. This is particularly true in Albania, Ireland, Poland and the United Kingdom. Similarly, women who live in households with below median income, and who have not completed secondary school have the lowest financial competence. Women are aware of their lack of financial knowledge. Studies (Lusardi

---

21 Fonseca, Raquel, Kathleen J. Mullen, Gema Zamarro, and Julie Zissimopoulos (2010) "What explains the gender gap in financial literacy." RAND Working Paper No. WR-762.

and Tufano, 2009)[22].show self-reported levels of financial literacy for women are lower in Germany, the Netherlands and the United States. Women also gave themselves lower ratings than men did when assessing their financial literacy over extending their financial ability to pay in a U.S. study about debt concepts. In addition, women tend to have lower financial literacy levels than men in their ability to deal with financial issues. The "*Women Understanding Money*" research campaign in Australia[23] in 2008 highlighted that women are confident in their day-to-day management issues like budgeting, saving, dealing with credit and managing debt. In addition to financial planning, understanding rights, risks and responsibilities when dealing with money matters, and ensuring money for retirement.

The evidence on self-assessed financial literacy and money confidence provides interesting insights. When compared to their male counterparts, women tend to show lower financial confidence remains consistent with their awareness of financial literacy needs. Therefore, if women can recognize their financial knowledge, they may be more prudent in their financial behavior. The combination of lower levels of financial confidence and literacy indicate that women are less likely to be willing to deal with financial issues, services and their providers. This also indicates that they may not necessarily take advantage of potential investment opportunities or income generation.

Men Overconfidence in Financial Skills

Men, in general feel more confident than women do in their financial decision-making. There is evidence that they tend to be over-confident both in general and in financial matters. On a survey analysis by (Lease,

22 Lusardi, A., and P. Tufano (2009) "Debt Literacy and Over Indebtness," NBER Working Paper, No 14808.

23 Australian Government and Financial Literacy Foundation (2008), Financial Literacy—Women Understanding Money, Australian Government, Financial Literacy Foundation (http://www.financialliteracy.gov.au).

Roland and Schlarbaum, 1977)[24] brokerage records in the United States show that men behave similar to overconfident investors than women do. Men spend more time and money on security analysis, less on their brokers, making more transactions, and believe that returns on investments are predictable. Therefore, they anticipate higher returns on their investments than women do. Another study of U.S. investors, (Barber and Odean, 2011)[25] show that men are more reckless than women are and that they tend to trade more securities than their female counterparts do. Evidence from this study adds that men trade 45% more than women do, and as a result, they reduce their net returns on their investments compared to women.

It is important to recognize that one has the confidence to make certain financial decisions and take specific actions. However, overconfidence in self-knowledge or ability concerning money matters can lead to error or disastrous mistakes. Overconfidence in financial decision-making has an impact upon the degree to which the reader seeks information and advice. Lower financial literacy and lack of confidence for women relates to the lack of interest in financial matters. If women are less interested than men are in finance, then it is natural that women may be less interested, and less motivated to learn the fundaments of financial literacy. However, it may also be that women show limited interest in money matters because they feel they have too little knowledge to engage in these issues.

In a survey of college students in the United States, young women expressed less interest in personal banking and finance than young men did. Although both young women and men thought that personal, banking and financial literacy would be helpful in improving their quality of life. Male students were most likely to feel that personal

---

24 Lease, Roland C., and Schlarbaum (1977) "The Common-stock portfolio performance of individual investors"

25 Barber, Brad M., and Terrance Odean (2011) "Boys will be Boys: Gender, Overconfidence, and Common Stock Investments," Quarterly Journal of Economics, 116, pp 261-292.

finance was important (Chen and Volpe, 2002)[26]. There are both experimental and survey evidence that women are less likely to invest in risky assets than men do, and are more risk reluctant. Using U.S. sample data, (Jianakoplos and Bernasek, 1998)[27] examine household holdings of risk assets to determine whether there are gender differences in financial risk taking. As wealth increases, the portion of wealth held as risk assets estimated to increase by smaller amount for single women than for single men, leading to the conclusion that single women exhibit relatively more risk reluctance in financial decision-making than single men do. Women financial education is essential to avoid unnecessary financial risk taking and to live happy lives. However, understanding how emotions influence financial decision-making is crucial to the intelligent use of money.

26 Chen, H., and R.P. Volpe, (2002). "Gender Differences in Personal Financial Literacy Among College Students" Financial Services Review," Vol. 11, No 3.pp 289-307

27 Jianakoplos, N.A., and Bernasek (1998) "Are Women More Risk Adverse?" Economic Enquiry, 36 (4), pp 620-630.

Chapter 3

Emotions and Financial Decision-making

Emotions are essential elements of financial decision-making, and arguably the most important to survival and peace of mind. Personal beliefs, values and emotions are the drivers of financial competence. It directs living within financial means, pre-planning expenditures, and guides building a financial safety net to manage the storms of life. Equally, certain behaviors triggered by emotions, such as anger, impulse buying decisions, and over-using credit, can reduce the peace of mind, affect the financial wellbeing and distress the stability of home life, immediate family and friends. In addition, emotions can alter perception, by those directly or indirectly affected by his or her day-to-day financial conduct.

This chapter will be focusing on giving the reader easy to understand and specific to apply information on a wide range of emotions and behaviors, with an emphasis on those facts that can increase or reduce his or her financial wellbeing, and peace of mind. To achieve this objective, the author and team of subject matter experts reviewed the core content of the financial behavior questionnaire, mandated by the Organization for Economic Co-operation and Development, in cooperation with the International Network of Financial Education. National and Regional authorities of the 28 countries of the European Union whom administered the survey sent to all households. These authorities, asked the respondents about their financial behavior using different question styles, in order to capture the maximum amount of financial literacy information. From the responses to these questions, the author and subject matter experts derived information about the ways in which the reader and a substantial number of Europeans manage their money, including:

- Do European residents consider carefully if they can afford to buy something?
- Do they typically pay bills on time, and
- Do they report that they keep a close watch over their finances?

In addition, determined whether there is an effort to save and set long-term goals, are respondents personally or jointly responsible for household financial management and budget? How Europeans choose financial products and if they have recently borrowed to make ends meet. Four of the questions used a qualitative scale, enabling respondents in all countries except Norway to provide more information about the frequency of their financial behavior. If the reader considers his or herself a financially literate person, will always have a relatively accurate idea of the amount of money it can afford to spend on a purchase, even if a higher income friend only needs to know approximately how much he or she is at ease to spend.

The first of the financial behavior statements on the questionnaire shows that respondents typically did consider whether they could afford potential purchases. This is especially the case in Norway, 14% percent of respondents put themselves below the midpoint-of the scale (ten being the outmost consideration of affordability, and one the least consideration) indicating that they tended not to consider their purchases; one in ten, United Kingdom residents answering the survey also put themselves at this end of the scale. It was found also interesting, that in Estonia and Poland, around one in five respondents, put themselves at the midpoint on the scale, suggesting that they were aware that they sometimes made purchases without considering the status of their personal finances or affordability. These findings indicate that personal banking and financial literacy requires organizational skills, in order to meet on time all financial commitments. In addition, these skills are necessary to avoid financial problems, for example reduced access to affordable credit or required to pay fines for late payments, or non-payment.

On the second financial behavior, the survey asks respondents if they pay bills on time. Most respondents reported that they did — putting themselves at four or five on the scale. Access to electronic payment facilities, has a double edge. It serves as support to be organized, or unwilling to meet responsibilities on time. In addition, in all cases, responses suggest that a sizeable proportion of European consumers could be either encouraged or supported to improve this poor financial behavior.

A third financial behavior statement asked European residents responding to the survey, how often they keep a close personal watch on their financial affairs. Keeping an eye on the reader personal banking and financial affairs is important for a variety of reasons. For those who use financial products, it is essential to be aware of anticipated withdrawals from his or her bank account and upon receipt, check the bank statements in order to investigate mistakes or fraudulent activity, such as duplicate amounts being withdrawn through computer error or unauthorized use of credit cards. Even if the reader at this time does not use financial products, he or she would need to oversee closely personal banking and financial affairs in order to keep savings at a safe level, manage expenditures and pay all bills on time. In same survey, few people claimed that they never keep an eye on their own finances — ranging from 1% in Norway, Ireland, and Germany to 8% in Hungary. However, in almost all the pilot countries where these inquiries were tested more than one in ten respondents put themselves in category three — suggesting that were aware they could do more, implying a considerable need to help people see the value of watching over their own finances.

The final statement in this set of questions relates to acting on longer-term plans. The survey asked if respondents set long-term financial goals and their plan to achieve them. It did not specify how far away the goal should be, or how easy it might be to achieve. Savings for specific objectives, for example paying for a comfortable retirement, education fees, a wedding or vacation expenses, purchasing a car or a house, are drivers for long-term financial goals. Alternatively, respondents to the surveys could relate to investment strategies, saving for retirement, business ideas or career development. The second phrase in the statement indicates that the respondent should be attempting to reach their goal, rather than simply thinking about it. Despite the fact that the reader can benefit from considering his or her longer term financial needs this particular financial behavior does not appear to be widespread.

For example, as many as one in five people in the United Kingdom (22%) said that they never set a long-term financial goal nor worked to achieve it. It appears that British Virgin Islanders (45%) are the most likely to set long-term goals. In the opposite direction, more than one in ten Estonians responded that they did not know whether this statement applied to them, perhaps indicating disengagement with long-term planning. A further (25%) placed themselves at one or two on the scale — suggesting that setting goals is not something that they do. A sizeable proportion of respondents in each country of the European Union (ranging from 12% to 26%) put themselves at the midpoint on this scale. Interpreted in this way, it indicates that people do not consistently work towards long term goals.

The behavioral questions asked on these surveys provided information about the responsibility an individual takes on household finances and budgeting. In addition, the combined responses assessed how many people report that they (a) have either personal or joint responsibility for day-to-day money management decisions in their household and (b) live in a household with a budget. Combining these two questions excluded someone using a budget if they do not take on any responsibility for household financial decision-making. Alternatively, contribute to the household income on a regular basis the grouping of these two sets of responses shows a wide variation across countries, with less than (25%) of respondents in Germany and Estonia being personally or jointly financially responsible and budgeting.

Saving financial behavior and reducing the reliance on credit are important indicators of financial literacy. This financial literacy measure focuses exclusively on whether or not respondents to the questionnaire save money. These surveys, asked, "In the past 12 months, have you been saving money in any of the following ways?" The questionnaire then lists a variety of ways in which people typically save, in order to prompt recollection of any type of saving. The country context was the driver to this question, but typically, included saving money at home, using informal savings clubs, putting money into savings accounts and buying investments.

For the purpose of transnational comparison, the author and team of experts derived a variable that counts all kinds of saving as active savings, except for the passive approach of building up a balance in a current personal checking account. This is an appropriate indicator of financial behavior, since it shows that saving was intentional rather than a default position due to income exceeding expenses. In addition, it confirmed that discussing savings is a cultural sensitive issue in some European countries. For example, in Poland a large proportion of the residents responding to the financial literacy survey claimed that they did not know if they had any savings, which almost certainly indicates an unwillingness to divulge such information. In Hungary, for example, respondents were unlikely to have been saving, (just 27% responded positively), although again, nobody refused to answer.

The way the reader behaves when choosing financial products is also an important aspect of his or her overall personal banking and financial literacy. If the reader attempts to make an informed decision by shopping around or using independent advice, it is more likely to choose appropriate products that meet financial needs in a cost effective way. Therefore, it is less likely to buy something inappropriate, and less probable to be subject to fraud. Readers do not typically choose financial products on a weekly, or even monthly, basis. The financial literacy survey, therefore asks about a product chosen in the last two years, excluding simple product renewals. It is important to note that this measure is specific to choosing financial products, and does not capture information about people who checked that their existing products were still suitable, unless they went on to shop for something new. Neither does it capture intention to behave — such as how do you think you might choose a product in the future?

This possible approach to choosing financial products may vary by country (and countries were able to add their own options to the survey), but shopping around cross-borders and gathering information are the financial behaviors that are most valuable for exclusive financial competence benefit. In the derived variable used in the final score of the financial literacy survey, respondents are considered to have made some attempt to make an informed financial decision, if they tried to compare across providers (even if they found out that there were no other providers), or if they sought information from someone outside their family circle. It is evident that consumers in Germany, Ireland and the United Kingdom, were most likely to have made active financial product choices by shopping around and using independent information or advice. As the reader, moves forward in his or her search for financial literacy skills, he or she will develop personal strategies to level income flows to avoid using credit for essentials such as paying for food and utilities. The success of these strategies will depend on the predictability of the readers' income, and emotional control when it comes to financial decision-making.

Recognizing however, that it is not always possible to prevent shortfalls in income such as periods of medical hospitalization or unemployment, but a reliance on credit for basic living expenses can become most dangerous and impossible to sustain over time.

Financial Literacy and Detours

Financial literacy has many detours during the reader lifespan, and it begins with the study of this book. It becomes a reality for the reader with a first "pay-packet"[28] from paid employment. It should last to the day when his or her family takes him or her to their final resting place. However, financial literacy deviations include knowledge about these important life-changing events:

- Social Security;
- Benefits in kind;
- Retired frontier workers;
- Work accidents and occupational diseases;
- Death grants;
- Invalidity—incapacity—benefits;
- Old age pensions;
- Unemployment benefits;
- Pre-retirement; and
- Family benefits.

Members of our "think factory"[29] group ware instructed to think about the facts and financial implications of each lifespan detour. Results indicated that most people have little or imperfect knowledge about financial life-changing matters.

For example, Social Security benefits are established in the European Union Regulation (EC) No. 465/2012 published in the Official Journal (OJL 149 of June 8, 2012) and in effect since June 28, 2012. This information and facts will serve the reader for life. The most important

---

28 The "pay-packet" consists of employee gross wages minus taxes and authorized deductions.

29 "Think Factory," term as used within the context of this book, is an interdisciplinary assembly of people of dissimilar level of financial knowledge and experiences coming together for a common pursuit of financial competence.

information he or she needs to know is that the social security systems of countries of the European Union are coordinated, granted under certain conditions, and determined at the national level, depending on the traditions and culture of each country.

Social Security

European law lays down rules and principles to guarantee the reader right of — free movement — in the European Union. Social Security Regulation applies to all nationals of a European Union country. The reader should also know that the legislation of the country of residence covers family members and his or her survivors. In addition, readers be aware that this regulation also applies to — third country nationals — living legally in the European Union. Whose situation connects them to several Member States? This Regulation also applies to members of their families and their survivors.

According to the — principle of equal treatment — nationals of an European Union country and persons residing in that country without being nationals of it are equal in terms of the rights and obligations provided for by the national legislation. Provisions of this regulation apply to — all the traditional branches of social security: — sickness; maternity; accidents at work; occupational diseases; invalidity (incapacity) benefits; unemployment benefits; family benefits; retirement and pre-retirement benefits; and death grants. This Regulation also recognizes the — principle of the aggregation of periods, — following periods of insurance, employment or residence in a European Union country are taken into account in all the other European Union countries. This means that the acquisition of the right to benefits in one State must take account of periods of insurance, employment, self-employment or residence in another European Union Member State.

Applicable Legislation

The reader, as the insured person is subject to the legislation of a single Member State only. The Member State concerned is the one in which he or she may seek to attain gainful employment. Particular rules are provided for — certain categories of workers,— such as civil servants who are subject to the legislation of the Member State to which the administration employing them is subject, and workers who are employed or self-employed in several European Union countries.

Benefits in kind

Benefits in kind include sickness, maternity and paternity, these benefits for frontier workers are subject and affiliated to the country in which they work, while residing in another European Union country. These workers have access to health care in both States. There are special provisions provided concerning benefits in kind intended for members of his or her family. The reader needs to know that when he or she is staying in a European Union country — other than their country of residence, in particular during holidays, he or she must be able to receive necessary medical benefits during their stay. It is the legislation of the State in which the reader is staying that determines the financial conditions for the award of the benefits. In addition, the costs are borne or reimbursed by the social security body of the country of origin. The European Health Insurance card certifies the reader right to benefits in kind.

Members of the retired worker's family in this case the reader — are entitled to certain benefits in kind, even if they reside in a Member State other than that of the reader who is holder of the pension.

Retired frontier workers

This category of insured reader can receive benefits in the last State in which he or she worked if it concerns the continuation of medical treatment, which began in that State. The reader as the insured person, as well as his or her family, can continue to receive medical treatment in the last Member State in which he or she worked. This medical treatment will be without restriction if the reader has pursued a frontier activity for two years during the five years preceding the retirement or invalidity—incapacity—provided the Member states concerned have opted for this.

Work accidents and occupational diseases

Readers should know that staying or residing in a Member State other than that in which he or she are affiliated to social security nevertheless benefit from the program covering accidents at work as well as occupational diseases. The institution of the place of stay or residence of the reader will provide the benefits in accordance with the legislation that is applicable there. The institution of the State in which the reader as worker is affiliated bears the costs of transporting him or her to their place of residence. The institution must have previously reached agreement on this form of transport, except in the case of frontier workers.

Death grants

Upon the dead of the reader as the insured person or when a member of its family dies in a Member State other than the competent State — State of residence — Member State, death is deemed to have occurred in the competent Member State. Later, the competent institution must provide the death grants payable under the legislation it applies even if the reader as the insured person entitled to receive benefits resides in another Member State.

Invalidity — incapacity — benefits

The reader should be aware regarding invalidity — incapacity — benefits. Member states may decide to determine the amount of the benefits based on the duration of periods of insurance or residence.

Old-age pensions

Reaching the age of retirement, and living on a fixed income requires the reader to have achieved financial competence. In addition, the reader needs to know that all Member States must pay an old age pension. The calculation of the amount of benefits — takes into consideration all the periods of insurance completed in another Member State. This Regulation also contains rules concerning the way in which the competent institutions calculate benefits and establishes rules to prevent overlapping. The total amount of the benefits must not be less than the minimum provided for in the legislation of the reader Member State of residence, if the State of residence has a minimum pension program. Otherwise, the institution of the Member State of residence must pay compensation.

Unemployment benefits

The reader level of financial literacy becomes a test during periods of unemployment. It forces one to live within a fixed income for a predetermined period. The competent institution of a Member State must calculate benefits based on periods of insurance, employment or self-employment completed under the legislation of any Member State where the reader has contributed. As an unemployed person he or she may move — to another Member State — in order to seek work while retaining entitlement to benefits for three months. The competent services or institutions may extend this period up to a maximum of six months. If he or she as the unemployed person does not return on or before the expiration of this period, he or she will lose all entitlement to benefits.

Pre-retirement

The reader becomes a statutory beneficiary of pre-retirement programs. These programs will cover his or her health care and family benefits in another European country. Based on the — principle of equal treatment — he or she must have the same rights and obligations as other citizens of the country. Since statutory pre-retirement programs exist only in a very small number of Member states, this Regulation excludes the rule concerning the aggregation of periods for the acquisition of entitlement to pre-retirement benefits.

Family benefits

The reader is entitled to family benefits in a competent Member State, including members of his or her family residing —in another Member State — as if they were residing in the former Member State. There are priority rules in place that determine—overlapping benefits for family benefits. The implication derived from this body of research is that secondary school students, Millennial Generation, and adults of all ages, are willing to be educated on the intelligent use of money if someone could only make the effort to teach it. The author and team of subject matter experts are committed to teaching the reader everything it needs to know and understand about how the reader beliefs, values and emotions determine his or her personal financial behavior and financial decision-making. Further, transfer to the reader the knowledge it needs to take advantage of these research and experience with personal banking, financial literacy, and consumer economics, and apply this newfound knowledge to their particular financial situation immediately.

Chapter 4

Building Lifelong Financial Survival Skills

Educating the reader to build lifelong financial survival skills is integral to the vision of this work. The author is sharing truthful, practical, and easy-to-understand information to enable the reader to apply it to his or her unique financial condition immediately. In addition, to help the reader build knowledge at his or her own pace, and provide a diagnostic framework to determine the emotional, behavioral, social, and psychological effects shaping personal banking and financial competence. The author and subject matter experts will be guiding the reader to initiate a new thinking process, by identifying significant personal banking and financial behaviors that will explain what makes him or her act the way it does about money. In addition, he or she will recognize the influence of emotional reactions and financial literacy in financial decision-making. These specialists will be accomplishing all the objectives for this book by using a self-motivated dialog format directed by the author in collaboration with Dr. O'Connor, and Dr. Golden. There is no one-size-fits-all personal banking and finance model.

The fact is there are substantial similarities of behavioral characteristics of all humans, regarding needs, wants and aspirations. However, the author is taking into consideration, cultural and linguistic differences within countries in Europe. Personal banking and finance practices within countries of the European Union are well established and accepted. In addition, there are transparent banking regulations, governing banking products and services. These regulations must meet global economic systems and transparency standards that are predictable and at the same time reliable and stable.

Research-based and Modular Organization

This book has its origin in advanced scholarly research. However, the author is sharing these important financial concepts with the reader in an easy-to-understand format, because he wants readers to have access to the underlying research. He has included at the end of the book a bibliography of works that have stood the test of time, including representative theses and recent studies about human conduct with money, and personality. The text includes a variety of reference entries to highlight the methodological aspects of each case. In addition, the modular organization of this book, CashMax^3, follows same pattern of effectiveness and reliability used in the book by the same author, title, "*Redefining Money.*" Its curriculum meets transnational personal banking systems standards. The content design centers on four core areas of financial knowledge, financial discipline, earning and saving, investing, and spending.[30]

To aid the reader understanding of the dynamic conversations regarding personal banking and the financial literacy progress, the author has added the correct answers to the questions asked. The purpose is self- evaluation and continuous improvement. In addition, to sustain a life-long knowledge of personal banking and finances, there is a glossary of personal banking and financial terms, under the title, "Resources," along with a comprehensive index located at the end of this book.

---

30 Rivera, J.CashMax^3 is a financial education proprietary program Model that uses the exponential power of 3 elements: (1) financial discipline; (2) earning and saving; and (3) investing and spending. The author incorporates three processes: microeconomics, human behavior and decision-making. Results are unified with mathematical theory and banking practices into a modular design for effective financial behavioral change of high school, college and university students; Millennial Generation and adults of all ages.

Thinking Purposefully About Money

A new thinking process about money and financial literacy begins with talking about it, no matter whether the reader is a school student, a Millennial Generation or an adult. No matter where he or she lives within Europe, no matter what the readers' social status is or what he or she does all day long, there is one thing the reader does engages in conversation. From the first, "Is it time to get up already? To the final "Good-night, I have to get some sleep," the reader speaks. In addition, talking about money is part of being a consumer.

Being an informed consumer requires a new thinking process. Thinking purposefully about money begins with understanding what role the reader plays in the European economy, from the moment he or she wakes up in the morning, the reader is a self-motivated economic equation. The reader is a consumer, at the same time an employer, and because of these activities an obligated tax payer. He or she consumes water, electricity, cable television, telephone, gas, toothpaste, bread, coffee or milk. Most of the time the reader does not think too much about his or her daily consumption habits, however well planned or spontaneous, these are equated with the wise or wasteful use of money.

The reader is an indirect employer; it pays a portion of the salaries of those people that produce the goods and services that satisfy his or her needs or wants. Each day the reader pays taxes and accumulates small tax liabilities. The reader is obligated to these tax liabilities in both the home country, and wherever the reader is working or had worked in the past twelve months. These become pain-staking realities, only on "Tax Day" of each year. However, the most startling fact is that readers seldom think purposefully about the financial impact of his or her day-to-day, money decision-making process. In addition, more often than not, the reader compares itself with those people he or she knows who are rich, or feel compassionate about those undergoing financial distress or are poor. Has the reader sometimes noticed that thinking about money occurs typically when it is time to reach for his wallet, or her purse to pay cash for something?

Has the reader at times noticed that when paying with a credit card is easy... and happens most of the time without much thought or consideration? Addressing these somber realities, is what the reader will be thinking and purposefully talking about, as he or she reads and studies this book. The reader will be engaging in a new process of thinking purposefully about money. Focusing on how intelligently he or she will use money. The intelligent use and movement of money within the European Union financial system, is what he or she will be thinking purposefully and talking about from this point forward, until the exit evaluation of this process. The result will put the reader in permanent control of his or her sustainable financial future. The terminology used in personal banking and financial literacy will give the reader a complete understanding of the meaning and precise application of these terms, to talk and communicate purposefully about money.

Knowledge Transfer Study-Play—Real Life Drama

To relate in personal banking and financial terms that are easy to understand, apply and have fun in the process. The author is formulating a real life drama, in the form a study-play style with the Comenius, Erasmus, Da Vinci, and Grundtvig members of the "think factory," as the main cast of characters. These players will become peers, as they are living examples of this real-life drama. The cast consists of students, single men and women; divorced men and women; and married couples with children to be the principal play characters on this "Bank on It!" production. Each member of the cast has similar needs, wants, expectations and dreams as the reader does, they are facilitating and making easy to apply this transfer of personal banking and financial knowledge to the reader. The players will be talking and giving examples about their day-to-day use of money and application of personal banking and finance terms. This lively dialog will make it easy for the reader to navigate the banking and financial systems of the European Union, and elsewhere, and lets him or her keep the profits generated by money.

The reader is self-governing in creating his or her own financial literacy level, to become the substance that will define and establish a new financial conduct. This new conduct will demonstrate ability to realize the benefits of applying financial discipline earning and saving, and investing and spending. These money skills, will give the reader the lifetime control it needs for a sustainable financial future.

Locations

To give readers an international perspective of today's financial illiteracy problem worldwide, the author is integrating locations of key financial illiteracy events that happened to real people in Europe, United States, Canada, Israel, and Saudi Arabia. Each participating member of the cast in this study-play has an international question or answer assignment. In addition, in conjunction with peers, the member of the cast has the knowledge transferring responsibility to help the reader build, expand, or recognize his or her level of financial literacy. The result of this knowledge integration will help the reader understand what makes him or her act the way it does about money. This study-play responds to the question of emotions and financial literacy to day-to-day financial decision-making. In addition, it will enlighten the reader to the reasons why Europeans are experiencing financial problems. This narrative incorporates answers to the questions of beliefs, values, emotions, and resulting behaviors that influence the reader financial decision-making and monetary survival skills needed for life.

The author and subject matter experts are collaborating in special partnership with the Military School of New York, a private secondary school; Kansas City Community College, Social and Behavioral Sciences Division; and the University of California San Diego, School of Medicine. The purpose of these collaborative partnerships is access to bring together an optimum pool of European ancestry human capital. The objective is to formulate and convene a cast for a study-play narrative. The mission is to help the reader to become financially competent for life. This cast is meeting eight consecutive times, for a period of two hours each time, to participate in topic specific focus groups of the reader peers. In addition, Dr. O'Connor and Dr. Golden are both serving as co-producers, medical, psychology and behavioral evaluators. The result of this collaborative effort and experiences of others will help the reader realize that he or she can become financially competent for life.

Principal Characters

The principal characters chosen for this "Bank on it!" production are people similar to the reader, each have comparable needs, wants and aspirations. None of the members of this cast knows each other, nor had any previous contact with one another. The purpose of this early introduction is to assist the reader during the upcoming discussions on factors shaping his or her financial personality. In addition, during the entire study-play, the reader will be able to identify with a given character, and reflect on the consequences of the actor's emotions, behaviors, and financial decision-making based on real-life events discussed throughout this book. This cast, in age, European heritage, personal circumstances and education reflects the four stages of the life-learning continuum. These four stages of financial education are priorities integral to the European Union as it anticipates meeting the needs of Europeans' lifelong knowledge building and financial skills development. The following cast of principal characters in this study- play represents the real needs and growth opportunities facing Europeans personal banking and financial literacy.

School students are the "Comenius." This casting consists of the following: Alexander, 15 year old, British native, and soccer player, going to school in Boston, Massachusetts ; Margaret, (16), Irish native, and violinist, going to school in Kansas City, Missouri; Carlos, (17), Spanish native, and basketball player, attending school in Miami, Florida; And Sofia, (19), Italian native, and cyclist, going to school in Chicago, Illinois.

University students are the "Erasmus." This casting consists of the following: Jacques, 19 year old, French native, and swimmer, attending Pre-medical school in New Orleans, Louisiana. Benjamin is (23), Scottish native, and golfer, going to Law school in Harrisburg, Pennsylvania. Catalina is (25), Portuguese native, and dancer, attending Dentistry school in San Diego, California; And, Albrecht is (29), German native, and tennis player, attending Engineering school in Pasadena, California.

Vocational adults are the "Da Vinci." This casting, consist of the following: Nicolaus, 33 year old, polish native, single and chess player, a vocational nurse at a Convalescent Hospital in Dayton, Ohio. Joseph, (35), Belgian native, divorced, serving as forest ranger in Bangor, Maine. Maria, (44), Spanish native, mother of two adult sons, singer, and vocational nurse, working at Children Hospital in Hollywood, California; Louis, (51), Hungarian native, soccer fan, a father of a 20 year old adult daughter, he is a plumber, working at an airline company in Atlanta, Georgia.

Adults of all ages are the "Grundtvig." This casting consists of the following: Juliet 41 year old, Austrian native divorced and volleyball player, computer programmer, working in San Jose, California. Britani, (58), Latvian native, baseball fan, crime intelligence analyst, working at the Police Department, City of San Francisco, California; and Larry and Laura, both (49), German natives, soccer fans, working as computer programmers in Santa Clara, California and married 12 years, parents of tween girls now 9 years of age.

The stories in this book are real. Each event unfolds to discuss factors that shape each character and their financial personality. In all cases, the main character of the story will represent a close similarity to the personal beliefs and values that consciously or subconsciously trigger the emotions of the reader. These emotions, whether anger, anxiety, fear, guilt, rejection, or an unforgiving heart, directs the reaction of the reader human behavior. In addition, the reactions that may turn good or poor activate financial decision-making, and resulting consequences. What are the basic factors the reader should know to build lifelong financial survival skills? This opening statement will initiate the study-play, led by the author in collaboration with Dr. O'Conner and Dr. Golden whom the reader met earlier.

Begin, the "Bank on it" study play.

Dr. O'Connor — "A basic factor of financial personality, is nature! The genes the reader inherits from his or her biological parents play a big part in determining his or her distinguishing characteristics or personality traits. However, the personality puzzle is much more complex than that. The reader begins to reveal his or her psychological makeup before he or she could walk — some people incline to be happy or caring. However, it does not mean the reader owes who he or she is solely to a few strands of *Deoxyribonucleic acid*, or DNA.[31] One thing that is becoming increasingly plain, though, is that the process, unlike that which governs many of the reader or anyone's physical qualities, goes far beyond merely matching up the genes in column (A) to the personality traits in column (B). It incorporates beliefs, values, and culture."

These financial decisions concepts will become clear and in context with an example that occurred last July. Charles Kluger is engaged to Clara Kellerman. Charles believes in his personal relationship with the Creator. Clara, in turn does not believe in anything, but her own nature and capabilities. This couple, friends of the author were in Brussels attending a European Commission, Internal Market and Services meeting. At closing of this event, the three socialized over dinner. Charles and Clara began discussing key financial aspects of their possible marriage.

The price tag proposed by Clara, including a priced engagement and wedding rings, number of guests, type and place of wedding reception,

---

31 DNA, or deoxyribonucleic acid, is the hereditary material in humans and almost all other organisms. Nearly every cell in a person body has the same DNA. Human DNA consists of about 3 billion bases, and more than 99 percent of those bases are the same in all people. The order, or sequence, of these bases determines the information available for building and maintaining an organism, similar to the way in which letters of the alphabet appear in a certain order to form words and sentences.

and honey moon plan. This wedding concept was far more complex than Charles could afford and openly said so. Charles excitement, about the wedding cooled off. He explained to Clara, that his personal values and beliefs were in conflict with her proposed plan. He further stated that for a marriage to succeed and enjoy peace of mind, a couple must agree in planning significant events and live within their financial means.

Clara quickly proposed a solution. Apply for a bank loan to pay the wedding. Charles strongly disapproved. Clara's emotions showed. Her face turned red, she stood up from the dining table and assumed a defiant body posture. Intentionally or not, her mixed emotions triggered anger. She stated, without much though or financial consideration: "I will ask for a bank loan and pay for the wedding expenses."

Charles, calmly explained to Clara, that his employment situation was not as stable, as he would like it to be. In addition, her proposal was in direct conflict with his personal values and beliefs — borrowing money for something that is not an urgent and unexpected need — but is something you want—without due consideration for the short and long-term financial consequences, was not of his pleasure. Clara's emotions of anger and others hard to define at that moment affected her proposed financial decision. However, it clearly demonstrates lack of financial literacy. Charles postponed the wedding.

A year and few months passed, Charles was attending a follow up meeting at the European Commission, Internal Market and Services. During the morning coffee break, he shared with the author he was anxious about the prospects of his bank closing its branch in Switzerland, where he works as a private client information officer. He feared for his financial capability to continue the wedding plans. He felt guilty of not measuring up. In addition, often thought, why did he not put a permanent stop to the relationship at the time of the first discussion with Clara?

Charles confided to feel a growing diminished self-confidence, constantly concerned with feeling of rejection for being inadequate to meet Clara's expectations. Does the reader ever wonder if he or she will ever be good enough to experience the desires of their hearts to become realities? Reflect on this statement for a moment...Charles became isolated from his work-related friends and focused on working hard to influence new people he met to like him. These feelings of anxiety, fear, guilt and rejection plagued Charles for the following six months. Until he could no longer be at peace and told Clara, it is over.

Clara, soon thereafter met someone else, and pressed on with borrowing money for her lavish wedding plans. Within a year, Clara was in financial trouble. She is filing a petition for bankruptcy and considering filing for divorce. This demonstrates the result of anger triggering poor financial decision-making. The result, is clear, anger is one of the most expensive and dangerous human emotions, affecting the reader human behavior and financial decision-making.

Dr. Golden — "Charles, is being so affected by this situation with Clara, that she fits the typical unobstructed personality.[32] That is a personality springing from self- assurance that she is capable of achieving her desires. However, Charles can become a game changer, by letting go of the suggestions that have tied him into a limited image of himself. History and society constantly press suggestions about one's intellectual, financial, physical or spiritual capabilities. These suggestions radically underestimate what the reader or anyone can be. Believing in limits creates limited people. Alternatively, as a famous poster puts it — "You can fly, but that cocoon has to go!"

Dr. O'Connor — "Many of the DNA strands that bind a person are unconscious suggestions. From the moment the reader is born, he or she begins to pick up suggestions from those around him or her on how to act. For example, mummy offers her arms to a child that responds with a bright smile. As he or she raises his or her arms, wanting to be picked up — And what you should be like — as this child grows, he or she hears ... sit up, straighten your body, do not speak while your mouth is

---

32 Unobstructed personality and self-assurance that one is capable of achieving desire goals. National Human Genomic Research Institute. Social and Behavioral Branch 10th Anniversary Celebration Conference. January 2014.

full of food. In addition, similar suggestions during the developmental stages of his or her life, made indelible imprints in his or her mind. In this case, Charles principles and determination saved him from being a party that led to a financial disaster."

Dr. Golden — "However, and this is most important, if Charles, is going to free himself from feelings of diminished self-confidence, feelings of rejection and added limitations. He has to take control of his life. This means to become aware of the true emotions that influence his human behavior, take on what he enjoys and unload the rest. The purest truth about Clara's existence is one she easily missed. Everyone needs LOVE to live, and Clara is starving for LOVE."

The reader financial failures may have set him or her emotionally to accept a low evaluation of his or her ability to learn, or to believe, he or she cannot become financially competent. Consequently, the reader might lack confidence. Through the years, comments from parents, siblings, teachers, friends and various authorities can bind the reader to the idea that he or she is not bright enough to do financially well. In addition, the reader might believe his or her ability lies in only one area. In early childhood for instance, a parent or a relative may have said repeatedly, "You certainly are hopeless in math." This negative suggestion — "you are not good at mathematics" — may have been accepted at face value by an uncritical child who then proved true. Math will then always be concern."

Failing school marks, poor showing in job tests, seeming inability to keep up an accurate bank balance — a variety of things that in this case, can reinforce Charles feelings about himself, or for that matter, feelings of insecurity within the reader. In addition, this emotionally charged uncertainty further reduces his or her chances of becoming financially competent. Based on critical reasoning[33] the reader might be skeptical of

33 Critical reasoning or critical thinking is the intellectual disciplined process of actively and skillfully conceptualizing, applying, analyzing, synthesizing and evaluating information. Sumner, W.G. (1940). ...A study of the Sociological Importance of Usages, Manners, Customs, Mores and Morals. New York. Ginn and Co. pp.632-633

his or her ability to learn the necessary fundamentals of personal banking and financial literacy. Alternatively, history shows people abilities can change. The second part of the logical barrier goes: "It might work for *other* people, but it will never work for *me.*" A third person may say, "I have never learned fast and easily in my life, so why should I now?" On the other hand, the reader may claim "I am already financially well off," Therefore, how much can he or she improved?

Dr. O'Connor — "The reader needs to know that it has a learning "norm" suggested to him or her by society and by his or her own experiences. Medical specialists continue to prove that as technology facilitates, humans are using less than ten percent of the minds' capabilities. The reader has all the brainpower he or she needs to learn. He or she can learn everything in this book about how emotions trigger human behavior and financial decision-making. The good news is that financial decision-making is not DNA inherited."

CHAPTER 5

HUMAN BEHAVIOR AND FINANCIAL PERSONALITY

Human behavior is one of the most enigmatic realms of science. In addition, the answers to its many secrets are as essential to identify the reader financial personality, as they are elusive. In a simple to understand language, this chapter will focus on the factors influencing human behavior that forms financial personality. In addition, how emotions influence financial decision-making. To achieve this goal with a comprehensive authority, and depth, the author will lead the discussion by asking Dr. O'Connor to identify and baseline this dialog. In addition, Dr. Golden to comment, interjects, or adds at will a critique or new dimension to the content. The entire dialog within this book is to assist the reader, in becoming financially competent for life.

Dr. O'Connor — "The objective of this dialog is to improve the understanding of the emotional factors that activate human behavior and ultimate financial decision-making. The basic element of our personality, whether related to financial behavior, playing piano, dancing, or playing soccer , begins with the much talk about by the media, but yet little understood, or for that matter, taken into consideration, as the key, when dealing with the reader as a unique person. It is an element called, DNA. It plays an immense part in determining traits and other emotional factors of human behavior and financial personality. However, the personality mystery is much more complex than is generally known by the average person."

Dr. Golden — "Family upbringing, values and beliefs, helps to shape emotions and human behavior. Parental education and family day-to-day conduct helps to shape the normal conduct of the reader. In addition, the cultural background, places of residence, social environments, work-related situations, financial literacy, and general education, among others — all together define financial personality."

Hereditary Descent and Financial Behavior

Dr. O'Connor — "The genetic qualities are the result of inherent qualities of biological parents. In addition, the remarkable qualities of one parent are neutral in the offspring by the opposite or defective qualities of the other. It is natural that contrast of qualities, in the parents' dispositions, should occur as frequently as in harmony. One of the many foundations of friendship and of the marriage union is a difference of character. Each individual seeking thereby to supplement the qualities in which he or she feels their own nature to be deficient."

Every special talent or character trait of a person depends on a variety of complex conditions. The analyses of these conditions have yet to be formally attempted. It is easy to conceive that the entire financial behavior might be considerably altered, owed to modification of any one of these conditions. Results of the author's investigation, at the University of Oxford show a biographical work, of manageable size, that contain the lives of the leading men of genius whom the world is known to have produced. Chosen was the work of Sir Thomas Phillips, in his well-known work of reference *"The Millions of Facts"*.

This work shows evident discernment, and without the slightest regard to the question on which the author was, investigating, specifically, hereditary factors that shape the reader financial personality. "The preface of Sir Phillips work reads" — "It has been attempted to record, in brief, only the original minds, who founded or originated. Biography in general is filled with mere imitators, or with men noted only for chance of birth, or necessary position in society." — The author, Dr. Golden, and Dr. O'Connor at the University of Oxford conducted three independent cursory examinations into the hereditary relationships of the notabilities of the 1800's. This effort purposefully center on determining the DNA of this genetic connections. The results produced an even larger relationship magnitude. For example, Walford's *"Men of the Time"* contains an account of the distinguished men of England, the European Continent and America, who were then alive.

Under the letter "A" only, there are 85 names of men, and no less than twenty five of these, or one in three and one half, have relatives also in the list; twelve of them are brothers, and eleven fathers and sons. These are:

(1) Abbott, Rev. Jacob (U.S.A.,) author on religions and moral subjects;

(2) Abbott, Rev. Carlos, younger *brother* of above, author on religious and moral subjects;

(3) A'Beckett, Sir William, author, Solicitor-Gen. of New South Wales, and *brother* of late Gilbert Abbott A'Beckett;

(4) Adam, Jean Victor, painter, *son* of an eminent engraver;

(5) Adams, American minister, *son* of Carlos Quincey Adams;

(6) Ainsworth, William Francis, editor, "Journal of Natural and Geographical Science," "Explorations in Asia-Minor and Kurdistan;"

(7) Ainsworth, William Harrison, novelist, *cousin* of above;

(8) Aïvazooski, Gabriel, Armenian, born in the Crimea, Professor of European and Oriental languages, and member of Historical Institute of France;

(9) Aïvazooski, Ivan, a marine painter, *brother* of above.

(10) Albermarile, Earl of (*brother* of Keppel);

(11) Albert, Prince (*brother*); and

(12) Aldis, Sir Charles, medical. Aldis, Charles J.B. medical, *son* of above.

In order to test the value of hereditary influence on financial decision-making with greater precision, the reader should consider extracting from the 12 biographical lists the names (they are 330) of those that have achieved distinction in the more open fields of science, economics, finance, and literature. The conclusion is there is no favor of heredity beyond the advantage of a good education.

Personality Traits and Money

Personality traits play a substantial role on the intelligent use of money. There are two types of major personality traits, identified among many theories of personality -- Extroversion and — Introversion. The terms introversion and extroversion, were popularized through the work of Carl Gustav Jung[34], and later became central parts of other prominent theories including the big five theory of personality (D.W. Fiske (1949)[35], (McCrae & Costa 1987)[36]. The 'big five' are broad categories of personality described as extroversion, agreeableness, conscientiousness, neuroticism, and openness. The introversion-extroversion dimension is also one of the four areas identified by the Myers-Briggs Type Indicator, (MBTI).[37]

Introverts, tend to focus more on internal thoughts, feelings and moods, rather than seeking out external stimulation. Introversion, is generally viewed as existing as part of a continuum along with extraversion.

34 Carl Gustav Jung, (26 July 1875-76 June 1961) was a Swiss psychologist and psychiatrist who founded analytical psychology. Jung proposed and developed the concepts of introverted and extroverted personalities, archetypes and the collective conscious.

35 Fiske, D.W. (1949) Consistency of the factorial structures of personality ratings from different sources. *Journal of Abnormal Social Psychology*. 44. PP 329-344.

36 McCrae, R.R.& Costa, P.T, Jr. (1987) Validation of the five factor model of personality across instruments and observers. *Journal of Personality and Social Psychology*. 52 pp 81-90 .

37 Myers, Isabel Briggs, Mary H. McCaulley, Naomi Quenk and Allan Hammer. (1998) MBTI Handbook. A guide to the development and use of the Myers-Briggs Type Indicator. Consulting Psychologists Press, 3rd edition ISBN 0-89106.130-4

Introversion indicates one end of the scale, while extraversion represents the other end, introverts have little difficulty talking to people they do not know if they can talk about concepts or issues. Extroverts enjoy social situations and even seek them out, they enjoy being around people. An Extrovert has the ability to make small talk appear to be more socially adept than introverts do. Extroversive behavior appears to be the standard in American society, while introversive behavior gives the impression to be the norm of European culture. On the other hand, northern Europeans fit the introverted version, while southern Europeans compare to the American extroverted behavior.

Dr. Golden—"However, extroverted behavior is simply a manifestation of the way an extrovert interacts with the world. Extroverts are interested in and are concerned with money in different ways than introverts. The elemental nature of the introverted-extroverted continuum is what makes it a core personality typing. For example, the Myers-Briggs test, devised during the 1940s by a Philadelphia homemaker, named Isabel Myers, with some help from her mother, Katherine Briggs, was one of the first psychological exams that focus not on diagnosing pathology, but in characterizing normal. Drawing from the noted psychologist Carl Jung's typological models, the self-schooled Myers and Briggs developed a detailed questionnaire designed to explore the particular preferences that make up each person worldview, and therefore his or her personality. The questions are simple, for example, do you regularly share your feelings freely or keep those feeling to yourself? Scores sort respondents into one or the four contrasts, or pairs of opposing traits.

The introverts-extroverts split figures most prominently, but Myers Briggs also divides between sensing and intuition, thinking and feeling, judging and perceiving; all of these are central to financial decision-making. The reader should consider taking this test, available for a small fee (€ 25 to 50)[38] to determine his or her personality, everyone has some degree of both introversion and extroversion. However, people often tend to lean one-way, or the other. Some people believe that an extrovert

38 This test is available from the following Email address: (coordinator@myersbriggs.org).

is a person who is friendly and outgoing. Carol Bainbridge, Psychologist, at Purdue University, offers this clear definition: "While that may be true, that is not the true meaning of extroversion. An extrovert is eager by being around other people. The introvert is happy to be alone.

Extroverts, Bainbridge asserts, tend to fade when alone and can easily become bored without other people around." When given the chance, an extrovert will talk with someone else rather than sit alone and think. In fact, extroverts tend to think as they speak, unlike introverts, who are far more likely to think before they speak. Extroverts often think well when they are talking. Concepts just do not seem real to them unless they can talk about them; reflecting on them is not enough.

The quest of self-knowledge has occupied humankind for more than 2,500 years. Hippocrates[39] the "father of medicine," lived some 400 years before Jesus Christ[40]. Hippocrates formulated the Greek theory. It places everyone precisely into one of four types—the sanguine or cheerful, melancholic or sad, choleric or angry, and phlegmatic or calm. However, the fact that everyone had to fit neatly into one of four personalities' pigeonholes was a fundamental weakness of the Greek theory. It left no room for shades of personality. They seem to combine features from two or even three of the basic Greek theory types.

A more sophisticated and flexible modern approach to the problem—and probably the best—has used "types" popularized by the Swiss psychiatrist, Carl Gustav Jung.

Self-knowledge continues to be at the center of humankind interest.

---

39 Hippocrates of Cos, or Hipocrates of Kos (460 BC-370 BC) was an ancient Greek physician of the Age of Pericles (Classic Athens) and is considered one of the most outstanding figures of medicine. He is the father of Western medicine and founder of the Hipocratic School of Medicine.

40 Jesus Christ or simply Christ (i.e., Messiah) is the central figure of Christianity, whom most Christian denominations worship as God the Son incarnate. Christians traditionally believe, based on the Scriptures, that Jesus was conceived by the Holy Spirit, born of a virgin, performed miracles, founded the Christian Church, die sacrificially by crucifixion to achieve atonement, rose from the dead, and ascended into heaven, from which He will return. The majority of Christians worship Jesus as the incarnation of God the Son, and the Second person of the Holy Trinity.

When it applies to financial decision-making, it focuses on eleven (11) fundamental characteristics of self:

(1) **Self-abasement** most people easily list excuses why they do not lead effective lives. Struggle with his or her identity, lack intimacy, often feel intimidated and worry about other people, and how they react towards one another or whether they will listen to what he or she has to say. In addition, often feel inferior as he or she compare themselves to others—even siblings and decided that they came short of expectations.

(2) **Self-acceptance** is a powerful personality characteristic. It is center on renewing the reader perspective of itself, releasing his or her past, and remembering his or her purpose.

(3) **Self-condemnation** is a personality trait that reflects on the value of age and experience, often temper young adult self-righteousness. Take an honest look at his or her financial past, present, and recognize his or her financial failures. In addition, look for ways to help others rather than hurt them.

(4) **Self-control** is superior to conquest. A person who lost control of his or her temper can ruin success in wealth building, business, school, or home life. The reader may risk exposing or losing what he or she holds the dearest representation of his or her hard work. Healthy self-esteem is important, because some people think too little of themselves on the other hand, some overestimate capabilities. The key to any honest and accurate evaluation knows the basis of oneself-worth—his or her identity. Readers must train each day to apply emotional and financial discipline to all relevant aspects of life dealing with money, compete with passion, and move forward with purpose, and master the banking and financial terms in this book, to lead quality personal banking and decision-making.

(5) **Self-deception** the way that seems right, may offer many options to the reader financial decision-making and require few sacrifices. Easy financial choices, however, should make him or her to take a second look and ask, is this solution attractive because it allows the reader to be

financially lazy? The right money choice often requires hard work and self-sacrifice. Do not be lured by apparent great deals, which seem right but end in bankruptcy.

(6) **Self-denial** the reader has the power and understanding within to do good, then he or she will look forward to profitable returns on his or her investments, with eager expectation and hope.

(7) **Self-exaltation** is perhaps the most dangerous enemy of financial success. Proud people take little account of their weakness and do not anticipate financial difficulties, or unexpected circumstances. They think they are above the fragility of common people. In this state of mind, they are easily to stumble. Ironically, proud people seldom realize that pride is the basis of their financial problems, although everyone around them is well aware of it.

(8) **Self-examination** when the reader does his or her best to follow the financial competency basis taught in this book, he or she feels good about the financial rewards of his or her behavior. There is no need to compare one with others. People make comparisons for many reasons. Some point out to others financial flaws in order to feel better about themselves. Others simply want reassurance that they are doing financially well.

(9) **Selfishness** is a demonstration by most financially competent people when they are not too preoccupied with their own financial needs, or to spending time working for charity. The reader is scheduled and personal concerns should not crowd out his or her service to and love for others.

(10) **Self-righteousness** even if the reader is innocent of poor financial behavior, his mouth would condemn him or her, in spite of his or her good life.

(11) **Self-will** sometimes-right actions or good financial intentions come too late. The reader must do what is financially right, but also do it at the right time. This means, that everyone including him or her—can find their niche somewhere on the scale running from extreme

extroversion or outgoing personality, to extreme introversion or withdrawn personality.

"Dr. Golden — "The outgoing personality or extrovert, is a person who values money, material and immaterial things of the world, for example, investments, real estate possessions, riches, power, and prestige. He or she is sociable, likes parties, has many friends, needs to have people to talk to, and does not like reading or studying alone. The extrovert craves excitement, takes chances, and often sticks his or her neck out by lending free money to friends and family. He or she acts impulsively and is generally an imprudent person. The extrovert moves home more frequently, changes jobs more often, and is low on brand loyalty.

The extrovert is one that enjoys practical jokes, always has a ready answer and generally likes to buy new things, meet new people, and creates new impressions. The extrovert is carefree, optimistic and likes to "laugh and be merry." He prefers to keep moving, and doing things, tends to be aggressive and loses his temper quickly. The extrovert does not keep his or her feelings under control, and he or she is not always a reliable person. It may often be subject to criminal or psychopathic behavior.

The introvert, on the other hand, is a quiet, retiring sort of person, introspective, fond of books rather than people. He or she is reserved and distant except with intimate friends. The introvert tends to plan, "looks everyday life with proper seriousness and likes a well-ordered before he leaps," and distrusts the impulses of the moment. He or she does not like excitement, takes matters of money and mode of life. The introvert keeps feelings under close control, seldom behaves in an aggressive manner and does not lose his temper easily. He or she is reliable, somewhat pessimistic and places great value on ethical standards. The introvert may also exhibit neurotic tendencies."

Discoveries and wonders of the automatic human mind are constantly growing. The rapid, automatic human mind and the gut-level decision making are equally in constant evolution. In addition, in reality, the subconscious mind is a mystery as well as a wonder. Nevertheless, it is also risky. The shortcuts that allow the reader to navigate each day with ease are the same ones that can potentially be impending the reader ordinary judgments and choices, in everything from health, to romance to finances.

Interpersonal Affinity and Money

Dr. Golden — "To explain interpersonal affinity and how this concept relates to what makes the reader act the way he or she does about money, emotional reactions and financial decision-making, the following story will place this concept in context. Carl Hanna's doctoral dissertation defended the Multidimensional Jungian personality types, as measured by the Myers-Briggs, Type Indicator, and response tendencies as measured by the Rorschach's Erlebnistypus (EB) ratio,[41] currently the most accepted methods to determine these relationships. To assist the reader in understanding how these relationships and tendencies serve as clues to his or her monetary conduct, it is necessary to explore how the introvert and extrovert differ in their perception of financial conduct. Are introverted thinking types predictably concerned primarily with one's own thoughts and feelings, rather than with the external environment? Moreover, are extroverted feeling types, predictably concerned primarily with the physical and social environment?

Dr. O'Connor — "In his latest edition of The Rorschach: "*A Comprehensive System*," American Psychologist, Carlos Exner, echoes Rorschach's 1921, claim that the Erlebnistypus score bears no relationship with a Jungian model of introversion-extroversion. Indeed, several recent studies, have failed to disprove the null hypothesis in attempting to correlate the Rorschach's EB, with Introversion-Extroversion, as measured by the Myers-Briggs, Type Indicator. Today, this indicator is the

41 Roschach Erlebnistypus (EB) Ratio. The Validity of Individual Roschach's Variables: Systematic Reviews and Meta-Analysis of the Comprehensive System. Psychological Bulletin 2013, Vol. 139, Number 3, pp 548-605.

standard psychometric instrument[42], to make use of Jung's personality theory. In addition, this indicator can be adjusted to determine why people act the way they do about money. A close reading of Exner's description of the personality features represented by Rorschach's EB leads us to wonder whether Rorschach's EB, might be instead capturing something represented by two dimensions of the Myers-Briggs, Type Indicator, a combination of Introversion-Extroversion and "thinking-feeling" scores. Data sample collected to test this question prove the hypothesis that a directional score toward "introverted thinking" on the Myers-Briggs, Type Indicator, would correspond to an introvert scoring direction on the Rorschach EB. Likewise, "extroverted feeling," to the direction of showing a predominance of color responses on the Rorschach EB test, and characterized by the urge to live in the world outside oneself."

Dr. Golden — "A comprehensive literature review was conducted, to set this hypothesis within context of personality logic between self-definition and interpersonal affinity. It is clear that despite apparent descriptive similarities, this evaluation produced no positive correlations between self-definition and interpersonal affinity for introverted thinking and extroverted feeling tendencies. Therefore, the interpersonal affinity, when applied to the way you act about money, centers on how competent the reader is about the intelligent use of money and correct application of personal banking and financial terms. In the same way, when studying how humans make financial decisions, this concept will become clear with this example, the reader starts his or her car, and the "check engine" light comes on, no big deal, it is not the first time it has happened, and the auto mechanic never found anything wrong with it. The author is interested in the process the reader goes through while making real-world decisions such as these or other decisions involving

42 Psychometrics is the field of study concerned with the theory and technique of psychological measurement, which includes the measurement of knowledge, abilities, attitudes and personality traits. Stevens, S.S. (1946) "*On the Theory of Scales of Measurment*" Science 103, pp 667-680, Michell, J. (1999) "*Measurement in Psychology*" Cambridge. Cambridge University Press.

money. Because they involve both "sensory" evidence — the reader sees the engine light come on. The other is "information based," — as he or she would when ready to write a check, it will check the balance on his or her check register, to verify he or she has money to issue the check."

DC Debit Card · ATM Teller Withdrawal · AD Automatic Deposit · AP Automatic Payment · BP Online Bill Pay · T Online or Phone Transfer

NUMBER OR CODE	DATE	TRANSACTION DESCRIPTION	PAYMENT, FEE WITHDRAWAL (-) $	✓	FEE	DEPOSIT, CREDIT (+) $	$ 500.00
AD	01/01	Payroll Deposit				300 00	800 00
BP	01/03	Home electricity	80 00				720 00
BP	01/03	Home Gas	20 00				700 00
T	01/08	Transfer to Savings Acct	400 00				300 00
DC	01/10	Grocery store	40				260 00
AD	01/15	Payroll Deposit				300 00	560 00
ATM	01/16	ATM Cash Withdrawl	100 00				460 00

The author is also interested in the process of measuring the perception of financial risk tolerance[43] and links to financial decision-making. He or she may tend to think that perception is a passive process. The reader sees, hears, smells, tastes or feels a stimulus that makes an impression upon the senses. The reader thinks that if he or she is objective, when recording what actually there is in his or her bank account, as cash available, and write it in the check register. Yet perception is evidently an active rather than a passive process.

Insight constructs rather than records "reality." Perception implies understanding as well as awareness. For example, has the reader ever questioned the validity of a non-sufficient funds notice? The process of perception links the reader to personal understanding of his or her financial situation. In addition, it is critical to an accurate understanding of the financial world around the reader.

Dr. O'Connor — "The following is a sample of how misperception of the financial world can affect financial decision-making. A wife, called

43 Gilliam, Carlos and Chatterjee, Swam and Grable, Carlos. "Measuring the Perception of Risk Tolerance A Tale of Two Measures" (2010) Journal of Financial Counseling and Planning. Vol.21. No 2. 2010.

Barbara, is fond of music. Her husband for her birthday gave her a Smart phone; Barbara perceived to be familiar with music applications and began downloading her favorite's songs several times a day. When the bank statement arrived and Barbara saw the balance, questioned a string of €.50 purchases. The husband was unaware of these charges and advised her to go to the bank and find out about what she perceived as fraud.

The banker reviewed the charges, and showed Barbara that charges shown on the bank statement were correct. She questioned the validity and negated knowing the source of charges. The banker assigned an assistant to call the providers and verify the nature of the disputed charges. "These corresponded to downloading music," the banker said. Then, Barbara realized that her perception of the costs of easily downloads of music was an inadequate understanding of her financial world, so it may also be case for the reader.

Think about this. Think about how often the reader might see a promotional program on television, for example, promoting a new wrinkle eliminating longevity pill. In addition, the distributor is selling it with a persuasive message, "buy now" at an attractive price of €30 for a 30-day supply. His or her first reaction may be, ah! It is just €1 a day...without much thought, the reader picks up the telephone, calls the number on the screen, places an order for two bottles of this longevity pills; and pays with a credit card.

After a faithful twelve months of disciplined intake, the reader meets his or her best friend on the street how says; "are you alright? Have you been sick? I am worried about you!" Without words ..., he or she may conclude, this miraculous pill has no health merits. The reader misperception of the financial world around him or her may be emotionally and physically devastating and to make things worse, financially debilitating because he or she has lost €720.

One particular and still unknown aspect of financial perception is selective perception. It is often life serving, but occasionally malicious.

The reader subconsciously selects scenes, events or happenings to perceive. He or she subconsciously choses to become blind and deaf to other obvious actions, such as the fact in this example that the miraculous pill has failed to eliminate Barbara's wrinkles on her forehead. These mental processes are rather unconsciously to block out any awareness of what his or her eyes see or the ears hear, in this case from her friend.

Dr. Golden — "That is known as selective perception[44], it is a mind device used to eliminate distractions and focus the subject's attention on things it feels are most important to his or her well-being, as when there is a need to solve financial problems, concentrate on immediate solutions, or rest the mind by daydreaming."

Personality-Financial Behavior and Money

The discipline of behavioral economics provides insights into the ways the reader may make financial decisions. While him or her are subject to prejudices that systematically lead them away from "rational" decision-making, those with limited resources bear the most serious consequences of poor financial decisions. Financial literacy, and the development of an awareness of prejudices, can help in improving decision-making. However, it is possible that cultural norms relating to debt and investments have a greater influence on his or her behavior. Experimental work, by academics such as Eldar Shafir,[45] finds that poor financial decision-making is widespread.

There are not many studies on the relationship between education and the quality of financial decision-making. However, those that are available do not suggest that individuals with high education, or high intelligence quotient (IQ,) are free from biased decision-making. Marianne Bertrand and others in the study: *"What's psychology worth? A field experiment*

44 MJ. Waller, JM. Conte, CB. Gibson and MA. Carpenter. "The effect of individual perception of deadlines on team performance" Academy of Management Review. Vol. 26. Issue 4. Pp 586-600.

45 Shafir, Eldar. Eldar Shafir and Robyn, A. LeBoeuf (February 2002) "Rationality." Annual Review of Psychology 53, pp 491-517.

in the consumer credit market" sponsored in 2005, by the Economic Growth Center, Yale University[46] reached same conclusion. Classifications such as income, education, family connections, race, nationality, color, or social class, provide little guidance on the quality of the reader financial decision-making. The fact is that he or she makes similar mistakes in financial decision-making. However, the main difference between the rich and poor is that generally, the rich have sufficient financial reserves to bear the consequences of poor monetary decisions.

Their main pain may in this illustration maybe a little social or neighborhood humiliation, when the rich has to sell his or her yacht, or trade down from a BMW to a more modest car. By contrast, the consequences for an hourly worker in the city or a person living in the suburbs, losing their only vehicle can be catastrophic. Furthermore, for many there is the crushing cost of losing their house because of unpaid mortgage. This wide spread phenomena of poor financial decision-making is an important point, for it suggests that the reader needs to improve his or her day-to-day financial practices, not as if it has some generally held wisdom or norms of good practice, which it can pass on to those who are struggling to save or to repay loans. Readers that are students and adults have a great deal of learning to do. Perhaps the current economic events in Europe and around the world provide the reader with an opportunity to improve financial behavior. He or she should never let nature, or other catastrophes go to waste, there is something to learn and consequently, improve management of emotions and financial decision-making.

Smart People Make Unintelligent Decisions

According to the U.S. Bureau of Economic Research, the Great Recession ended in June 2009. However, the recovery has been slow to materialize. Unemployment in the U.S. hovers around seven percent,

46 Bertrand. Marianne and Karlan. Dean S. Mullainathan and Shafir, Eldar and Zinman, Jonathan. "What's Psychology Worth? A field Experiment in the Consumer Credit Market (July2005) Yale University Economic Growth Center, Discussion Paper No. 918.

and many Americans continue to struggle financially in same manner as Europeans. In the U.S. the critical time from 2006 to 2012 — a period of financial mishaps have provided examples of poor financial decision- making on a scale that exceeds all experience since the 1930s — the author refers to severe worldwide economic down turn or Great Depression. [47]The crisis in Europe or Great Recession of 2009[48] generally progressed from banking system crises to sovereign debt crises, as many countries elected to bailout their banking systems using taxpayer money, an unintelligent decision. Greece was different in that it concealed large public debts in addition to issues within its banking system. Several countries received bailout packages from the "troika"[49] consisting of the European Commission, European Central Bank, and the International Monetary Fund, which also implemented a series of emergency measures.

According to the *"U.S. Central Intelligence Agency, Fact Book,"* from 2010 to 2012, the unemployment rates in Spain, Greece, Ireland, Portugal, and the United Kingdom increased. France and Italy had no significant changes. Germany and Iceland the unemployment rate declined. Eurostat the statistical office of the European Union reported that Eurozone[50] unemployment reached record levels in September 2012 at 11.6%, up from 10.3% the prior year. Unemployment varied significantly by country.

---

47 The Great Depression was a severe worldwide economic downturn in the decade preceding World War II. The timing of the Great Depression varied across nations, but in most countries, it started in 1930 and lasted until the late 1930s or middle 1940s. Bermanke, Ben (1995)."The Macroeconomics of the Great Depression. A Comparable Approach." Journal of Money, Credit and Banking (Blackwell Publishing) 27 (1) pp 1-28.

48 The Great Recession describes the general economic decline observed in world markets. In Europe generally progressed from banking system crisis to sovereign debt crisis. United Nations (January 2013) World Economic Situation and Prospects. P 200. ISBN 978-92111091663.

49 Troika a Russian term meaning "a set of three" or three of a kind.

50 Eurozone is a geographic and economic region that consists of all the European Union countries that have fully incorporated the euro as their national currency.

The men and women charged with making these critical decisions in the United States, the European Union and other countries are amongst the wises and best educated yet, made some unintelligent financial decisions. Equally, people with degrees from the best business schools in the U.S. and Europe — Harvard, Oxford and Wharton included — have behaved recklessly on Wall Street as well as on Main Street. For example, who among the readers of this book would buy a used car sight unseen? Alternatively, who would invest in shares of a company without knowledge of physical location, business plan, or debt ratio? Who would buy an investment product at a cocktail party? Nevertheless, that is exactly what mentally bright and well-educated people were doing when they traded in collateralized debt obligations in both the U.S. and Europe and similar opaque instruments. A used car dealer would say they did not even kick the wheels.

How Do Emotions Drive Money Decisions?

Chapter 6

Money and Stress Silent Killers

This chapter will show the reader with a dialog between the author and subject matter experts how money and stress may turn into silent killers. The discussion will add a new perspective on how generosity can change lives. In addition, the reader will clear his or her perceptions of charitable and volunteer services by Americans as perceived by European residents. Even though answers to these questions are complex, they are most common among European residents and residents of other nation's victims of financial illiteracy.

On a Saturday morning, last summer, Dr. O'Conner and the author left Los Angele's Union Station, to attend a meeting at the University of California, in La Jolla, 130 miles south of Los Angeles. La Jolla, is consider one of the natural jewels of Southern California. This was Dr. O'Connor first time visit to La Jolla. The purpose of this trip was to accomplish some work on the content of this chapter and at the same time enjoy the beautiful scenery of the Pacific Ocean as a distressing mechanism from the recent work in Canada and Saudi Arabia. At the arriving station in Solana Beach, Dr. Golden, Professor of Behavioral Sciences and Psychology, former Chief Psychologist, Department of Behavioral Science, Israelite Defense Forces, was waiting to join and attend the meeting at the University of California. After the usual and customary courtesies, the threesome walked to nearby Chrystal's Eatery for breakfast. At breakfast, the author briefed Dr. Golden on the issues regarding money and stress discussed with Dr. O'Conner during the train ride.

Educating the reader, whether he or she belongs to the Comenius, or secondary students; Erasmus, or university students; Da Vinci, or vocational students, or Grundtvig adults reading this book, on the effects of stress, caused primarily by the mishandling of money and lack of financial literacy. However, most importantly, how these stress conditions affects the reader. How these also affect his or her intimate life. Further, as a direct result of poor financial decision-making. Taking advantage of the relaxed environment, the author asked Dr. Golden, does one inherit a tendency to suffer from stress over money?

Dr. Golden — "Yes, unfortunately one does. The person physiological or psychological makeup contains some of the factors that make a person susceptible to anxiety over money or conflict over finances. Many scientists believe that many of these factors are genetically determined."

"Please share an example." The author asked.

Dr. Golden — "There is clear evidence that some of the major psychoses run in families as the same way as do tendencies towards particular physical diseases or financial conduct. On the other hand, a condition of chronic stress is not merely dependent upon the young adult or the adult man or woman's make-up but also upon the forces that operate in their school, social life, work environments, and most importantly, day-to-day domestic lives. Therefore, even a person who comes from a family with a long history of stress may lead a relatively peaceful life, if he or she lives in an environment that does not provoke conflict situations such as disagreements over money. One might add here, that one should never lose sight of the fact that stress in the short term is a natural and healthy response."

Dr. O'Connor — "No one unfortunate enough to be born without the capacity to react in a "stressful" way would last long in our essentially dangerous world. Stresses are silent killers!"

This short but somber statement regarding danger promoted by the deadly combination of stress and money worries prompted the author's next question. Can the reader suffer from stress over money and not know it?

Dr. Golden — "Yes one can suffer from stress and not know it. More importantly, this is often the most damaging and upsetting sign of the problem. It has physiological and psychological indicators of the states of alert that each person can describe in words. The school student, the Millennial or the adult can easily identify itself with specific moments of distress in the reader life. The following life example will bring this concept to a clear alert to the reader. A young Israelite Officer, pilot, named CAPT. Bob and his wife an Officer and communications expert, CAPT. Kimberly. They are married for five years, and may apparently have a normal and "satisfactory" marital relationship and yet major conflicts about money may arise which relates to unconscious likes or dislikes, conditioned by some neurotic behavior pattern or by attitudes carried over from the past.

From here onward, CAPT. Bob and CAPT. Kimberly will simply be Kimberly and Bob. Kimberly may devote an abnormal amount of time shopping during off duty time, which could be her way of concealing basic anxieties, about her husband's fidelity. Bob in turn, may spend little of his off duty time at home, because his psychological immaturity, makes him wish to deny and reject the marriage, to which he is religiously, militarily and socially committed."

Reasoning from human behavior shown by opposing parties during strategic planning and negotiations, both sides may have unconscious goals — Kimberly is to retain her husband's love, and Bob is to escape from what he believes to be a trap. In addition, Kimberly and Bob might not be conscious of their secret goals and might even deny having any knowledge of these. This will indicate that a state of chronic stress will exists. The stress will remain largely at the psychological level, and the bodily "state of alertness" will persist at a low level, but over a long period. However, psychologists believe that it is from these unconscious stress situations that most major neurotic behavior patterns stem and if not resolved may become silent killers! In this case, Kimberly may devote all her energies and channel her stress into a compulsive concern with off duty shopping, consequently affecting the wise use of money. Bob may use his psychic energy on heavy social drinking, recreational gambling, and drugs consumption or other essentially wasteful activities, thus creating double financial jeopardy.

Dr. O'Connor — "Unless the stress-inducing conflict is somehow resolved, the neuroses may escalate, so that Kimberly becomes an obsessive shopaholic or depressed. While Bob, may push his social drinking into alcoholism, his recreational gambling and drugs consumption into chemical dependency. In addition, the resulting combined high-energy cocktail will turn into verbal abuse, followed by financial abuse, leading to physical or sexual abuse, which ultimately will carry a heavy financial burden and the potential destruction of innocent lives, as a direct result of financial illiteracy, and poor money management. These are examples from real life situations. However, they indicate one classic point, in understanding stress and money: emotions, body and finances should act in harmony, and any disruptive stimuli, when it occurs, should encourage prompt corrective action or may in due course become silent killers! When emotions are on edge, tension remains, and the reader in this case will seek out a channel of escape, when action or correction turns inadequate. Stress and money problems are at their worst, when the reader cannot identify his or her origins."

Breakfast concluded and the trio departed to attend the meeting at the University while enjoying the scenic drive. The meeting title, "Stress and Money in the Military." The breakout session attended dealt with the effects of financial distress in the lives of military men and women returning from the theater of War, who are unable to secure gainful civilian employment within a year from the date of discharge from military duty. Upon conclusion of the lecture, Dr. Golden extended an invitation to go up the hill, near his home, to the Hilton Hotel, where the south garden overlooks Torrey Pines Golf Course, and at the edge of the fifth fairway, the Pacific Ocean. This vista point it is spectacular! There, the threesome, continued with the content for this chapter, and enriched by the outcome of the session on stress and money in the military returning from war. To rekindle the flow of the previous conversations of this day, the author posed this open question: Are there different kinds of stress at it relates to money?

Dr. O'Connor — "Yes, stress can be either short-term or long-term, and may have physical or psychological bias. For example, stress duration — short-term stress is the kind of situation that arises when the reader is briefly startled or shocked by something — a loud noise, a sudden earth shake, or a pain in the finger, these stress-states are mostly short-lived, because corrective action is easily taken, generally automatically by the body. The reader should be alert to distinguish between stress and the things that cause it."

Consider these examples: Kimberly receives a call from her bank regarding an overdraft on her checking account, or Bob gets another bad news, about the state of his overdue car payment and potential repo effect on his credit and military records. These types of situations generate stressors that require corrective action of some kind. Even thinking over the problem will be helpful in finding a solution, and when a solution is clear, the stress will vanish. Unfortunately, overall, psychological stressors are more difficult to deal with in comparison to stressors with a physical base. These are chronic stress. Chronic stress becomes a byproduct of sustained series of shocks or unpleasant events, or by cruel psychological pressures such as marital problems, employment related worries or money difficulties. Stresses of these kinds are not easily removed and apart from his or her direct debilitating effects on the sufferer's mood and personality, the persistent physiological and biological changes which go hand in hand with it tend to build up and make even longer-term side effects affecting communications, relationships and intimacy.

Dr. Golden — "Does stress over money affect our physical performance and intimate lives?"

Dr. O'Connor — "Yes, it can affect intimacy in a number of ways. A young person or an adult, when afflicted by anxieties due to stress over money, a normal intimate life is often one of the first casualties. When under stress, the mental energy of an individual may be side tracked into a constant search for solutions to the most pressing, and often time-sensitive money problems, great or small, in which he or she had become entangled. Little of this effort remains to feed the powerhouse of the sex drive. A tense mind about money tends to prevent intimate performance. Temporary impotence in men and coldness in women may be a consequence. Sometimes however, there is a curious inversion of this rule."

Dr. Golden — "People with one or more of the major psychological conflicts, bringing a prolonged state of stress over money, may attempt to deny to themselves the existence of conflicts and thus distract surplus psychic energy into alternative channels. This denial can lead to an abnormal involvement with sex enhancement drugs, or other preoccupation, which can cause disruption of one's domestic life. Because one or the other of the partners, dissatisfied with the marital relationship, embarks on a series of "affairs" or even working life, which occasionally can become an overwhelming concern with money and sex. It also means that these conflicts because they are "denied" remain unresolved. Moreover may in due course become costly, by poor management of money. Then, how important is financial literacy? Financial literacy is important enough to change your life — forever!"

Can Love and Generosity Change Lives?

People across many countries of the world, are searching for love, happiness, health, wealth, and that truth that change lives. Where is that truth or how can one experience it? Not everyone knows where to look, so they wander from relationship to relationship, idea to idea, from one diet to another, one exercise program to another, in search of reducing or eliminating that feeling of distress, arising from a sense of guilt from past personal and financial mistakes. Sometimes giving away, what the reader has treasured or worked hard to earn, feels as the equivalent to a sacrifice. Even sincerely wanting to make a difference for others — sharing his or her time, money, resources, or emotional energy, are challenges when counting the cost. Then, the reader may realize he or she does not need to become smarter materialist, but needs to change his or her mind and become smart manager of money. In this book, the reader will learn to focus on validating his or her own financial progress, based solely on measurable evidence.

Europeans and Americans Generosity

Europeans charity and voluntary service are alien concepts in a society conditioned to rely on the welfare state to look after the poor and needy. In addition, provide a multitude of services from cradle to grave. All these benefits paid by the European Union taxpayers. Therefore, it should not come as a surprise that when European working people pay higher tax rates, they have little incentive for charitable ideals. What is frustrating, however, is that the "socially aware" United Kingdom and the European residents as a whole often rebuke the Americans for being greedy and selfish as they trumpet the virtues of government enforced income redistribution policies. Daniel J. Mitchell presents the Organization for Economic Co-operation and Development data to argue that Americans are far more compassionate than "socially conscious" Europeans are. In addition, that the virtue of the European system of central government controlled redistribution is a myth.

To illustrate this charitable concept, the reader may want to take a tour about what Europeans perceived as America the charitable, the rich and famous. One of the most surprising, and perhaps confounding facts of charity in America, are the statistics compiled by the U.S. Internal Revenue Service. These data show, that people who can least afford to give, are the ones who donate the greatest percentage of their income. In 2012, the wealthiest Americans — those with earnings in the top 20 percent — contributed on average 1.2 percent of their income to charity, by comparison, Americans at the base of the income pyramid—those in the bottom 20 percent — donated 3.5 percent of their income. The relative generosity of lower-income Americans is accentuated by the fact that, unlike middle-class and wealthy donors, most of them cannot take advantage of the charitable tax deduction, because they do not itemize deductions on their income- tax returns.

This financial minority is the one, who like Peter, 5 year old, asked his father for money to buy him a birthday gift. The father is happy, by the love behind his present, yet in actuality, he is the one who provides the creative and financial resources for him to give. The same could be true for the reader. The Creator is the provider of the resources he or she is committed to give to the poor and needy. There is no escaping from the fact that poverty is everywhere and is here to stay, even in the wealthiest nations of the world, still find people and families in dire circumstances. It is important to remember the poor and the needy, and to help in any way possible. However, not those who lack material wealth are the most impoverished.

At some point, will all be call to engage in an inner battle, whether initiated by money failures or other outside financial circumstances or within our own hearts. In those difficult moments, the dark suggestion that the Creator cannot be trusted is never far from our minds. No matter what the reader does, he or she cannot seem to shake the thought that despite all of his or her prayers, faith, money giving and devotion, the Creator would not come through. The reader greatest fears and anxieties over money come to surface, and suddenly feel as though the ground is eroding beneath his or her feet. What does the reader lack?

Is it generosity? Is it faith; is it peace, because he or she has failed to help someone in desperate need? Is it acceptance or forgiveness for having caused grief to someone the reader loves? Does he or she need strength to face disappointments of loss dreams, or feel disappointed for failing to meet his or her part to achieve a worthwhile cause? On the other hand, does the reader need to resolve issues from broken personal or financial relationships? Whatever the need, material, emotional or financial, everyone has a Redeemer, who can met it — in his way, and in his timing. He is the way and that truth that forever change lives.

Chapter 7

Emotional Intelligence and Money

This chapter advances the reader understanding of his or her emotional intelligence and use of money. A classic study by Jay L. Zagorsky of Ohio State University[51] states, "It is still not well understood, why some people are rich and others are poor." Parents, upbringing, culture, place of residence, religious beliefs, social environments, choice of spouse and many other emotional factors may play important roles in shaping his or her personal circumstances and relationships between intelligence scores, earning capacity and wealth. Focusing the attention on a quantifiable measure of income as the baseline, it shows that people with higher intellectual quotient (IQ)[52] earn higher income. However, income alone is not a measure of financial literacy.

The relationship between emotional intelligence and the wise use of money completes the picture by addressing the differences between these two financial measures: Is there a relationship between IQ scores and wealth? In addition, is there is a relationship between IQ scores and financial trouble? Zagorsky tries to challenge the question of whether

51 Zagorsky J.L., "The Impact of IQ on wealth, income and financial distress," Intelligence vol. 35. No. 5, pp.489-501, 2007

52 Intelligence Quotient (IQ) is score derived from one of several standardized test designed to assess intelligence. The abbreviation "IQ" comes from the German term Intelligence Quotient, originally named by psychologist William Stern. Approximately 95% of the population IQ scores between 70 and 130.

better IQs, lead to sudden increase in bank accounts and less bankruptcy. Statistical tests show that the answer is no. Being more intelligent does not confer any advantage along income and net worth, two of the five key dimensions of financial literacy and the wise use of money, these five measurements are: (1) income, (2) savings, (3) investments, (4) net worth and (5) financial distress.

Income corresponds to the amount of money earned each paid period, for example a weekly, bi-monthly or monthly amount shown on the reader "pay-packet". The stream of money off which he or she lives and pays for food, rent or mortgage, clothing, transportation, telephone and other necessities. The net worth represents the sum of available cash, savings, plus investments, minus his or her liabilities. It represents the cash reserves the reader has available to fall back upon to meet large expenditures, unexpected emergencies, and periods when income is absent, such as unemployment. The financial difficulty becomes evident when he or she is getting into a situation where credit is at risk by not paying bills on time or charging credit cards to their authorized maximum limit. These situations will prevent or reduce his or her ability to borrow money in the future. Emotional intelligence and financial wellbeing is a combination of all three measures; (1) having a steady income stream; (2) an accumulation of wealth to respond effectively to unexpected circumstances of life, and (3) not being worrying about money, or being close or beyond your financial limits.

"Your IQ has really no relationship to your wealth. In addition, being very smart does not protect you from getting into financial difficulty. Financial success for most people means more than just income; you need to build up wealth to help buffer life's storms and to prepare for retirement. You also shouldn't have to worry about being close to or beyond your financial limits." Zagorsky said.

These results confirmed research by other scholars (Ceci and Williams

(1996)[53] that show secondary school graduates earn U.S. currency 212,000 more than non-graduates did over their lifetimes. For example, university graduates will earn U.S. currency 812,000 more than secondary school dropouts will. People with higher IQ scores tend to earn higher incomes. In related studies, each point increase in IQ scores was associated with U.S. currency 202 to 616 more income per year. This means the average income difference between a person with an IQ score in the normal range (100) and someone in the top two percent of society (130) is currently between U.S. currency 6,000 and 18,500 a year.

However, when it came to total wealth and the likelihood of financial difficulties, people of below average and average intelligence did just fine when compared with the super-intelligent. The study could find no strong relationship between total wealth and intelligence. How could high-IQ people, on average, earn higher incomes but still not have more wealth than others have? Zagorsky said this data cannot provide an answer, but it suggests that high-IQ people are not saving as much as others are. He is currently finishing a study that is exploring that question.

These findings revealed mixed results when it came to the links between emotional intelligence and measures of financial distress. For example, the percentage of people who have maxed out their credit cards rises from 7.7 percent in those with an IQ of 75 and below to a peak of 12.1 percent among those with an IQ of 90. Then the percentage falls in an irregular pattern to 5.4 percent among those with an IQ of 115 before rising again. This irregular pattern repeats among the bankrupt and people who missed bill payments. "In these measures of financial difficulties, it seems that those of slightly better than average intelligence are best off," Zagorsky said.

---

53 Ceci, Stephen J., and Williams, Wendy M. Cornell University. "Schooling, Intelligence and Income" American Psychologist, American Psychological Association, Vol. 52 No 10 pp 1051-1058.

Just because the reader is smart does not mean that he or she does not get into trouble. Among the smartest people, those with IQ scores above 125, even six percent of them have maxed out their credit cards and 11 percent occasionally miss payments. Emotional intelligence and wealth are not necessarily representations of wealth. Professors tend to be smart people. However, if the reader looks at university parking lots, he or she does not see a lot of Mercedes Benz, Porsches or other expensive cars. Instead, he or she will see a lot of old, low-value vehicles. Thus, smarts are not a symbol personal banking and financial literacy.

"The lesson is simple; intelligence is not a factor for explaining wealth. Those with low intelligence should not believe they are handicapped, and those with high intelligence should not believe they have an advantage." Zagorsky said.

The following real life story validates these findings. The name of the person is fictitious to protect his identity. On his 22 birthday while working as a member of the "Young Ambassadors" internship program, assigned to the Latin America, Special Projects, U.S. Atomic Energy Commission, Atoms for Peace Exhibit, Alberto Holguin was required to submit to an intelligence test, administer by the U.S. Department of Defense. These tests consisted of general science, arithmetic reasoning, cognitive ability, word knowledge, paragraph comprehension, numerical operations, and coding speed. He passed, and ranked on the top five among thirty-seven on his class who took same test. This event launched his Foreign Service career. However, what good is it for Holguin to be smart and have a better salary if he ends up broke or spending it all on credit card bills?

"I have been there." Holguin said.

"At age 28, I was earning a six figure income, as a Washington Representative, for The International Atomic Energy Agency, with Headquarters in Vienna, Austria. However, I was in financial trouble. I can remember such a time in my life. I have never felt so alone. Perplexed and unable to discuss my financial difficulties with others, I would get out of bed; kneel in my dark, quiet room; and cry out to the Creator to help me, strengthen me, and change the situation that was causing me pain. I would ask, 'Father, please do not leave me like this. Show me what to do.

It was in those difficult, lonely times when I realized that my advanced academic degrees were not enough. I needed understanding that was greater than my own. I needed the Creator's insight, thankfully, I believed in his promise as written in the Epistle of James.[54] I was in deep financial trouble; because over a period of five years, I charged my credit cards and consumer-revolving accounts to their authorized maximum limits, spent U.S. currency 187,891 and 39,145 in attorney fees, and end up broke. A regretful lesson I learned for a life time."

If Holguin was so smart, why did he end up broke?

That was the key question asked by Zagorsky. Income does dimly correspond to emotional intelligence test scores; an income increase of €346 per year does not reflect a one point higher in IQ. The same one-point increase in IQ, leads to a net worth increase of at most €83. In addition, when it comes to financial distress, smarts are no help at all either. People with 130 IQ scores (a score of 100 is average) missed payments and maxed-out their credit cards more often than their lower IQ counterparts maxed-out. This evidence indicates to the reader the need of a systematic personal banking and financial model. It will help the reader to take advantage of his or her IQ and use it to manage money intelligently.

Personal Banking and Finance Model

This systematic personal banking and finance model will assist the reader to benefit from all personal banking and financial services. In addition, upon application, of his or her newfound financial discipline, earning and saving, investing and spending, this model will help him or her to become financially competent. Using this model, it will show

54 James 1:5-6. The Holy Bible, New King James Version.

the reader how to choose a bank; open appropriate bank accounts; distinguish profitable uses of these accounts; and keep a positive cash flow; the reader will learn how to set realistic and sustainable financial goals. He or she will know to develop, implement and test his or her spending plans and keep track of his or her money. The reader will also learn how to manage his or her emotions, and apply financial discipline to earning and saving, and investing and spending; he or she will know the reasons and purpose of paying himself or herself first, buy his or her pre-retirement and make money grow. The implementation of this mathematically tested personal banking and finance model begins with the reader. In addition, the rewards and sustainable financial benefits start with self-discovery, his or her willingness to truthfully acknowledge and admit the current level of financial literacy.

What is financial literacy? The reader may ask. In essence, financial literacy is the application of personal banking and financial terms of reference to the intelligent use of money. Financial literacy is the process that allows him or her to gain the emotional knowledge, discipline and survival skills needed for life. To empower the reader in understanding the skills he or she needs to become financially competent for life the author will be using the "Mastery Learning" method. This alternative method of teaching and learning involves the student reaching a level of predetermined mastery on units of instruction before the student is to progress to the next unit. Mastery learning is not a new concept (Block 1971)[55]; introduced into American education over 70 years ago.

Mastery learning is a process whereby students achieve the same level of content mastery but at different time intervals (Arredondo and Block (1990)[56]. The review of literature indicates positive effects of mastery learning on students, especially in the areas of achievement, attitudes toward learning, and the retention of content. This teaching tool will apply to this personal banking and finance model. It will

---

55 Block, J. (1971) *Mastery Learning: Theory and practice.* New York: Holt, Rinehart & Winston.

56 Arredondo, D., & Block, J. (1990) Recognizing the connection between thinking skills and mastery learning. *Educational Leadership.* 47 (5), pp.4-10.

assist the reader to enjoy life-enduring value of emotional intelligence, financial discipline; earning and saving his or her money; and investing and spending in their future. There has never been a greater need for Europeans to develop effective habits of earning, budgeting, saving, spending and investing than now. Job stability and income security fluctuates and are increasingly difficult to assess. When jobs are lost, replacement jobs could be hard to find, sometimes impossible to secure, these uncertainties, are creating newly defined economic contributors — the Millenial Generation, adults, and retirees, who are becoming micro financiers — and the new breed of micro-entrepreneurs.

Moving Forward To Financial Competence

Young persons of all age, need to become financially literate, and quickly! Adults of all ages should face the economic realities of the time and become financially competent now. Moving forward towards gaining personal banking and financial competence, the author will be guiding the reader to implement this solution, by showing him or her how to use CashMax³ a self- paced, modular learning tool, centered on mastering three core concepts: financial discipline, earning and saving, and investing and spending. Expected results over a pre-determined time will be emotional intelligence, self-reliance, social impact, sustainable and scalable wealth building. CashMax³ is an easy way for the reader to learn the financial system fundamentals. In addition, the essentials of banking services, importance of managing emotions, financial discipline and earning, savings, smart money management, using credit responsibly, investing, and wealth building. The reader that embodies the teachings in this book will be financially literate for life.

Whether it is opening a checking account, avoiding identity theft, paying for private four year college, buying a car, applying for a loan, establishing credit card value, starting a small business or becoming a micro financier, CashMax³ will provide real world, life-long lasting skills, and knowledge the reader can use immediately. Each CashMax³ module will range in understanding and application from 20-60 minutes when study in its entirety. However, the content of each module will be layered so that it can be self-taught in two or more parts, to help the reader build financial confidence and to tailor each module and understanding speed to his or her specific need, time availability and financial condition in order to realize mastery learning. Financial education is the catalyst of freedom. However, there is no freedom without the intelligent use of money. In addition, there is no happiness and peace of mind without money. The reader can use this personal banking and financial model now, follow and it, and at the same time make it flexible to replicate repeatedly, to become an integral part of his or her personality, emotional intelligence and financial discipline.

Chapter 8

Personal Banking and Financial Discipline

This chapter discusses the fundamentals of personal banking and principles on the application of CashMax[3] module to financial discipline. It introduces fundamental banking concepts and norms applicable to the financial systems in Europe and the world. The narrative will lead with the basics of how banks and financial institutions operate as financial service providers and business entities within the European Union and the world. The study-play will discuss banks and financial institutions obligations to operate in a safe and transparent manner to manage risk and protect money as their main responsibility. In addition, the dialog will show what bank services are available to the reader from various financial institutions. The resulting narrative will demonstrate to the reader the benefits of applying emotional intelligence to manage money and his or her relationship with the bank. In addition, the study-play will show and illustrate with real-life examples the responsibilities of bank employees in a customer focused financial services scheme.

From this point forward, after the introduction of the participants the author will lead the discussions executed by the think factory cast. These will cover the reader earning and saving with banking services, investing and his and her financial future decisions, who shall be pay before non-essential obligations. He or she will learn the importance of borrowing and the value of credit scores, and the fundamentals of home ownership. This book is innovative in its guidance, quality and substance. It is responsive to the reader personal banking and finance critical needs for financial literacy and competence. However, the publisher nor the author is engaged in rendering legal or professional accounting or tax services or advice. Should the reader needs require these services, he or she should seek the services of an appropriate professional, licensed to practice in the country of residence and the European Union.

Good morning every one, this is a special day to all.

"I am Albert Jenkins, member of the United States, Financial Literacy and Education Commission, and your host. You are virtually together from coast to coast, by the wonders of mobile and computing technologies. You are present from Washington, D.C and New York to Kansas and Southern California.

This is a unique collaboration opportunity to bring a practical solution to the personal banking and financial illiteracy crisis, equally present in Europe, the United States, and for that matter in the World!

You are here to help formulate personal banking and financial literacy education solutions for the benefit of the reader whether he or she is a secondary school student or Comenius, university student or Erasmus, Vocational Student or Da Vinci, an adult or Grundtvig residing in Europe.

Thank you for considering, and accepting this invitation and for your time commitment, this exclusive group will constitute the "think factory" and cast of a unique study-play. You will become catalyst to changing the lives of millions of Europeans. They are your peers. You may never meet them in person or you might. I hope you will. Perhaps you would see them holding a copy of *"How Do Emotions Drive Money Decisions? EURO"* a draft copy of the book you have in front of you. You might see these people while traveling to or touring in Europe, hear them around school campus, the university, at the office, at the shopping mall, a coffee bar or in the bank, talking about how personal banking and financial literacy education is transforming their lives — one at a time.

Please welcome Dr. Sean O'Connor. He is a former Professor of Neurobiology, at the University College Dublin, Ireland, and a research Psychiatrist. Also, please welcome Dr. David Golden. He is a Professor of Behavioral Science and Psychology; and former Chair of the Department Behavioral Sciences of the Israel Department of Defense.

It is my pleasure to introduce the author of this unique and powerful life-changing book, Dr. Jorge Rivera. He is an Economist, and he holds a dual specialty. He is a Behavioral Science Specialist, and Adjunct Professor of Transnational economics and Strategy, United States Department of Defense, and member of the United States Council of Economics and Financial Literacy.

Dr. Rivera, Welcome!"

"Thank you, Dr. Jenkins.

It is my privilege and an honor to be virtually here with you. Thank you for accepting this challenge. Thank you for agreeing to be members of this cast of principal characters in this study-play production, named "Bank on It!" It will become a once in a lifetime experience, for the participating peers and for the reader. The reader and the think factory cast are now an integral part of a mastery learning critical process, and together will be communicating to others on the urgent need for financial literacy education in Europe. In addition, the reader and think factory cast together will be making an impact on the future of the secondary school and university students, vocational students and adults of all ages. I trust, than when the reader, and peers participating as members of the cast focus groups, leave the eight-session program, all will be equipped to inspire others, in a similar ways to become financially competent.

I will be leading you to become the movers and shakers of the next generation of financially worry-free persons within Europe and your own circle of influence. Without further delay, let us move to the study-play plan."

Think Factory Cast and Study-Play Plan

Members of the think factory cast received a pre-publication copy of the book title *"How do emotions drive money decisions? EURO"* This reference book will be a thematic sample, for critical thinking, and a subject guide. It will serve as foundation for this financial study-play and sequence of events, creating real-life scenarios and relevant stories, to move with ease in applying the mastery-learning tool to the personal banking and finance model. Also, with this material is a glossary of personal banking and finance terms, working agenda, and rules of engagement. These rules are ground rules or rules of play. These are instructions to the "cast" by the author, the medical and behavioral subject matter experts participating with the reader, and cast as team co-leaders. These rules are to delineate the circumstances and limitations under which the author will initiate and or continue the focus group engagement, within the natural behavioral forces encounter.

Mainly, these behavioral forces are the natural resistance of humans to accept new concepts or thought processes. However, most realistically, there is a natural inborn resistance to a "new," when change requires a conscious acceptance of responsibility. The word "responsibility" falls on young ears like a curse. For most adults, too, the word responsibility means "unwelcome duty" and is something the reader is tempted to deny or avoid. However, there cannot be financial freedom without emotional control, neither happy lives without financial discipline and responsibility — the code of unwritten guidelines that govern his or her financial conduct — and how we relate to the banking and financial system and society as a whole. That code is just as important as the European Countries Laws.

A sport example will illustrate this concept. In a soccer game, the referee monitors the written rules on the playing field. While the technical director, keeps an eye on how each player is measuring up to his responsibilities to the team. Every team player has to do his or her job to make the offence and the defense solid. Few of these guidelines exist on paper; they are just in memory, drilled into habit by repeated practice, so it is the reader emotional intelligence and financial discipline, in order to maximize the benefits of optimum use of his or her money.

The governing "Personal Banking and Finance Terms" to implement this learning experience, are located at the end of this book under the heading: "Resources." The only difference in the application of these terms is the fact that if the reader is under 18 years of age, he or she must have the signature and consent of his or her parents or legal guardian, to open a bank account. With this notice, and from this point forward, no longer will be a distinction between the secondary school students, university students, or adults. The author will be treating this personal banking and financial literacy education strictly as an adult subject, with the relevant legal weight and consequences it demands. The reader will use terms that are applicable to the specific discussion, emotional intelligence, financial discipline, earning and saving or investing and spending.

Freedom is not free it has a price. The reader is investing the most valuable asset all humans poses, time. The time he or she is investing in becoming financially competent and the self- commitment the reader is making to learn, apply and embody the governing terms of personal banking and finance, to these terms the reader will be referring most often. The application of emotional intelligence to the use of the reader money is the road to financial freedom. This freedom begins with financial discipline.

Core Concept — Financial Discipline

The reader is about to take the first step into the core concept of this book, "financial discipline," it is easy to begin ... start ... There is something refreshing and optimistic about these words. Whether they refer to the dawn of a new day, the first day of school, the first day of college, the first day of work or a family vacation. Free from financial problems and full of promise, beginnings stir hope and dreams of the future, a future where money is the catalyst of freedom. If freedom to fail matters to the reader, where is there evidence of this in the countries of Europe? Is it within the Bankruptcy Courts? Is the solution with the Divorce Courts? Is freedom in the school or universities remedial courses?

Therefore, if the reader is free to take chances and fail, he or she is free to try again. This gives the reader the opportunity to succeed whatever current level of personal banking and financial literacy, whatever financial mistakes he or she has made or are making, there is a way to correct this financial conduct and apply immediately the principles of emotional intelligence and financial discipline contained in this book. The first core concept of financial discipline is the reader truth about his or her financial condition and financial literacy. The truth is what corresponds to what actually is, because this truth is a vital part of his or her financial conduct and true freedom. These truths will guide the reader and serve him or her as financial protection. These truths will also help to understand with ease, what mastery learning is. How it works, and how to apply it, both to the core concept of financial discipline and to incorporate this process within his or her personal banking and financial literacy needs.

Pre-Learning

This process will begin with introducing to the reader a cognitive behavior concept or in simple terms pre-learning. It will be asking the reader truthfully and openly respond to a few questions about his or her characteristics and attitudes about money; how does he or she feels about financial discipline? What does the reader know about money? What motivates him or her to be reading and ready to study this book? In addition, why is the reader willing to invest his or her time and learn to become financially competent?

The reader should write down his or her answers to these questions on a note pad as he or she responds to each of the statements; the reader will be noticing there are some questions he or she knows the answer already. Questions may appear basic. However, be patient; as there are some answers the reader may not be too clear about or totally unfamiliar with their meaning or application. The goal here is to master all aspects of the subject before he or she moves from this to the next module. This is how the reader will achieve mastery learning of personal banking and finances to achieve financial literacy.

Self-evaluation and Strategic Thinking

To assist the reader in self-evaluation about how much he or she knows about personal banking and finance now, a member of the cast will address each question assigned, and their assigned counterpart will respond. If there is a consensus with the answer, the study-play will move forward without delay. If there is lack of consensus, any member of the cast may interject and provide the correct answer. This dynamic format is designed specifically with the reader in mind; it promotes the development of consistent strategic thinking about the intelligent use of money, will help him or her to understand why he or she acts the way it does about money, and how his or her emotions influence their financial decision-making and resulting consequences.

Bank on It! — Production

The reader, the cast and peers are the principal characters of this financial literacy study-play.

This is a real life drama! The plot is composed of real life stories; the names of the protagonists are fictitious to protect their identity and privacy. The events are taking place in Europe, United States, Canada, Israel, and Saudi Arabia. The euro is the currency of reference. The time is now.

The location is the privacy of the reader-selected environment, anywhere, anytime.

The reader chooses the place and pace of play, based on his or her particular financial literacy needs.

The plot thickens as the reader anticipates the outcome of his or her exit evaluation and self-assessment.

On that day — the reader final evaluation and assessment — he or she will know it is financially competent, ready to enjoy the money skills him or her has learned — and benefit from the intelligent use of money for the rest of their lives.

This is the reader first step to financial freedom. He or she can rely on it!

Let it roll...Action!

Alexander — "Which of the following are considered financial institutions? Are these (a) **Banks;** (b) **Credit Institution;** and or (c) Pawn shop?"

Margaret — "Who is assigned the opening story?"

Carlos — "My friend Dario, from my school, learned that his father Juan, got €1,000 from a pawn shop, and gave as a guarantee a 1.5 karat diamond ring belonging to the family estate, as the ring was inherited from his grandparents. The due date to recall the ring arrived, and Juan was in the hospital due to a scheduled nose correction surgery. Three days later, Juan went to the pawn shop to recall the ring, to find out the ring was already sold. Juan sued the owner of the pawnshop for €75,000 that was the certified appraised sale value of the ring. The Court ruled that pawnshops are not financial institutions, and thus not regulated, like banks. Juan lost the ring, attorney fees in the amount of €7,000, Court costs and loss time from work, another €2,827. This ordeal according to Dario, is affecting his health, and his family relationships; in addition, Juan total loss was €84,827 as a direct result of lack of financial literacy."

Sofia — "Why should the reader keep his or her money in a bank? Select the answers that applies: (a) To keep his or her money safe and insured; (b) Have fast and easy access to money; (c) Because it is cheaper than using any other business; (d) To cash checks and pay bills; (e) To help the reader to get a future loan or line of credit; or (f) **All of the above.**"

Jacques — "The answer is all of the above.

Benjamin — "When the reader applies to open a new bank account, the bank will first: (a) Withdraw money from his or her new account; (b) Give him or her an account number; (c) **Ask for his or her European Country issued identification (ID)**; or (d) Offer him or she a credit card."

Catalina — "The answer is (c.)"

Albrecht — "Why is (c) the correct response?"

Nicolaus — "The reason is because the bank, once accepts the reader money in deposit, now this bank, is legally responsible to keep his or her money safe; and in case of fire or loss, this bank must positively identify the account holder, the reader. It would only be able to claim his or her money from the bank or the deposit-guarantee scheme by presenting his or her personal valid identification, the Country issued identification card or the reader National driver's license."

Joseph — "Which of the following steps will help the reader from overdrawing his or her bank account? (a) Open the bank account; (b) Make deposits and withdrawals; (c) Balance his or her checkbook one time every year; or (d) **Record all transactions in a check register.**"

Maria — "The correct response is (d.)"

Louis — "Britani, show Maria's response and demonstrate evidence with a real case story."

Britani — "Last week my father almost had a heart attack! When he received a nonsufficient funds notice from the bank, that five checks he wrote totaling €93.20 would cost him €125 in bank charges. The worse of it all was that he wrote a €25 check to my grandmother, my mom's mother for her Birthday and another €25 to my grandfather, my mum's father for Father's Day. You can imagine the emotional heat around the house and the demining comments during dinner celebration that evening. All of this because my father is so busy at all times with his work that he forgot to record these five checks, including the two checks issued to my grandparents, in the check register.

Lesson learned: record all transactions in the check register immediately, each time you write a check, make a deposit, make an ATM withdrawal or debit card purchase; calculate the math and keep an accurate balance. That is the good news, the bad news is that since my father has made same mistake several times before, yesterday, the bank sent him a letter. In short, the letter made clear that next time a nonsufficient charge shows the bank would close his account. Wow! On that day I am afraid my father would really have a heart attack!"

Larry — "Two types of deposit accounts are: (a) **Checking and savings** (b) Money orders and Automated Teller Machines (ATMs); (c) Stocks and bonds or (d) Overdraft protection and checking fees."

Laura — "The answer is (a.)"

Alexander — "Margaret, please show evidence that validates Laura's answer."

Margaret — "Well my dad deposits €2,000 each month in my checking account for me to pay monthly room and board, schools supplies and incidental expenses; and also he has deposited €75,000 in my savings account to ensure that upon graduation date, I will have starting money for private university studies. As I understand it, both of these deposits are demand deposits. I can draw these funds any time from my checking or savings accounts."

Carlos — "Which account would the reader use to pay bills and buy goods? (A) Savings account; (b) **Checking account** or (c) Non-deposit account."

Sofia — "The answer is (b.)"

Jacques — "Laura, demonstrate evidence why Sofia is or is not correct."

Laura — "I am managing the money in my family since Larry and I got married. Larry is a salesperson, travels at least 60% of the time; therefore, I pay all bills and purchases over €50 from our joint checking account. Two weeks ago, I received a collection letter from car dealer in Hamburg, Germany claiming that we owe them €1,416 for an engine repair the dealer performed two years ago. At that time, we were living in Hamburg, and since then we have moved to the U.S. Santa Clara, California. I searched my records and could not find a canceled check to prove I had paid the dealer. I wrote a letter to the dealer explaining the move from Germany to U.S. and asked that they give me some time to ask the bank for a copy of the check. Their response was "an attorney in Santa Clara would move forward with legal action unless we receive payment within ten days."

I almost panicked. That night, Larry called from Milan; Italy and after calming me down, he told me to call the bank in Hamburg, simply ask them to do the search and send me a copy of the lost check so I could avoid the legal action. I sent an e-mail to the bank relating the situation and requesting a copy of both sides of the missing check. The following day I received the much-needed electronic copy of the check, called the dealer and sent a certified letter, signed return receipt requested. Within my transmittal letter I sent a copy of the both sides of the canceled check."

Benjamin — "Why should the reader copy both sides of the check?"

Laura — "Because his or she cancel check is the only legal proof it has to show evidence of payment."

Alexander — "In which situation below would the reader needs to speak with a bank's customer service representative? (a) Apply for a mortgage loan; (b) Cash a check; or (c) **Ask a general question.**

Margaret — "The correct answer is (c.)"

Carlos — "Which of the following are ways to prevent identity theft? (a) Protect your National Citizenship Card (b) Protect your credit card number; (c) Protect your mail; (d) Sign up for direct deposit; or (e)

All of the above."

Sofia — "The correct answer is (e.)"

Jacques — "Debit cards can be: (a) A quick way to get a small loan; (b) A way to delay having a purchase come out of your account; (c) Paid off over time; or (d) **Used at many retailers.**"

Benjamin — "The answer is used at many retailers or (d.)"

Catalina — "With online banking, the reader can access his or her accounts at any time to: (a) View your account balance (s); (b) Conduct multiple transactions, for example, transferring money between accounts, paying bills, or ordering checks; (c) Download information, including your monthly statement; (d) Change account information; or (e) **All of the above.**

Albrecht — "That is easy: (e.)"

Nicolaus — "If the reader wants to get a loan at the bank, he or she would most likely work with the: (a) Loan officer; (b) Teller; (c) Customer service representative; or (d) Bank Manger.

Joseph — "The answer is (a.)"

Maria — "Which of the following is similar to a check, a document used to pay bills or buy goods? (a)Would the reader use a loan; (b) **Money order;** (c) Remittance; or (d) Money transfer.

Louis — "The answer to these questions is (b.)"

Juliet — "Britani, please give the reader a description of a money order.

Britani — "Now I am going to show that I am paying attention to what is being taught. I will be sharing with the reader and the cast what is a money order, it is a financial instrument, similar to a check that can be easily change into cash by the payee, named on the money order. The money order shows the date, amount, and lists both the payee and the person who bought the money order, known as the payer. It is also, a document issued by a bank, post office, or Money Gram, or duly authorized business entity. The reader can use a money order to pay bills or make purchases when checks or cash is not accepted."

Larry — "Where can the reader find information on how a financial institution handles and shares his or her personal information? (a) It is listed in the Deposit-Guarantee Scheme; (b) In the Terms and Conditions listed on your account statement; (c) **In a Privacy Notice sent to you by the financial institution**; or (e) On the back of your checks.

Nicolaus — "The correct answer is (a.)"

Joseph — "No, no. no that answer is incorrect. Who has the assigned correct response?

Maria — "The correct response is (c.)"

Louis — "Juliet, why is "c" the correct answer?

Juliet — "Because, the bank has many affiliate businesses, who market goods and services to its clients. Therefore, the bank, by Law must give the reader a written copy of the privacy notice and give him or her a choice to accept sharing personal information or opt out.

Britani — "The following overview of banks content is designed for the reader to confirm how much he or she knows, how much the reader did not remember, or how much it has learned about personal banking and finances on the road to personal financial competence, by examining why the reader should keep his or her money in the bank."

Why keep your money in a bank?

Larry — "A bank is a business that offers the reader a safe place to keep money, and uses his or her deposits to make loans to business and other customers of the bank. Some of the reasons to keep his or her money in a bank may include safety — the reader money is safe from theft, loss, and fire; convenience — he or she receives money rapidly and easily. Using direct deposit, for example, saves the reader time and allows him or her quicker access to their money."

Laura — "Funds that are electronically deposited in the reader account these are available faster than if he or she deposited a paper check. It can also use Automated Teller Machines (ATMs) to get fast access to money; other reason to keep the reader money in the bank is cost. Using a bank is probably cheaper than using other businesses, similar to a check cashing service, to cash your check or pay bills; security—The Deposit-guarantee scheme, insures the reader deposits in the bank up to the maximum amount allowed by law, which as of the time of printing this book is €100.000,00 per depositor, per insured bank. This means that the Deposit-guarantee scheme will return his or her money up to this limit, if the bank closes and cannot return the reader his or her money in deposit."

Alexander — "The most important, the reason to keep the reader money in the bank is his or her financial future — paying bills on time and having a savings account are conditions necessary for securing a loan."

Types of Financial Institutions

Margaret — "The reader knows from the pre-learning exercise, that there are two types of insured depository financial institutions: Banks and Credit Institutions. These financial institutions operate under European Union Directives, laws, and regulations. Banks and Credit Institutions make loans, pay checks, accept deposits, and provide other financial services, for example, provide investments offerings, life insurance and home owners insurance."

Carlos — "Credit Institutions are nonprofit financial institutions, owned by people who have something in common, for example, teachers, firemen, policemen, country or municipality employees, may join a credit institution. Credit Institutions offer many of the same services as banks. If the reader wishes to keep his or her money with a credit institution, he or she has to become a member of that particular credit institution to keep money there."

Activity 1: Identify Financial Institutions

Sofia — "This assignment requires to describe two types of financial institutions, and at random call a name from the cast for the answer. Here is the situation. Golden Gate, financial institution insured by the Deposit-guarantee scheme. It must follow European Union Directives and Member State laws. The reader could get a loan, a credit card, or open a checking or savings account there. Which one is it? Laura."

Laura — **"It is a Bank or Credit Institution."**

Jacques — "The Big Apple, financial institution, requires account holders to be a faculty or staff member or student of Big Dreams University. The account holders are also the owners. Which one is it? Britani."

Britani — **"That describes a Credit Institution."**

Establishing Banking Relationships

Benjamin — "When in search of a financial institution, whether a bank or a credit institution, to establish a banking relationship, it is most important that the reader make a list of questions, about the institution services, and costs of banking there. Answers to these questions will help him or she to choose a financial institution that is right for the reader. The first set of questions relates to the bank or credit institution. What services the financial institution offers the reader to meet his or her banking needs. Does it have branches that are located near home, school, work or place of worship? This is as important as ATMs locations. The reader needs convenience.

He or she needs access and peace of mind. What are the institutions operating hours? Are they open on Saturday? How late? Do employees speak other languages, in case the reader needs to help someone that does not speak his or her native language? Does the Deposit-guarantee scheme insure this institution? To facilitate understanding of this subject, from here onward both, a bank and a credit institution, will simply be named a bank, unless there is a consumer responsibility distinction."

Catalina — "The reader would want to ask a second set of questions, these relate to the types of accounts; bank requirements for him or her to open and keep each type of account; if a checking account, what is the minimum opening balance? What is the minimum monthly balance without charges? What are applicable bank fees? Are fee waivers available? Number of withdraws per month without a fee? Does the reader account earn interest? What is deposit hold in business days, when he or she deposits a check from another bank?"

Albrecht — "The reader third set of questions, are linked to overdraft programs. Does this bank offer free mobile and smart phone applications? In the event his or her account reaches, a low balance of less than €25 does the bank offers mobile phone or text alerts. What are the overdraft fees? If the reader links his or her checking account to his or her savings account, is there any fee in the event of an overdraft?"

Nicolaus — "The reader fourth set of questions, relate to his or her savings account. What is the minimum opening balance and monthly balance? What is the annual percentage yield? What are if any fees? Does the bank imposes a maximum number of withdraws the reader is allow to make per month?"

Joseph — "The fifth set of questions, relate to ATM and Debit Cards. What are the fees for using the reader debit card at non-bank ATMs? What are the fees when he or she uses the debit card to receive cash at the store, gas station or another bank? Consider whether the prospective bank offers rewards for using debit cards to pay for goods and services."

Maria — "The last set of questions, relate to mobile and online banking. Are mobile and smart phone applications and online services available, and are these free of charge? Is online bill pay free? What are the transaction types and limits? The reader is in control of choosing a bank and where it is located for him or her to establish a profitable banking relationship. Profitable, because by the nature of the reader questions, the customer services representative of the prospective bank will know that the he or she is financially competent. Therefore, the bank representative in his sales effort to bring the reader in as a new customer, may give him or her some free services that otherwise carry a charge."

Opening and Maintaining Bank Accounts

Louis — "The reader is in the process of realizing that financial discipline begins with the banking power of knowledge. Opening and maintaining a bank account, is not as difficult as he is or she might think. Four basic things the reader has to do open the account; make deposits and withdrawals; record interests and fees; and at all times, keep an accurate track of his or her available balance. The first thing the reader needs to do to open a bank account is to go through a process called account verification. This account verification is for two important reasons. First, the bank must make sure that the reader is whom he or she says it is. In addition, that the reader is permitted under the law to open a bank account.

Moreover, the bank may want to make sure the reader will be a responsible bank customer. For these reasons, the bank will need his or her full name as stated in a valid Member State issued identification, (ID) card, driver's license, European Union passport, or European Union resident alien card. In addition, the bank will ask for the reader residence address, and date of birth."

Activity 2: Deposits and Withdrawals

Juliet — "The purpose of this exercise, is to practice making deposits to and withdrawals from the reader bank account, and keeping track of the money, by maintaining at all times an accurate account balance. Before he or she embarks on this activity, there are legal elements of a bank deposit or commonly known as, "Deposit Slip."

The deposit slip, must bear the name of the bank, prominently displayed the word "Deposit," it must indicate if the money is to be deposited into a checking account, savings account or pre-paid card.

DEPOSIT/DEPÓSITO

Your Bank DEPOSIT/DEPÓSITO

CHECKING/CHEQUES ☒
SAVINGS/AHORROS ☐
CHASE LIQUID ☐

Today's Date/Fecha 01/14/14

R/T 500001020

Customer Name (Please Print)/Nombre del cliente (en letra de molde) John Do IV

CASH/EFECTIVO ▶ 20.00

CHECK/CHEQUE ▶ 80.00

Sign Here (If cash is received from this deposit)/
Firme aquí (si recibe efectivo de este depósito)
X

TOTAL FROM OTHER SIDE/TOTAL DEL REVERSO ▶

SUBTOTAL ▶ 100.00

Start your account number here/
▼ Empiece su número de cuenta aquí

LESS CASH/MENOS EFECTIVO RECIBIDO ▶

001 234567890 0 TOTAL $ 100.00

⑈0570693795⑈ ⑆50000█⑆

The reader must complete all applicable information on the form. He or she will use this information as evidence and legal recourse to show him or she made a deposit on certain day and amount. When the reader needs cash-back, he or she must sign the deposit slip, where indicated on the form. The reader signature is the bank's legal evidence that he or she received cash from that particular deposit; and the final and unique element of the information required for a deposit is the reader account number. At the bottom of the deposit slip are two electronic printed numbers, one corresponds to your specific deposit and the other is the routing number of the bank. These two numbers are for the bank internal control, to balance the teller's cash box; each day at the bank closing of business."

Britani — "The reader second exercise, part of this activity, is to know the legal elements of a bank withdrawal or commonly known as, "Withdrawal Slip."

The withdrawal slip is simple, the basic legal elements are same as the deposit slip, except that it requires that the reader signs the withdrawal slip in the presence of the bank's teller as an indication that he or she actually received the cash it is withdrawing."

Your Bank WITHDRAWAL/RETIRO

CHECKING/CHEQUES ☒
SAVINGS/AHORROS ☐
R/T 500001017

WITHDRAWAL/RETIRO

Today's Date/Fecha: 01/14/2014
Customer Name *(Please Print)*/Nombre del cliente *(en letra de molde)*: John Do IV

If Purchasing a Cashier's Check Provide Payee Name/Si desea comprar un cheque de caja, escriba el nombre del beneficiario aqui

N13063-CH (Rev. 07/12) 30485131 10/13

Customer Signature/Firma del cliente
X John Do IV

Start your account number here/
▼ Empiece su número de cuenta aquí

AMOUNT/CANTIDAD

0 0 1 2 3 4 5 6 7 8 9 0 0 TOTAL $ 100.00

⑈0266822813⑈ ⑆50000███⑆

Real Life Scenario

Larry — "Margaret, please formulate a real life scenario that will bring home the concept of establishing a banking relationship. Please do not name the bank, for this book is not a bank sponsored.

Margaret — "I opened a bank account at a Small Plaza Bank, a neighborhood bank located near where I live, go to school, work part-time, and also attend church. Actually, this is what I did: I made a list of all those questions we discussed, and printed it; selected three banks, within one half mile from my "best meeting point"—that is, where I spend most of my free time with my classmates, and friends. I visited each bank on my own, and determined that Small Plaza Bank was the one I felt best met my banking needs. Then, I asked my mum to go with me to open the account, because I will be 18, next month, so I could not legally open the bank account on my own.

My mum and I went to Small Plaza Bank; it has a European Union wide network of ATMs, and suitable banking hours. My mum and I met the customer service representative, an "attractive young man." I introduced my mum; pull out my printed list and begin asking the "choosing a bank questions," one by one; after a little while, half way down the list, my mum, visibly embarrassed, asked the young man at the bank to excuse us for a moment. My mum took me aside said to me: "what are you doing? Did you not see the poor man is about to run...?" He has taken four tissues to dry up his hands. This poor young man is not on a courtroom stand, please take it easy or I will leave.

To her treat, I responded: very well mum, would you please sign the authorization, leave and wait for me in the parking lot. My mum and I returned and mum said to the "attractive young man:" I just remember I have something to do and must leave. Is it there anything I need to sign, so Margaret can complete the paperwork to open her account?

At this point, the branch manager came, introduced himself and ask if there was anything he could do to make our first experience with Small Plaza Bank a pleasant one. Yes, I responded, can my mum sign her consent for me to open my bank account and leave? The branch manager, a little surprised with my direct statement responded, yes, as he asked the "attractive young man" for the authorization form. My mum signed, and politely left... to sit in the car and wait for me to finish. I opened my first bank account with €100 cash; no monthly fees as I signed for direct deposit of my monthly allowance."

Carlos — "Sofia, using Margaret's new opening balance of €100, please talk with Margaret for a moment, and with her information, continue with the scenario that reflects what making deposits, withdrawals and keeping an accurate balance are all about?

Sofia — "According to Margaret, the next day after opening her bank account, she withdrew €40 from an ATM, at the end of the same week she deposited her part-time "pay-packet" of €75."

Jacques — "Benjamin, what is the balance in Margaret's bank account after she made her ATM withdrawal, and deposit?"

Benjamin—"The balance is €135."

Deposit and Non-Deposit Accounts

Joseph — "Bank accounts that allow the reader to add money to his or her account are called deposit accounts. Banks call deposit accounts "products." Samples of these products are checking and savings accounts. A checking account allows the reader to pay bills and buy goods with the money he or she has deposited. Therefore, when the reader writes a check, use an ATM, debit card, pre-paid card, or bank online to pay for goods or services the bank takes the money from his or her account and pays it to the designated person or business. Banks make a daily and monthly record of customer checking and savings accounts deposits and withdrawals. It makes these available to the reader either by mail or online, a compilation of his or her banking activity; this is a bank statement.

A savings account is a safe method for the reader to save money. He or she will be paid interest by the bank on the money in a savings account. However, the reader cannot write checks from his or her savings account; it can often open a savings account with as little as €25, but the reader might pay a monthly fee, if the balance is below a certain amount, this requirement varies with financial institutions. He or she can keep track of the account balance by reviewing the account statement."

Banks vs. Check-Cashing Services

Maria — "Even though, a bank may charge the reader a monthly fee, it is much cheaper to use a deposit account at a bank, than a check cashing service. When the reader compares banks to check-cashing services, other benefits include: financial institutions provide the convenience of Internet banking, access to his or her account information 24 hours, 7 days a week, all year around; and peace of mind. No worry about cash being lost or stolen, it is insured. Using a bank account responsibly can help the reader to develop a positive banking relationship, which may be helpful if he or she needs to apply for a loan in the future, for example, when buying a car; or the reader can easily save for his or her future."

Non-Deposit Accounts

Louis — "Many banks also offer non-deposit accounts or products that are not insured by the Deposit-guarantee scheme. For example, stocks, bonds and mutual funds are investment products. These carry some level of risk, meaning, that the reader could lose some of all of its money that he or she invests in these products. Law obligates the bank, to provide the reader with a written explanation that states these products are not insured, and there are some risks of losing value."

ATM and Debit Cards

Juliet — "An ATM card allows the reader to make deposits to and withdrawals from a checking or savings account; he or she can check the account balance, print statements and transfer funds between accounts. The reader can use his or her ATM card in stores that accept ATM cards. It works just like a debit card; however, their acceptance is limited outside the issuing bank's network.

Maria — "Debit card, also known as a check card, usually displays a Euro Card or VISA logo. It has all the functions of an ATM card, and allows the reader to pay for goods and services at locations that accept Euro Card or VISA credit cards. A debit card immediately withdraws the reader account for each purchase."

Louis — "When the reader uses a debit card to make a purchase, the retailer may ask him or her to choose whether to process the transaction as a "debit" transaction, where you input a Personal Identification Number, (PIN), or a "credit" transaction, where you sign a receipt in place of entering your PIN. Either way, it automatically withdraws his or her checking account. Check with his or her bank to find out whether there are any fees or incentives for credit card transactions versus debit transactions."

Juliet — "Another kind of card, which can be confused with ATM or debit card, is a store value or prepaid card. Stored value cards, often have the logo of one of the major payment systems, for example, American

Express, Euro Card or VISA displayed on the card. These cards do not link to the reader bank account. Therefore, money must be preloaded onto these cards, and the value goes down with each purchase."

Britani — "Common types of store value cards include: General purpose cards—purchase from retailers. Some come with a set value others require the reader to "load" or add money to the card after obtaining it. Gift cards — are purchased in fixed amounts. Unlike most other stored value cards, these gift cards often can only be redeemed for purchases from particular stores or restaurants."

Laura — "pay-packet" cards — are used by an employer to pay wages instead of giving the reader a paper check. "pay-packet" cards are different from other types of store value cards. Because he or she does not need to purchase them or pay activation fees since his or her employer provides the card."

Larry — "Government disbursement cards are similar to "pay-packet" cards, except these are provided by government agencies to pay benefits, for example, unemployment or Social Security benefits."

Activity 3: Additional Banking Services

Alexander — "Banks provide additional services with some deposit accounts, and may charge a fee for these services. It is most important that the reader keep track of the fees charge, if any. The following are common services that banks offer: ATMs, debit cards, direct deposit, loans, money orders, money transfers, remittances, and telephone online banking."

Margaret — "Banking services differentiation will bring mastery learning to an experience. It will help the reader determine what he or she has learned. I call on Britani a member of the cast to describe a banking service from the list of questions on the agenda. What is the method of electronically transferring money from one bank to another?

Britani — **"It is a money transfer when it is within the European Union. It is a remittance when money is send abroad."**

Carlos — "What is another name for a kiosk or terminal where the reader can deposit, withdraw or transfer money from one account to another 24 hours a day?"

Sofia — "It is also called drive-in banking."

Jacques — "That is not the correct answer. Who can help?

Laura — "It is called an **ATM.**"

Benjamin — "What is the term used when you call your bank to check your balance?"

Catalina — **"It is called a telephone inquiry."**

Albrecht — "What is the function that allows the reader to check his or her account balance from a computer, or Smartphone? It may also include the ability to pay bills. Or transfer funds between his or her checking and savings accounts."

Nicolaus — **"It is known as online banking."**

Maria — "What is the negotiable document that is used like a check to pay a bill?

Joseph — **"It is called a money order."**

Louis — "Juliet, name the method that the reader employer or a government agency might choose to issue a "pay-packet", or unemployment benefits?

Juliet — **"This method is known as government disbursement cards."**

Britani — "What is the term used when the reader borrows from a bank with a written promise to pay back later?"

Larry — **"It is called a bank loan."**

Laura — what is the name of the card, that when you use this card to buy something from a store or another business, the money comes out of your bank account immediately.

Alexander — **"It is called a debit card."**

Margaret — "Is there another card that works identically to a debit card?

Carlos — "Yes, some ATM cards can be used as debit cards, provided that the store specifically accepts ATM within the reader bank network.

Alexander — "This example will illustrate Margaret's question and Carlos response. Three weeks ago, my uncle opened a bank account, and because he had no previous credit or banking relationship, the bank issued him an ATM card, which did not display the **Euro Card or VISA logo.** Two weeks later, he went to a store to buy some items, when he presented his ATM for payment, it was not accepted. My uncle almost lost his temper, upon inquiring; the store manager explained to my uncle that the store was not in my uncle's bank network. Therefore, this store was unable to accept ATM cards."

Sofia — "What is the type of card onto which the reader can load money to be used for future purchases?"

Jacques —"It is called **stored value or prepaid card**; however, these cards do not link to your bank account.

Privacy Notices and Opting Out

Nicolaus — "The reader personal financial information is private. Privacy notices explain what information the bank collects, how financial institutions and affiliated companies handle and share the reader personal financial information. The reader can limit what information he or she will allow the bank to share with others. Privacy notices also explain how the financial institution protects the reader personal information. Upon opening a bank account, the reader receives an initial privacy notice and every year thereafter. European Union law requires financial institutions to keep the reader personal financial information private; the public does not have access to the reader personal financial information. European Union privacy laws give him or her a right to stop or "opt out" of some sharing personal financial information."

Opting Out

Joseph — "The reader might prefer to limit the promotions it receives, or if he or she does not want marketers and others to have his or her personal financial information. The reader should review the privacy notice. This will determine whether the financial institution shares information with others, and if so, how the reader can opt out. In addition, the reader can prevent credit reporting agencies from sharing information with lenders and insurers. If the reader opts out, he or she limits the extent to which the financial institutions can provide personal financial information to non-affiliates, or groups outside of the financial institution."

Catalina — "The reader cannot opt out and completely stop the flow of all personal financial information. The European Union Directives and individual counties laws, permit financial institutions to share certain limited information about the reader, without giving it the right to opt out. Among other things, financial institutions can provide to non-affiliates information about him or she to firms that help promote and market the financial institution's own products, or products offered under a joint agreement, between two financial companies. For example, Small Plaza Bank, credit card with Euro Card, or VISA logos. These affiliates record the reader transactions, including loan payments and credit card or debit card purchases. The bank provides this information to firms that provide data processing and mailing services for financial institution where the reader has an account. Information about the reader in response to a Court Order, including payment history on loans, and credit cards share to credit reporting agencies."

Protecting Yourself from Identity Theft

Maria — "Identity theft occurs when a criminal steals the reader personal information, for example, his or her European Union Identification Number, birth date, or credit card numbers, and uses it to commit fraud or other crimes such as defamation of character. The following are common forms of identity theft: Phishing, pharming and skimming."

Phishing, is when criminals send out unsolicited e-mail that appear to be from a legitimate source: perhaps the reader bank, school, well-known merchants, his or her internet service provider or even a trusted government agency. For example Europol; or when criminals attempt to trick him or her into divulging personal information, such as Social Security, age, profession or home address.

Pharming is similar to e-mail phishing as follows: criminals seek to obtain personal or private information by making fake websites appear legitimate; the reader web browser will even show that he or she is at the correct website. This makes pharming more difficult to detect than phishing.

Skimming happens any time criminals steal credit or debit card numbers by using special storage device when processing the reader card.

Online Shopping Security

Louis — "My assignment is to show tips to help the reader to do business safely online: make sure the Internet site is secure before he or she uses a credit card or enter personal information. Most web browsers will have a secure symbol, for example, a "padlock," or "Site Lock Secure" to identify whether the site is secure. When shopping online, deal with reputable merchants and be wary of unbelievably low prices. If the reader is uncertain about an online merchant, he or she can search online for complains about that particular business firm."

Identity Theft Tips

Juliet — "My task is to present tips to avoid identity theft that may include: protect the reader Country Identification Document Number, credit card, or debit card numbers; Personal Identification Numbers, PIN(s) pass words. Or any other confidential information, and never give out information in response to an unsolicited e-mail, text message, or phone calls, regardless of who the source supposedly is. Legitimate organizations, would not ask you for these details, because they already have the necessary information, or can obtain it in other ways. Do not respond to these calls, emails or advertisements."

Britani — "The reader should ignore online "friend" invitations, from people he or she does not know. Because the reader does not know, may be covers for fraud artists. Be careful about the profile and contact information the reader posts on social-networking and employment-related websites, because in the wrong hands it can lead to identity theft and other crimes."

Larry — "The reader is to protect his or her computer. For example, install a free or low cost firewall to stop intruders from gaining remote access to his or her personal computer. Download and frequently update security patches offered by the software manufacturer operating system and authorized software vendors to correct weakness that a computer hacker might exploit."

Laura — "The reader should consider using pass words that will be difficult for a hacker to guess. For example, use a mix of 16 characters numbers, upper and lower case combinations of letters and symbols instead of easily guessed words. Also, shut down your computer when you are not using it.

Alexander — "The reader may want to seek free tips to help him or her guard against Internet fraud, secure his or her computer and protect his or her personal information. This free service is available from the online U.S. website "www.OnGuardOnline.gov". Guard his or her mail outgoing mail, by depositing letters in locked mailboxes or directly at the post office; and your incoming mail, by picking up your mail as soon as possible or use a locked mail box. Keep the reader financial trash "clean." Shred old bank statements or other documents containing personal information before throwing them away. The reader may be selling, donating or disposing of his or her personal computer. He or she should use special software; completely erase files containing financial records, tax information, and other personal sensitive data."

Margaret —. "To the reader, beware of offers that seem too good to be true, con artists often pose as charities or business people offering jobs, rewards, or other "opportunities." Be extremely suspicious of any offer that involves "easy money" or "quick fixes." Be careful if the reader is under pressure to make a quick decision. Also, beware of any transaction for which you receive a cashier's check made out for more money that the amount due to you with a request to wire back the difference—you could lose a lot of money if the check is fraudulent."

Carlos — "To the reader, be alert to signs that require his or her immediate attention; these include bills that do not arrive as expected, unexpected credit cards or bank statements, and calls or letters about purchases you did not make."

Sofia — "The reader should review his or her bank statements upon arrival. He or she should also review bills, and credit card statements for suspicious activity. Monitor his or her bank statements and all credit card bills upon arrival each month, and contact the financial institution immediately if he or she notices something suspicious, for example, a missing payment or unauthorized withdrawal."

"Jacques — "While European Union and Countries laws may limit the reader loses if he or she is victim of fraud or theft, to fully protect itself, the reader must report the problem quickly. Contact his or her financial institution if a bank statement or credit card bill does not arrive on time. Missing financially related mail could be a sign that someone has stolen the reader mail or account information, and may have changed the reader mailing address with the intention to run up large bills in his or her name from another Country or location."

Benjamin — "The reader should review his or her credit report, no less frequent that twice a year. He or she should do this even if he or she does not have any loans or credit cards — to look for accounts or inquiries the reader did not authorized. If the reader suspects he or she is victim of identity theft, he should contact his or her creditors immediately and then go to the police and file a police report."

Activity 4: Identity Theft Warnings

Catalina —"I am assigned the task of bringing mastery learning to an additional level of experience. It is to help the reader, decide his or her own level of progress and to confirm by self-determination that he or she knows the subject taught thus far. I am calling on any member of the cast to describe a potential identity theft and warning from the list of questions on the agenda."

Alexander — "The reader answers the phone one evening at home from a stranger; the voice on the other end is offering him or her a free weekend trip to a popular sky resort, but to get the low price coupon the reader has to give a credit card number."

Britani — "Does the reader gives the caller the number?"

Larry — "No, the caller could use the credit card number to commit fraud."

Carlos — "The reader receives an e-mail from someone who says they are a student in his or her math class but the reader does not know the sender. The e-mail states that the sender needs to get on the school network to check homework, but they lost their password. The caller wants to "borrow" yours. Should you give it to them?" Please Maria, expand on this warning."

Maria — "A similar event happened to me last week, I work for a large hospital with 783 employees; last Friday, I received an e-mail from a person who stated to be one of the night security guards, and that he had forgotten his password to login the hospital's network."

Louis — "Would the reader be so kind and help either the math student or the night security guard?"

Laura — "Under no circumstance I will help either person; it could be a hacker or anybody trying to damage Carlos's login account, or a potential competitor trying to access business information from Maria's hospital."

Britani — "The reader calls his or her bank to find out if a deposit was posted to his or her account. The bank's customer service representative asks the reader for the European Union Identification number to verify his or her identity. Does the reader gives it to the customer service representative or hang up?"

Albrecht — "That is a difficult question. I learned never to give my European Union or Country Identification over the phone to anyone. However, I placed the call to the bank I know it is legitimate. In addition, because I need to know about my deposit I will give the bank the last four digits of my Country Identification Number. If the person on the line asks for the complete number, I hang up."

Laura — "I had just paid all the family bills for the month, and my husband Larry hands me a stack of "paid" counterfoils and asks me to throw them away. What should I do? Should I trash them away because I want to follow my husband's instruction, or shred them away so no one else can get financial information from them?"

Joseph — "I am assigned to ask Larry to give a real life scenario that brings this important point to be remembered by the reader and the cast participants."

Larry — "I am a computer programmer and work for a multinational software company with 532 employees. The company Security Chief, called for a general departmental meeting to inform programmers that the customer support department continues receiving multiple phone calls from customers. Complaining about the exaggerate bills they received in the mail. In addition, asking why were they to send payment in the form of a cashier's check or credit card only, to a post office address located outside Europe. The Security Chief launched an investigation. The result showed discarded computer generated reports containing customer-billing information and tossed away by programmers on waste paper baskets. Then, these documents throw in the company general trash bins for collection by the trash Company."

Juliet — "What is a safe action the reader should take in all cases, regarding the safeguarding of private and financial information?"

Margaret — "Always, and I mean always! The reader must shred all papers not needed. Especially those papers that contain his or her private or financial information before you throw them away."

Sofia — "This is another scenario; the reader receives a letter in the mail from a well-known Credit Card Company. It says they are "concerned about recent activity on his or her account" and they want to protect their customers. However, you have never had a credit card with that particular company. There is a toll free number to call to speak with a fraud service representative. Should you call it?"

Jacques — "What should the reader do?"

Benjamin — "The reader should not call. Because the letter may be a method to illegally, obtain his or her private information. I am learning to manage my emotions, discern the financial cost of my decisions, and take into consideration why not to give personal information out."

Did Someone Steal Your Information?

Catalina — "No matter how carefully the reader protects his or her personal information, if his or her wallet or purse is stolen or someone obtains his or her personal information, then the reader may become a victim of identity theft. This is what I am learning to do should I think I am a victim of identity theft: I will file a report with the local police, as soon as possible, keep a copy of the report in case the bank or insurance company needs evidence of the reported crime. I will inform the bank as soon as possible. I may have to close my account, cancel the ATM or debit card, open a new checking or savings account, and request a new ATM or debit card with a new number and use a new password. I will place a fraud alert on my credit report by calling each of the major credit reporting agencies in my Country of residence. Further, I will contact the major check verification companies to request that they notify all the stores that use their databases not to accept my lost checks. I can also ask my bank to notify the check verification service with which it does business."

Activity 5: Key Personal Banking Employees

Albrecht — "Financial institutions have various employees to help the reader with different banking services. Understanding their roles helps him or her know who he or she should talk to when visiting the bank. While the exact job title of these employees varies from bank to bank, the job duties are similar in all banks. Some key bank employees the reader needs to be familiar with are customer service representative, teller; loan officer; and branch manager. Members of the cast are assigned specific bank employee role to show what each employee can do for the reader."

Nicolaus — "As the Customer representative, of this bank, I can help the reader open an account; explain services; answer general questions; refer him or her to a person within the bank that can help the reader with a particular situation; and provide him or her with written information explaining the bank products."

Joseph — "As a bank teller, I would deposit the reader money in the bank for him or her; cash their checks; answer questions; and, refer the reader to a person within the bank that can help with other bank services."

Maria — "I am a loan officer, and if you need money I can take an application for loans offered by this bank; answer questions; provide written information explaining loan products; and help him or her to fill out a loan application for consideration and approval."

Juliet — "I am the branch manager, and my job is to supervise all the bank operations that take place at this branch. I help fix the problems that other employees cannot solve. Here are some key points to remember: ask for help, if the reader does not know whom to talk to at the bank. Feel free to ask questions until he or she is clear on the understanding on all information. Most important, do not sign not anything the reader does not understand. Ask for written information to take home to review. In addition, always use the "Choosing a Bank and a Bank Account Checklist" to help the reader choose a bank and the account that is right for his or her personal needs."

Module Summary

The reader has completed "Personal Banking and Financial Discipline" module. With the assistance of the cast, he or she has learned the fundamentals of personal banking and the application of finance terms. He or she has experienced the first core concept—financial discipline,—types of insured financial institutions, opening and maintaining a bank account. The reader should have learned from real-life scenarios presented. In addition, he or she has learned the differences between banks and check-cashing services. Distinguish between deposit and non-deposit accounts; privacy notices and opting out. The reader has learned to protect itself from identity theft, types of banking services and bank employees and their roles.

Mastery Learning and Knowledge Check

Mastery learning in action is as dynamic as other learning concepts, it continues to develop and evolve as the reader, assisted by the author and cast journey together to fulfill his or her need for personal banking and financial competence. This need can only be realized when the reader openly and truthfully participate in the following knowledge check. It consists of thirteen questions. These will represent the reader aptitude, the length of time it takes for him or her to learn. Everyone can learn given the right circumstances. How much of the material to this point the reader knew; how much he or she was not sure about, and how much of the content the reader did not know.

The purpose of this knowledge check is to build the reader personal banking and financial confidence, and experience a sense of the security it needs to move successfully forward. The reader would go through the private process of self-discovery about what repeated emotions trigger behavior that makes him or her act the way they do about money. It will bring to light insights about emotional attitudes towards money and his or her motivation to learn financial discipline.

The result of this exercise would help the reader in building sound personal banking and financial knowledge, security, and a feeling of hope in basic financial competence to this point. When he or she is responding to these questions, jot down the answers. Thirteen correct answers indicate the reader is ready to move on to the next module; seven correct answers indicate the reader is to review those responses that he or she missed. Less than seven correct responses indicate the reader needs to return to those themes him or her is experiencing difficulty. When the reader becomes proficient at all thirteen questions, he or she is following the roadmap towards meeting a personal need for financial competence.

Knowledge Check Questions

(1) Which of the following products is not Deposit-guarantee scheme insured? (A) Stocks and savings accounts; (B) Savings and checking accounts; (C) Stocks and mutual funds, or (D) Checking accounts and mutual funds.

(2) Which type of financial institution requires the reader to be a member in order to keep his or her money there: (A) Banks or financial institutions required membership; (B) Credit unions required membership; (C) Money markets requires membership; or (D) Individual Retirements Accounts (IRAs).

(3) What type of account is typically insure by the Deposit-guarantee scheme: (A) Deposit account or (B) Non-deposit investment type?

(4) Deposit accounts generally offer which of the following banking services: (A) Direct deposit; (B) Telephone and online banking; (C) ATM and debit cards; or (D) All of the above.

(5) A store value card is (A) Card onto which the reader can load

money to be used for future purchases (B) Money transfer that goes to a bank or a person in another country (C) Document that is used like a check to pay a bill, or (D) Method of electronically transferring money from one bank to another.

(6) Who is the best person at the bank to help the reader deposit or withdraw money from his or her account (A) Customer service representative (B) Loan Officer, or (C) Branch manager?

(7) During the account verification process, the bank will: (A) Withdraw money from the reader new account; (B) Give him or her and account number; (C) Ask the reader for his or her Member State issued ID; or (D) Offer a credit card to him or her.

(8) A debit card: (A) It is used to make purchases at retail locations and ATM cash withdrawals; (B) Has a "buy now, pay later" feature, like credit cards; or (C) It is similar to a gift card from a retail store.

(9) Two types of non-deposit accounts are: (A) Checking and savings; (B) Money orders and ATM(s); (C) Stocks and bonds; or (D) Overdraft protection and checking fees.

(10) Debit cards can be: (A) A quick way to get a small loan; (B) A way to delay having a purchase come out of your account; (C) Paid off over time; or (D) Used at many retailers.

(11) The five advantages of using a financial institution are safety, convenience, cost, security, and financial future: (A) True; or (B) False.

(12) European Union Directives and individual countries privacy law give readers the right to stop or "opt out" of some sharing of his or her personal financial information: (A) True; or (B) False.

(13) How can the reader protect itself from identity theft? Select all that apply: (A) Keep copy of his or her PIN in his or her wallet or purse should you forget the number; (B) Use secure mailboxes for incoming and outgoing mail; (C) Review his or her bank statements upon arrival for any suspicious activity; or (D) Accept incoming call or an email from a stranger.

Self-evaluation

The reader should consider his or her progress and self-evaluation as the truth of his or her financial literacy regarding this module on the fundamentals of personal banking. He or she should not be satisfied with the reader self-assigning a grade on his or her first attempt, and then move onto the next module, unless he or she responds to thirteen correct answers. Therefore, it is critical that the reader not proceed to the next chapter until it has become proficient with the essence and content of the current module. To verify that the reader is in his or her truth, taking ownership of this teaching and on the right road to financial competence, at the end of this book are the correct answers to each question asked in this and subsequent modules. The reader will find the title "Resources" to validate his or her answers.

One word of caution, as the reader proceeds with his or her self-evaluation try to regard the financial literacy progress record as his or her personal rating. The only valid comparisons are between the reader present, past and future financial progress. What he or she has accomplished to this point, is all to his or her credit and something to build on. The reader only objective now is to unlock his or her better self. In addition, apply from now on the first core concept in this book, financial discipline, to all future money related decisions.

In education, the idea that learning can be fun is still innovative. Play, is the mode in which children discover their world. However, the moment they step into the classroom the joy of discovery ends. "We are through playing now," is the message from some teachers. "We have got to get down to work," states another. The assumption is that anything that is good ought to cost the learner something. He must "give it very last ounce," "keep his nose to the grindstone"—or "kill" himself.

Dr. O'Connor — "Sad to say, such sacrifice diminishes rather than improves progress. The child who cannot play is destitute of a learning experience and an essential educational process. Children who cannot laugh are needy of an important physiological releaser of tensions, as well as philosophical perspective. Such children grow to be adults bewildered as to why their serious efforts to learn a new discipline have not gained them maximum rewards. The reader financial discipline training is a joy when is done in a way that is right for him or her; improvement is immediate."

Dr. Golden — "Early financial conditioning is the process of preparing oneself step-by-step for focusing on financial discipline activities. These foundational activities are the center of paying attention and producing order from chaos in the reader daily financial conduct. As a child, the reader hears from his or her parents and grammar school teachers to "pay attention!" In more or less seasonal ways the reader may have be receiving the same message ever since. Even though he or she may have grown accustom to this command and shrug it off, there are a few things in life more important."

For paying attention is how the reader prepares itself psychologically to be in the right frame of mind and give his or her best to the task at hand, to determine the kind of financially competent self he or she is cultivating. When the reader gives his or her full attention to become financially competent, it is really attending; he or she is calling on all his or her natural resources of emotional intelligence, feeling and ethical sensitivity. This can happen at home, at work, or at play, in interaction with people the reader sincerely cares. At such moments, the reader is not thinking about itself because him or her are completely absorbed in what they are doing — attempting to understand how personal banking and financial literacy will give the reader a peace of mind. Although such moments of contemplating peace of mind because of the reader financial literacy are enjoyable, it does not seek them because of pleasure, because they are things he or she really want to do in terms of a larger context of life and that of his or her immediate family.

The reader wants to be free from financial distress, free from living at the edge of financial precipice, free from leaving beyond his or her means. — However freedom is not free, it requires devotion and purpose. These "make sense." The new organization of financial knowledge is available to the reader. Advantages include the fact that the reader has a place of awareness for what it is — a tool to be used and thought to others — as an effective method for the self-study of his or her financial behavior. However, a new model of personal financial behavior is terribly hard to accept as valid. Comenius and Erasmus students as well as Da Vince and Grundtvig adults are so tied to the world picture they were taught as children that any suggestion of other — or, in the present case that the one growing up with is valid for only one part of reality and others are needed for other parts—is automatically judge as foolish.

For example, Euclid's geometry[57] considered the valid geometry for 2000 years. Mathematicians such as Bolyai[58] and Lobachevsky[59] presented systems of geometry different from Euclid's in the hope that these systems were worth considering in connection with the actual properties of space. These mathematicians attempted to show that Euclid's system was valid for only small part of reality and that other systems needed for other parts. At first they regarded by other mathematicians as neither serious nor sane. The reader first instinct is to reject the new, particularly if it implies a number of word pictures, and to say with complete conviction, this commonsense financial model is the true description of reality.

Producing order from chaos in the reader daily life involves the exact same procedure as training for a championship —the soccer World Cup. First, stop everything and wait for a moment. Next, take a deep breath and relax. Then, determine the reader top financial priority task

---

57 Euclid (300 BC), Euclid of Alexandria, a Greek mathematician referred as the "Father of Geometry" His "Elements" is one of the most influential works in the history of mathematics, serving as the main textbook for teaching mathematics, especially geometry from the time of its first publication until the 20th Century.

58 Johann Bolyai, Hungarian (15 December 1802-27 January 1860. A Hungarian mathematician was one of the founders of non-Euclidian geometry—a geometry that differs from Euclidian geometry in its definition of parallel lines.

58 Nikolai Lobachevsky, Russian.(20 November 1792-24 February 1856) mathematician and geometer, known for his work on hyperbolic geometry.

— balance your check register — turn to it and set the other priorities aside. He or she is not going to be able to do them all, the readers tell themselves. However, financial discipline calls to initiate one task at a time and do it well.

Chapter 9

Earning and Saving

This chapter will use the CashMax[3] module to help the reader identify ways he or she can earn and save money. Earning and saving will teach the reader what it needs to know to open a checking account and maintain a positive balance, responsibilities involved with maintaining his or her checking account and ways the reader can use it to earn and save money. What are the objectives for this module? The reader will be able to state the benefits of using a checking account; determine which checking account is best for his or her particular needs; identify the steps involved in opening a checking account; add money and withdrawal money from their checking accounts. In addition, and critically important correctly reconcile the reader check register with his or her bank statement. The definitions and application of pre-learning established in the previous chapter, along with the self-evaluation and strategic thinking about the intelligent use of money will remain for the rest of the study-play.

Let it roll on again…Action!

Laura — "Which of the following statements is NOT true? (a) Checking accounts are convenient; (b) **Checking accounts are only for rich people;** (c) Using a checking account is generally less expensive than using a check-cashing service; or (d) Using a checking account helps keep the reader money safe."

Alexander — "The correct answer is "b."

Larry — "Which of the following is NOT an example of a common type of checking account: (a) Free checking; (b) Interest-bearing checking; (c) **Per-transaction fee checking;** or (d) Electronic-only or automated Teller Machine (ATM) checking."

Britani — "I am not certain, free checking is the answer."

Louis — "No, that is the incorrect answer."

Maria — "The correct response is per-transaction free checking account."

Joseph — "When the reader writes a check and the check bounces, the bank will charge a fee. What is that fee called: (a) ATM fee; (b) Stop payment fee; (c) Minimum balance fee; or (d) **Overdraft or non-sufficient funds fee?**"

Nicolaus — "The fee is called non-sufficient funds fee, or commonly known as NSF fee."

Albrecht — "Select all that apply to withdraw money from a checking account, he or she can: (a) **Use an ATM card at a machine; (b) Write a check out to "cash" and go to a teller;** (c) Use a credit card; or (d) Purchase items using a store value card."

Catalina — "I would say that (a) and (b) are the correct answers."

Benjamin — "To open a checking account, the reader will most likely need to provide the bank with: (a) **European Union Issued photo identification (ID);** (b) **Country Identification Number (CIN) and money to deposit;** (c) Name, address, and CIN; (d) A good credit history and a deposit; or (e) Photo ID, address, and a good credit history."

Jacques — "The answer is "a" and "b."

Sofia — "Direct deposit is a way to keep money safe because: (a) He or she has the check sent directly to a check-cashing location; (b) The reader cannot withdraw it once he or she deposits the check. In addition, (c) It waives the fee at a check-cashing store; or (d) **the reader check goes**

directly to his or her bank account and there is no risk of misplacing it."

Margaret — "The correct answer is "d."

Alexander — "Electronic banking services include all of the following EXCEPT: (a) Electronic bill pay; (b) Text message alerts about banking transactions or the reader account balance; (c) **Calling the bank on the phone;** or (d) **Debit/ATM card transactions."**

Margaret — "Electronic banking excludes "c" and "d."

Carlos — "Which of the following statements are false? (a) The check register is a tool for the reader to keep track of his or her account balance; (b) **If you make a mistake in his or her register and overdraw the account, the bank will not charge the reader.** In addition, (c) The reader should enter all withdrawals and deposits in his or her check register. Alternatively, (d) Checks that he or she has written not cashed yet will not show up on the reader bank statement."

Sofia — "I understand this statement to be false: "b."

Jacques — "From the following statements, indicate which two of these will best help the reader determine if a particular checking account is right for him or her: (a) **Ask the bank what the fees are so the reader knows if he or she can get a better deal elsewhere.** Alternatively, (b) Find out if the bank has checks with the reader favorite team logo on them. In addition, (c) **Ask about different services to see if the bank offers the ones the reader needs;** (d) Negotiate monthly service charges with their bank."

Benjamin — "The answer is: "a" and "c."

Catalina — "Select all that apply. In order to add money to a checking account, the reader should: (a) **Fill out a deposit slip and give its deposit to a teller; (b) Cash his or her "pay-packet";** (c) Write a check out for "cash."; or (d) **Deposit cash at the ATM."**

Albrecht — "To add money I will select: "a" and "d."

Nicolaus — "Reconciling a bank account means: (a) **Comparing the monthly bank statement with his or her check register to make sure**

they match; (b) Comparing monthly deposits with his or her bank withdrawals; (c) **Entering bank fees in the reader register; or (d) Listing outstanding checks."**

Maria — "My response is: "a," "c" and "d."

Joseph — "A debit card is: (a) **Similar to an ATM card, but the reader can also use it to make purchases at retail locations and funds are withdrawn directly from his or her checking account;** (b) The same as a credit card — buy now pay later. However, he or she can use a checking account with it; (c) Similar to a gift card from retail store, since the reader buys the debit card and can replenish the funds once a month; or (d) only used to get cash from an ATM if the reader does not have a checking account from which to withdraw funds."

Louis — "My answer is "a."

Juliet — "The best way to avoid overdrawing an account is to: (a) Limit the number of checks he or she writes; (b) Check its account balance regularly; (c) **Record all of his or her transactions in a check register;** or (d) Use electronic payment services."

Britani — "The answer is: "c."

Larry — "All of the following are key steps to balancing and reconciling your checking account EXCEPT: (a) Keep it up to date; (b) Account for any differences between your statement and your check register; or (c) **Compare your checking and savings account balances."**

Alexander — "My response is keep it up to date."

Laura — "That is the wrong answer!"

Margaret — "The correct answer is: "c."

Carlos — "When the reader takes more money out of an account than he or she has in it, that action is called: (a) A debit transaction; (b) Balancing your account; (c) **An overdraft;** or (d) A monthly service fee."

Sofia — "The correct answer is: "c."

Benefits of Checking Accounts

"Jacques — "A checking account allows the reader to deposit money into its account, withdraw money from his or her account and write checks or use it as debit card to pay bills or buy goods and services."

Convenience

Benjamin — "Checking accounts are convenient because the reader has a quick and easy access to his or her money. The reader can use checks and debit cards to make purchases instead of carrying cash."

Catalina — "The reader can also have money from his or her employer or government agency. For example, the reader can receive a "pay-packet" and other type of government benefit or assistance, directly deposited into his or her checking account."

Cost

Albrecht — "Using a checking account is usually less expensive than using other type of services, for example, check-chasing services, money orders, or store value cards."

Activity 1: Comparing Costs

Nicolaus — "The purpose of this activity is to understand and compare costs of a checking account with several other services. Each member of the cast has an assigned real-life scenario in order to make the answer vivid to the reader to compare costs and determine who saves most money. The following scenarios take place in the United States and Canada. Nevertheless, to make calculations easy to apply, by readers residing in Europe, the euro (€) is the currency of reference."

Real Life-Scenarios

Maria — "My friend Tony, who resides in White Rock, Surrey, British Columbia, Canada, comes across the U.S. Border to Blaine, Washington

State, to work two days per week at a souvenir store, near the Peace Arch, International Monument, Tony is not a U.S. resident, thus not able to open a regular bank account. Consequently, each week he works he cashes his weekly "pay-packet" at "Fees4Cash," a check cashing service. "Fees4Cash" charges Tony €5,00 to cash every check. How much does Tony pays this check cashing service each month to cash his "pay-packet"? How much does Tony pay each year?"

Joseph — "Leaving the issue of the legality of Tony's right to work in the U.S. aside; and as he works four weeks each month, then the math is this:

(5,00 X 4 weeks) = €20,00 per month. My next assumption is that Tony will work 50 weeks during a year. Then, the math is this: (5,00 X 50 weeks) = €250.

Store Value Cards

Maria — "Store value cards, or prepaid cards, generally allow the reader to spend only the money deposited on the card."

"Pay-packet" Cards

"Louis — "Pay-packet" cards are one of the main four types of store value cards. An employer uses these cards to pay wages instead of giving the reader a paper check or "pay-packet," this cards are unique from other types of store value cards because the reader does not need to purchase them or pay activation fees since its employer provides the card.

Real Life Scenarios

Juliet — "My sister Liza, works part time at a boutique in the Santa Clarita mall, near San Jose, California, in the U.S. and opts to have her salary or "pay-packet" deposited onto a store value card that she purchased for €5,00 because her employer does not offer "pay-packet" cards. Money can be "loaded" onto the card via direct deposit or by going to certain stores to reload. It has a VISA logo on it, so she could use it anywhere as with a credit or debit card. Liza can use her store value card at an ATM, but the card issuer charges €2,00 for every ATM transaction. Liza mostly uses her card at stores where she slides her card through the point of sale (POS) terminal, however this month she used the ATM four times. How much did Liza pay this month in fees when using her store value card at an ATM? How much would Liza pay each year in fees if she used her store value card at an ATM four times each month?

Britani — "The math equation rational is: Liza paid an initial €5,00 to purchase the store value card; plus €2,00 per ATM transaction fee and she made four transactions during this particular month.

Therefore, €5,00 + (2,00 X 4) = €13,00 this is the amount Liza paid in the first month, due to the price she paid for the store value card.

Thereafter, Liza would only pay (2,00 X 4) = €8,00 per month or (8,00 X 11) = 88,00+13,00 = €101,00 for the first year in fees.

The second year and thereafter, Liza does not have to buy a new card, thus she would only pay:

(8,00 X 12)= €96,00 a year in fees."

Carlos — "My girlfriend Marina, has a checking account in the Trusted Bank, in Madrid. Her bank charges a monthly fee of €6,00 unless she uses direct deposit or her debit card more than five times per month. If Marina uses direct deposit, her debit card frequently and uses no more than one box of checks every year, which cost her €18,00, how much does she pay per year to maintain her checking account?"

Sofia — "The way Carlos described the personal banking relationship of Marina; I am making two separate assumptions. One, Marina did not make use of the direct deposit checking account feature, thus she would pay €6,00 per month service charge, twelve times a year, or

(6,00 X 12) = €72,00 Marina would pay to maintain her checking account.

Second assumption, Marina will use direct deposit. With this decision, the bank will not charge her monthly fees. As a result she would only pay €18,00 per year which is the cost of a box of checks to maintain her checking account."

Jacques —"Keep in mind, that some banks are eager to bring in a customer and may offer free checks. By the power of personal banking knowledge in progress, the reader will improve the value of his or her financial competence, and therefore obtaining a free checking account."

Activity 2: Comparing Scenarios

Jacques — "How much can Tony save each year if he opens a checking account and pays what Marina does? Even if Tony pays a €6,00 monthly fee for twelve months, for a total of €72,00 a year, plus €18,00 the cost of a box of checks,

(72+18) = €90,00 how much could Tony save each year?

Benjamin — "Leaving aside the issue of legality of Tony's right to work in the U.S., if Tony opens a regular checking account, and taking Sofia's assumption "One" Tony will be earning from his financial literacy knowledge and thus saving (250-90) = €160,00 per year. Under the "Second" assumption Tony will be saving

(250-18) = €232,00 per year!"

Larry — "In the same way that Juliet evaluated Liza's store value card, (5+ (2 x 4) = €13,00 for the first month. Then, for the next eleven months Liza will pay (8 x 11) = €88,00. Adding the first year total costs: (13+88) = €101. Comparing these scenarios and realizing the application of earning and saving, Tony would have saved

(250-101) = €149,00 per year."

Joseph — "It is clear that earning and saving begins with the reader financial discipline and emotional control knowing how to select the right bank product that best meets his or her needs, at a cost that advances the reader goal of becoming financially competent for life. This concept applies to all personal banking transactions regardless of type."

Albrecht — "These responses point out to savings as a direct result of financial discipline, personal banking and financial education. This financial literacy is what few people realize how close fantasy is to reality."

Core Concept — Earning and Saving

Nicolaus— "This core concept, earning and saving is the second most important element of the reader financial competence foundation. Therefore, to realize its benefits, it is most important at this point in his or her progress to take a quick assessment at current levels of personal banking and financial knowledge. How the reader does accomplish that? It is quick and easy, has he or she understood financial discipline as stated in the previous Module?"

Britani — "If the reader truthfully responds with an affirmative Yes! Then, he or she is following the roadmap to build upon to reach financial competence that will last you for life."

Earning and Saving with Bank Products

Larry — "Selecting the appropriate bank product that best meets personal needs is what earning and saving with bank products is about. Using a checking account can help the reader manage money, and intelligently earn and save from his or her decisions, meet the second core concept in this book. To take advantage of the benefits of this banking relationship, it requires discipline to record all transactions in a check register, including deposits, cash withdraws, issuing a check or using a debit card to pay bills or make purchases. In addition, having funds directly deposited into a checking account is one way of saving in account monthly fees. These actions will earn and save the reader money each month."

Safety

Laura — "Keeping money in an insured financial institution means money is safe up to the Deposit-guarantee scheme insured limit, per depositor, per insured bank."

Types of Checking Accounts

Alexander — "There are four types of checking accounts most financial institutions will offer the reader. One type is free of monthly charges; low cost checking is another, it varies from bank to bank. In addition, the most common type is a regular checking account and the least common is interest bearing checking accounts. The application of lessons learned from real life scenarios presented by the cast and his or her own responses will make a difference between earning and saving or wasting money."

Free and Low Cost Checking

Margaret — "If the reader does not plan to write many checks per month, a free or low-cost checking account might be ideal. However, it might limit the number of checks he or she can write in a month. Some banks offer special checking and savings account products for students and for the "Grundtvig" adults. These may include a waiver of monthly fees, or a minimum automatic transfer of a specific amount from the reader checking to savings account. In addition, the bank may require the reader to maintain a lower minimum balance, and might offer free personalized printed checks."

"Ben," — " If the reader is under 18 years of age, when shopping for an account, he or she should ask the customer service representative of the financial institution if it offers a student account. If it does, the reader should find out before he or she opens the account, what happens when he or she turns 18, or is no longer a student. For example, what kind of account will the financial institution assign?"

Electronic/ATM Checking

Carlos — "This type of account, usually requires the reader to use direct deposit and his or her ATM or debit card. If they do not plan to use teller services often, an electronic checking account might be right for the reader. This type of account normally allows him or her to write an unlimited amount of checks per month without incurring a fee for each check it writes. However, the reader may have to pay a fee for in-person teller services."

Regular Checking

Jacques — "With a regular checking account, there is usually a minimum balance required to waive the monthly service fee. This type of account normally offers unlimited check-writing privileges."

Interest Bearing Checking

Benjamin — "With these accounts, the reader typically has to maintain a high minimum balance in order to earn interest and avoid a monthly service fee. The minimum balance varies from bank to bank, but is usually at least €500. There are also different forms of interest-bearing accounts: the Negotiable Order of Withdrawal (NOW) account or the Money Market Deposit Account, (MMDA)."

Activity 3: Types of Checking Accounts

Catalina — "The purpose of this activity is to conduct a quick knowledge check, to assist the reader in understanding with certainty the types of checking accounts financial institutions might offer; and to have a defensible position, to reason the choice of account he or she may recommend to a friend or relative. The following real-life scenarios will make each answer powerful to the reader. Each scenario will help him or her to verify by his or her response to it, how much the reader has advanced to this point in his or her personal banking and financial competence."

Real-life Scenarios

"Laura," — "Carolyn, is a single mother who works as a physical therapist in a local hospital. Her working hours vary, and she often cannot get to the bank during normal banking hours. Carolyn pays most of her bills online. For example, she pays her mortgage, utilities, and telephone bills. In addition, she uses her debit card to make many purchases. Robert, her ex-husband uses direct deposit to transfer his child support monthly payment into Carolyn account. What type of banking account you would recommend to Carolyn and why?"

Albrecht — "I would recommend that Carolyn open an electronic ATM checking account for the following reasons: Robert pays his child support by direct deposit to Carolyn, this will qualify Carolyn for a no service fee checking account. In addition, due to Carolyn type of work hours at the hospital, she seldom goes to the bank in person."

Nicolaus — "Roy, works in a local auto parts warehouse distribution center. His mother, Martha, does not work. They rent their home; utilities including water, heat and electricity are included in their monthly rent. Martha does the household groceries shopping and pays using an ATM card she also uses this card for other purchases. They do not write checks because their property owner accepts electronic payments for the monthly rent. What kind of banking account would you recommend to Roy and why?"

Joseph— "I would recommend that Roy asks his employer at the auto parts distribution center to deposit his "pay-packet" directly to his bank. Then, with this condition met, I would make same recommendation to Martha, for her to open an electronic ATM checking account. Because the transactions described by Nicolaus are the type that meets the description of electronic banking, and would be, free from monthly service fees. In the absence of direct deposit from his employer, then my recommendation would be for Roy to open a regular checking account and pay the usual and customary monthly service fee."

Maria — "My father and mother own their business in Barcelona. It has grown from small grocery store to a medium size supermarket with 107 employees. They work hard and are careful not to spent money needlessly. They pay themselves a regular salary, which they deposit in a joint checking account to pay for their household and living expenses. In addition, they often make purchases with a debit card, but my parents pay most of their bills by check. What kind of banking account would you recommend and why?"

Louis — "Given this scenario it shows that even though Maria's parents have successfully grown their business from small grocery store to a medium size super market, their personal banking needs attention. Because they deposit their respective "pay-packets" instead of arranging for their business to make, direct deposits to the joint checking account, thus saving in monthly service fees. My recommendation for this couple is to open a regular checking account, make direct deposits of their "pay-packets" and maintain a minimum balance, thus saving money on bank service fees."

Juliet — "Choosing a bank and a checking account that is right for the reader is an important personal banking decision, for it has bearing in his or her financial future. He or she is now more knowledgeable of the products offered by financial institutions, and the options available to the reader. Therefore, the choice of checking account should reflect what he or she has learned to this point. It is equally important that the reader meet with the customer service representative, to establish a personal banking relationship where he or she will be able to ask for reliable advice on his or her banking options before making account changes or decisions affecting his or her selected products and banking services.

Understanding Bank Fees

Britani — "An integral part of the decision-making process about choosing the type of checking account that is right for the reader, also requires that he or she asks the customer service representative at the bank to give him or her a copy of the bank fee schedule. It must list the fees the reader will pay for certain activities. Some of the most common fees include:

Monthly service fee, also called a maintenance fee. The bank may charge the reader a fee each month, just for having the account.

Minimum balance fee, some accounts may require that a certain amount of money be in the account. If the account goes below that amount, the bank automatically charges a fee.

ATM-use fee, the bank will charge the reader a fee each time he or she uses another bank's ATM card, in the same manner if the reader uses another bank's ATM expect them to charge a fee as well.

Overdraft fee, also called Non-Sufficient Funds, (NSF), fee. The reader will pay a fee when he or she does not have enough money in the account to cover a specific transaction, for example, a withdrawal, purchase or payment.

Stop payment fee, in the event the reader loses a check, or needs to stop payment for any other reason, he or she will pay a fee for this type of service. Be aware that the bank may not be able to catch the "target" check before it is paid. Therefore, the reader must keep in mind its timing of this request to prevent the bank from paying the "target" check in question."

Activity 4: Savings on Bank Fees

Larry — "To test the understanding of different fees bank charges, members of the assigned cast will use the EURO Friendly Bank fee schedule to answer the following questions. It is important that he or she pay attention to the value of his or her growing knowledge!"

Real Life Scenarios

Laura — "I have received from the customer service representative at the EURO Friendly Bank, a copy of the checking account fee scheduled, and it reads as follows: Monthly service fee €5,00. (This fee is waived if you keep a minimum daily balance of €500.) ATM transaction fees, EURO Friendly Bank FREE, other banks €2,00. Overdraft or NSF fees €35,00 per item. Stop payment requests €35,00 per item."

Alexander — "Clark has his checking account with EURO Friendly Bank, last month he used the bank's ATM three times. He also used another bank's ATM twice. How much will EURO Friendly Bank charge Clark for using his ATM card last month?"

Margaret — based on Alexander's description of this bank fee schedule and the fact that Clark used another bank's ATM twice, the math looks like this: (2,00 X 2) = €4."

Carlos — "My friend Tamara also has a checking account at EURO Friendly Bank. Two weeks ago, Tamara wrote a €350,00 check to pay for sky trip. She gave the check to Mr. Rogelio, the trip organizer. Someone stole Mr. Rogelio's computer case, where he was keeping the ski-trip checks until he could deposit them in the bank. Tamara wants to make sure no one can cash her check, so she contacted the customer service representative at her bank and makes a stop payment request. How much Tamara pays in fees for requesting a stop payment?"

Sofia — "Tamara paid a fee of €35,00 for this service."

Jacques — "For the past eleven months my survival training instructor, Mr. Boyer has kept not less than €600,00 in his checking account every day. This month, a medical emergency came up and he had to use most of the money in his account. Now he has only €100 left in his account. How much will Mr. Boyer pay for monthly service fees in the twelve-month period?"

Benjamin — "Based on the facts given by Jacques, Mr. Boyer kept a minimum daily balance of €600. This balance he kept for eleven months out of the twelve-month period. Therefore, Mr. Boyer only paid €5,00 for the month, that his account fell below the €600,00 minimum daily balance required by the US Friendly Bank to maintain a free checking account."

Larry — "Adali, the girl that helps Laura babysit my twin girls when she needs to go to medical or dental appointments, deposited in the bank her babysitting "pay-packet" totaling €75. Adali already had €100,00 in her account. The next day, thinking she had a lot of money, she went to the mall and made four purchases; two for €35,00 each, one for €50,00 and one for €60,00. The following day she checked her checking account balance and discovered that her account showed a negative balance of €40. Why did that happened? And how can she avoid same mistake in the future?"

Alexander — "Apparently the reason behind Adali situation is that she failed to keep track of her deposits and checks written on a real-time basis. Adali, and for that matter the reader, can avoid wasting money in NSF fess by keeping its check register balanced at all times, that means, making sure that the opening balance is accurate, deposits are added and checks, ATM withdrawals and purchases are subtracted as these are occurring. I can relate to this with pain for until now I kept on paying NSF fees because I seldom balance my check book register."

Opening a Checking Account

Margaret — "What is needed to open a checking account? The reader already knows from the subject of establishing a banking relationship, which he or she will be asked by the customer service representative of the bank for a European Union or Country Issued Identification; and initial money as the opening deposit. The customer service representative of the bank will also ask the reader to sign a document that is traditionally a "signature card." This document identifies him or her as the rightful owner of the checking account."

Account Verification

Carlos — "The bank will perform a mandatory account verification activity because it wants to make sure the reader will be a responsible bank account holder and ensure identity and avoid identity theft. In addition, if in the past the reader mishandled a checking account or performed poorly as a banking customer, the bank may not want to risk accepting him or her as a new customer. The bank normally may access the Euro Chex Systems database, to help assess the risk in accepting the reader as a potential new customer. If the reader is unable to open a bank account due to past credit-related problems, he or she should ask the bank if they are eligible for "second chance" checking programs. These programs may allow the reader to open a checking account after completing a bank sponsored check-writing workshop. In addition, the bank may require a direct deposit and will charge twice the amount of monthly service fees for one year. This price the reader will pay because of his or her financial illiteracy."

Activity 5: Checking Account Management

Sofia — "Based on the material covered this far, and focusing on the first two key concepts of this book, financial discipline, earning and saving, my first question to the reader is, does he or she has an income from a job or other source that pays the reader by check? If the reader's answer is yes; then my second question, does he or she has bills to pay that writing a check would be convenient? If also the answer yes; then does the reader buys money orders? Has the reader ever lost cash, finds it disappearing, or continues to spend it quickly? If his or her answer is yes, to three of these questions, the reader is a perfect candidate to open a checking account using a direct deposit, thus earning and saving money by not paying monthly service fees."

Jacques — "My question to the reader is: does he or she regularly keep track of the money earned or is allocated to him or her from any source and have a record of how the reader spends it? If the answer is NO, then the reader might not be ready to open a checking account. Because, the reader must have an income in order to aspire to a financial future. He or she must first have the desire to become financially competent. He or she should also be willing to embody the principles of financial discipline he or she is learning in this book. In addition, the reader must keep track of the money earned or is consistently pledged to him or her and how he or she spends it. By taking positive action in this direction, the reader would be developing a banking relationship for a favorable financial future and avoiding wasting money on non-sufficient funds fees."

Benjamin — "This book, provides a model for financial order and banking relationships, essential to understanding what makes the reader act the way he or she does about money, his or her emotional reactions and financial literacy. At the same time, it also points with hope to the future by equipping the reader with the money survival skills needed for life. At a minimum, if the reader does not think having a checking account is right for him or her at this point, he or she should consider opening a savings account. A savings account earns interest. The reader may still be able to use a direct deposit of its "pay-packet" or funds resulting from a legal relationship, into his or her savings account to avoid check-cashing fees. Remember to ask the customer service representative at the bank, what fees and transaction limits are associated with the savings account under consideration."

Laura — "Using a checking account has been easy for me because before marriage my previous job was that of a teller at a local bank. However, being a bank teller, and managing family banking and finances is not by comparison an easy task. When the reader opens a checking account, he or she receives an ATM or debit card that arrives in the mail within a few days after opening the bank account. Alternatively, the reader might receive a debit card issued by the bank on same day. The reader also receives a book of temporary checks and checkbook register until personalized checks arrive in the mail."

Alexander — "Adding money to a checking account is equally easy. When making a cash deposit with a deposit slip, he or she needs to make sure that the deposit slip has all the required information and that his or her account number is accurate. As the reader learned earlier, the deposit slip has specific legal information components designed for his or her benefit. It is also the bank's internal daily cash control. It serves as evidence of the composition of the reader's specific deposit transaction, for example, how much in cash, what denominations; how many checks and for what amount each check. Therefore, all applicable information must be accurate. Including, total cash, plus the total of checks deposited."

Margaret — "What happens when the reader needs cash back? The teller must verify that a subtotal shown is correct, less cash and then the net deposit is accurate. In this case, the teller will ask him or her to sign the deposit slip. The reader's signature signifies that he or she has received the exact cash back from the bank's teller as stipulated on the deposit slip. However, other key aspects of this activity are obvious to the reader, not too clear to others and plain new to some."

Carlos — "One of these aspects relates to depositing a check or cashing it. In both cases, the check is a negotiable instrument. The reader is negotiating with the bank the check he or she is depositing; it may be a "pay-packet" or a check the reader received from another person. In order for the bank to accept legal authority from the reader to negotiate this check, he or she must endorse it on the reverse side of the check. This action represents the reader's legal consent for this particular check to be transacted by the bank, with the issuing bank, either accepting it as a deposit to the reader's bank account or be converted into cash by the teller."

Sofia — "Another key aspect of deposit deals with checks the reader wants solely for deposit, and no cash back is to be demanded. In this case, he or she would endorse the check and write "For deposit only." These words indicate to the bank that no other person may negotiate this check. In addition, this check is exclusively for deposit to the account."

Jacques — "In the event that the reader receives a check and he or she cannot go to the bank to negotiate it, he or she may endorse the check to someone else, a parent or a friend. To make this endorsement valid, the reader must endorse this check by writing on the reverse "Pay to the order of" (person name...) and his or her signature below that statement. Other key aspects of the deposit activity that need attention, for example, deposit by mail. He or she can mail its deposit slip and checks to the bank for deposit to his or her account. However, he or she must not send cash."

Benjamin — "Direct deposit, occurs when an employer or government agency directly deposits his or her "pay-packet" or benefits to his or her bank account electronically. He or she can also make an ATM deposit. An ATM allows the reader to make deposits and withdrawals 24 hours a day 7 days a week. He or she can also use the ATM to check balances, make transfers between savings and checking accounts for these activities the reader needs a Personal Identification Number or (PIN). That is a secret code usually four digits that he or she enters with the keypad to access your account and conduct limited personal banking transactions."

Catalina — "In the event someone uses an ATM card without his or her permission, the Deposit-guarantee scheme law protects the reader. However, to benefit from this protection, and to minimize loses, report lost or stolen ATM/debit cards. In addition, report all unauthorized charges to his or her bank immediately."

Carlos—"Margaret is showing special interest and real-life application of the core concepts in this book. She is experiencing the benefits of financial discipline, and is demonstrating that earning and savings begin with financial literacy. Margaret will be showing with a life-scenario how the reader should take money out of his or her checking account and avoiding wasting money from lack of financial discipline."

Margaret — "I am now a bank customer, a checking and savings accounts holder. Therefore, I can speak with the reader how valuable this book is, and my learning experience continues to grow. First, the more I read, the more I realize how little I knew about personal banking and finances. Being a member of the cast has brought me to understand the value of banking interrelationships. In addition, I am experiencing the power of financial literacy. The reader should consider taking money out, it is an easy activity. However, before he or she does, he or she should make sure that the check register balance is accurate, and up to date, all deposits, checks and fees have been properly accounted for and that after this mathematical proof he or she has enough money in the account."

As an illustration of this simple but important issue, let me share what happened last week to my best friend Lynn. She is an 18 year old, popular at school and has rich parents. They give her money for almost anything she asks; Lynn has a checking account, an ATM, and a VISA credit card. She is always generous and invites some of us for coffee and goodies. Last week, Lynn wrote a check for €80,00 to buy by mail, two tickets, for a play at a local theater. To her surprise, she received a letter from the Company returning her NSF check and no tickets. Lynn called me immediately and asked me what to do. I told her to come to my house and bring her checkbook. When she arrived, she was in tears, for the last day of the play was the date for which she intended to purchase the tickets. She was in tears, because her boyfriend was also upset about not being able to go see the play, both had been longing to see together.

Based on what I am learning about personal banking and finances I proceeded to review Lynn's check register. Immediately noticed she had not kept a running balance for over two months. Only because she did not know how much money she really had in the account, at the time she wrote the check to the Company for the tickets, she incurred a €35,00 NSF fee.

After I helped Lynn to calm down, I gave the same tips I am sharing with the reader, he or she may find some of these obvious, some not so clear and some valuable. For example, upon issuing a check, record it in your check register immediately, enter the check amount in the appropriate column and deduct it from the previous balance. Most often than not, the arithmetic of this transaction could be the culprit to send all future transactions into error. Thus, double check the math and I mean double check it every time. If the reader makes a mistake in the process of writing a check, the best solution is to write "Void" across the face of the check. In addition, always tear it up to prevent thieves from stealing your financial information. Immediately, draw a line across the transaction in the check register, and write "Void," complete the math and initiate the new activity again."

Carlos — "The reader should know that writing a bad check or doing so with fraudulent intent, is a crime in every Country in Europe. For this reason, if he or she ever does mistakenly write check without sufficient funds, the reader should correct it as soon as possible. Contact the person or company he or she issue its check and give a reasonable explanation of the circumstances leading to this error, and state a specific plan to correct the situation. If he or she repeatedly overdraws his or her account, the bank might close the account and report negative checking account activity to the credit bureaus. This financial conduct can make it difficult to cash or write checks, or open a bank account in the future.

Opt-In Rule — ATM/Debit Card Transactions

Sofia — "The bank will ask the reader how to handle certain overdrafts generated by ATM withdrawals; and one-time debit card transactions at store point-of-sale, (POS), terminals. If the readers "opt-in" to a bank's overdraft program the bank can charge a NSF fee — perhaps €35,00 or more — to process POS or ATM transactions that exceed its account balance. Alternatively, if the reader does not "opt-in" and does not have sufficient money in the account to cover the withdrawal or purchase, the bank will decline the ATM withdrawals and debit card transactions at POS terminals."

Opt-Out and Account Overdraft Programs

Jacques — "If the reader decides to "opt-out" and opt-into an overdraft program he or she should learn the options he or she has. These may include linking his or her checking account to a savings account so the overdraft amount is automatically transfer from savings to checking account, linking a savings account to a line of credit or enrolling in an overdraft program. All financial institutions, must disclose on the monthly bank statement the total euro amount of all overdraft and NSF fees charged to his or her account. The monthly statement must include separate total amounts of fees for the statement period and the calendar year to date. How should the reader avoid overdraft fees?"

Benjamin — "I will be illustrating the answer to this question with a personal story. I am a golfer at heart and for the Scottish; golf is a passion and almost a way of life. To play golf successfully it mandates to manage one's emotions and exercise discipline to end with a par score. The same applies to avoiding paying NSF or overdraft fees that can be costly in more ways than the fees charged. The reader should at all times manage his or her emotions and exercise financial discipline or it may cost a banking relationship, affect his or her credit score, and potentially upset the relationship with family and others.

The reader can avoid these costly mistakes by keeping an accurate track of how much money he or she has available in a checking account. He or she can accomplish this by simply keeping a check register up to date. Particularly, paying attention to track and record in the reader's check register, all ATM transactions, debit card purchases and online transactions; remembering to record automatic bill payments and checks he or she writes. The reader can also avoid charges by reviewing the bank statement as soon as it arrives in the mail, and reconciling it against the check register."

Catalina — "Another way to avoid costly overdraft fees is to ask the bank if it offers e-mail or text alert messages when his or her account reaches a low balance. The safest and best savings are the result of keeping extra money in its account as a safety cushion. In the same way the reader needs to be aware of ATM fees his or her bank charges when another bank's ATM card they used; be alert not to exceed his or her available funds or overdraw the account for it always incurred NFS fees."

Albrecht — "Electronic banking is becoming more popular as mobile applications are turning user friendly and free. With electronic banking for example, the reader can use either a computer, electronic tablet, or smart phone to deposit money, and move money between a checking and savings account. It is important that the reader makes sure that the bank offers this product free of charge; some banks may charge a fee for electronic banking."

Protection — ATM-Credit Card Charges

Nicolaus — "How does the reader protect itself when someone not authorized uses his or her credit card? In addition, what is the meaning of temporary hold? The most important information the reader should know is that European Union Directives and individual European Country Law protects him or her. The liability cap for unauthorized credit card transactions in Europe is €50. However, the reader should be aware that in the case of an ATM withdrawal, or debit card charges, the transaction in question most often has completed and deducted from the reader's account. By Law, the bank will issue a credit for the amount in dispute to the reader's account; further, the bank will charge a fee of €50,00 while the card issuer investigates the matter, when the case is resolved the bank will reverse this €50,00 charge. In addition, the bank must credit the reader's account within ten days from the date the bank receives notice from the reader."

Joseph — "Based on the lessons in this book, there are certain things the reader should do: first, upon discovery of the unauthorized charge and within 48 hours, notify his or her bank by phone, write down the date, time and name of the person notified at the bank. Then, follow up with a written notification to the credit card issuer, for example to VISA or Euro Card, stating only the facts, date and time you discovered the amount of unauthorized charges, and facts about you notifying your bank. If the reader fails to notify the bank within 48 hours of discovering the unauthorized charges, he or she becomes liable for the entire unauthorized amount of charges."

Maria — "I am going to communicate with the reader about "temporary holds" with a personal example of what my sister and I encountered when we devoted a weekend at a golf resort following one of our Spanish golfing idols at a golf tournament. We arrived at the Costa Brava Club and Golf resort, and boy what a treat! Valet service to park our car, our luggage was whisked away before we got off the car, how can we make your stay a memorable one, one porter asked me; another, may I help you with your hand luggage? Both, my sister and I were excited and felt like queens. At the reception desk, upon checking in, the front desk attendant asked for a credit card, and he explained that the charges for our reservation were approximately €300,00 per night, and that the hotel as a matter of policy will be placing a hold on an initial amount of €500,00 to cover incidental expenses during our stay. All was going wonderful, our "golfing idol" was playing good and we both were excited and happy to be there, until the second day when we decided to go to the gift shop to buy some souvenirs to bring home the following morning. We selected our gifts, and gave the sales clerk my credit card to pay for these.

After a few minutes waiting, the clerk politely stated, "may I have another form of payment?" This credit card transaction shows denied. If either my sister or I wished, could speak to the credit department. I responded we would. A polite woman at the credit department explained that even though we had the money, it was the policy of the hotel to place a "temporary hold" on funds greater than anticipated amount to be incurred, and posted for the closing bill to the account. Now what do we do? My sister asked.

I responded; let us ask the credit woman. Look, I said, as I was nearly whispering to this good-mannered person, since we are leaving tomorrow, and check out time is eleven o'clock, can we close the account now, to know the current charges and determine what to do? She was gracious and proceeded to do a preliminary closing of the bill. Surprise, we only owed the hotel €248. After this finding, the credit person removed the temporary hold, called the gift shop, and authorized the sales clerk to accept the credit card without calling the card issuer for authorization. All ended well. This successful conclusion was a direct result of the financial training I am receiving, from both studying this book and participating as a member of the cast.

The same good experience could happen to the reader, if he or she knows what to do under similar circumstances. With this illustration the reader may know, how it could end when him or her exercise financial discipline. When the reader knows what actions to take, and how to earn and save with its personal banking and financial literacy knowledge."

Keys to Your Financial Future

Louis — "My assigned activity is to share with the reader, my peers and others, one of most important aspects of financial discipline. It is to record all transactions in his or her check register immediately upon issuing a check, paying for purchases with a debit card or withdrawing money with an ATM card. Financial discipline is the key to a financial future."

Juliet — "By consistent application of financial discipline the reader will build a good banking relationship; safeguard his or her credit score; and develop solid a foundation for his or her financial future. Another important issue for the reader to consider is to use electronic bill pay; this service automatically takes money from a designated account each month to pay his or her bills. The benefits include saving the reader's time, gas money and postage, payments will always be on time, thus consistently improving their credit score. It is a key element for building the reader's financial future. Depending on the services offered by the reader's financial institution, and wireless phone service provider, he or she may be able to execute the following banking transactions from your cell phone, smart phone or electronic tablet: receive text message alerts when his or her account balance reaches a certain low level, or when certain transaction occurs."

Britani—"The reader can also access its bank online to check account balances. He or she can pay bills and transfer funds between accounts; locate his or her bank's closes ATM to where he or she is at a particular time and place. The reader can pay for purchases at stores, and as with a regular telephone landline. He or she can contact the bank to conduct many other transactions, for example to determine whether a particular check has cleared. Lastly, keep all passwords on his or her Smart phone protected and accessible elsewhere in case of emergency."

Safe Electronic Banking

Laura — "My assigned activity is to communicate with the reader on safe electronic banking. It involves making wise choices that will help him or her to avoid costly surprises, frauds or identity theft. To bank safely online use a secure encrypted connection to the internet, ignore, delete, or report fraudulent e-mails asking him or her to send an account number, password or any other personal information via e-mail. Legitimate financial institutions do not ask for any of this information via e-mail. Confirm that the subject online bank is an authorized financial institution. How can you do that? The reader can verify an online financial institution authorization to conduct business in Europe by calling the reader's Country, Department of Financial Institutions, the European Union, Member State agency that regulates operating financial institutions."

Larry — "To maintain a safe electronic banking the reader should monitor account activity closely and keep his or her financial information private. He or she should contact the bank to find out additional precautions it can take with online banking or mobile banking services they offer. Consider using anti-virus software, keep it up to date in order to detect and block spyware and other malicious attacks; use a "firewall" to stop hackers from accessing his or her computer."

Carlos — "My assigned activity is to communicate to the reader the importance of keeping an accurate record of his or her checking account transactions and monthly bank statement. Financial discipline is the key to a solid financial future! In personal banking, the most important issue is recording and keeping an accurate record of all checking account transactions in the reader's check register including deposits, monthly maintenance fees, and interest earned, ATM cash withdrawals, debit card purchases and other bank charges. By keeping an accurate record of the reader's checking account activity, it helps him or her know at all time the exact amount of money he or she has available to spend. Therefore, it would also save money by avoiding unnecessary NSF fees.

Sofia — "Equally important, is how promptly, and accurately the reader reconciles its monthly checking account statement, whether paper format or electronic format. It shows all the checks he or she wrote and cleared the bank. In addition, the statement must show cash withdrawals, ATM or debit card cash withdrawals. Further, the statement shows debit card purchases and fees the bank charges for the stated time. Particularly, the reader should be aware of errors or transactions he or she did not make. If it notices something in error, or have other questions about the reader's bank statement, immediately contact its bank's customer service representative and report the error on the statement."

Juliet — "The content, format, and layout of checking account statements may vary from bank to bank. However, by regulation, checking account statements must show the following elements: bank name and address, the time cover by the statement and the reader's name and address. It must show his or her account number, a list of all transactions by date, a detail of all cashed checks in numerical order; some banks may not offer this feature, In addition, a statement summary including interests earned and fees charged."

Reconciling Your Checking Account

Jacques — "My assigned activity is to communicate to the reader another key issue of personal banking and that is reconciling a checking account, one of the most neglected today caused by financial illiteracy. Further, this is one of the causes of major concerns and financial distress in Europe, and stems from not knowing, having inadequate knowledge or not being timely, to reconcile his or her checking account. Actually reconciling a checking account is a perfect activity for me to talk about with the reader, and the cast, because it is a source of monthly disagreement in my home! My father is a pilot for a French commercial airline Company, he is absent from home at least 17 days each month. My mother is a homemaker, caring for my three brothers, they are six, eight and a ten year old. My mother does volunteer work at a local hospital and is active every day. Each day she checks the mail, and upon arrival places it in a basket.

My mother on Saturdays separates the stack of mail. She separate bills by due date, discards advertisements and places bank statements to the side. When my father gets home, he remains home for a few days and then when he is ready to take off again, he normally asks mother, what is my spendable cash available? She responds, "I think it is €700?" What do you mean by you think?

This statement brings chills to my spine. You think, my father repeats in a loud voice! Starts the argument, about why mother has not reconciled the bank account as the statement arrives, her response is immature at best, and it takes at least two hours of verbal exchange to resolve the same issue repeatedly.

Yesterday, when the bank statement arrived, I picked it up from the basket and asked mother if she would give me some private time to go over something important, she immediately said, "What is it?" I responded, I have been participating as a member of a "think factory" on financial literacy study-play and I would love to share with you what I am learning about reconciling a bank account. My mom was excited, and said let us do it on Saturday! I responded no. That is what I believe is causing my father to be upset every time he is ready to take off. Her faced turn red, as if she was embarrassed, paused for a moment, and said lets go to the office upstairs and do it now. All right, with this example, it will also help the reader, the cast and mother to experience how easy is to reconcile the bank statement."

Benjamin — "First, the reader should have been balancing their check register with every transaction that is the foundation for reconciling the bank statement. Therefore, he or she will know on the spot how much money it has available in the reader's checking account. That is the first issue the reader, and Jacques mother needs to resolve. The reader should keep the check register balanced at all times. When he or she receives a monthly bank statement, reconcile the checking account as promptly as possible, do not wait until some other time as Jacques mother does. When the reader receives its monthly checking account statement, there may be a difference between the statement balance and his or her check register balance. Reconciling the checking account helps the reader to find the exact reasons for the differences."

Catalina — "Based on the facts I am learning regarding personal banking and finance I am going to make it easy to communicate my assigned activity, reconciling the reader's bank account. I will break the process in two parts. First, whenever he or she reconciles a check register, the reader must compare line by line with its monthly checking account statement. In order to do that, I am going to ask the reader to go along with me in performing the following exercise as he or she looks at his or her check register.

Did he or she write all check numbers, ATM cash withdrawals, or debit card purchases and the corresponding transaction dates? Did the reader note a brief description of each transaction, for example, the purpose of the expenditure, books, lunch, movies tickets? Did he or she enter the amount under the column titled: payment/debit (-)? Did the reader enter all deposits under the column titled: deposit/credit

(+)? Did he or she enter a balance on each line with the corresponding transaction?

Did the reader check the math? When each entry is arithmetically correct, then the reader should look at its bank statement, to determine his or her checking account balance (see "New Balance" or "Ending Balance") on the statement. Does this balance match the balance on the reader's check register?"

Albrecht —"To reconcile the two balances and to find out why they are different, the reader should do the following: compare the check register with the monthly checking account bank statement. Does this balance match the balance in the reader's check register? It is unlikely that these balances are the same. To reconcile the two balances, and find out why they are different the reader should do the following: compare the check register with each entry on his or her monthly statement; place a small check mark besides each item in the check register that matches an item on the reader's bank statement. The next step is for him or her to determine if there are any items that are listed on its bank statement that are not in the check register. If so which one, if more than one, add the missing transactions to the reader's check register below the last transaction; calculate the balance by adding all deposits; and deducting all checks issued, cash withdrawals made at the bank, ATM cash withdrawals and debit card purchases. What is the new balance in the reader's check register and does this match the checking account statement balance?"

Nicolaus — "Is the reader finding the account reconciliation process easy? It is not as complicated as I first feared. Next time the statement comes in the mail, I will reconcile the account as promptly as possible. My assigned activity is to explore the second part of the process, using the tool already provided by the reader's bank. Using the reconciliation form provided by the bank, as an integral part of the bank statement to reconcile with the reader's check register, in four easy steps:

First, the reader already has compared the check register with the monthly statement, and placed a check mark besides each transaction listed in the monthly statement. Second, did any deposits shown in the check register are not present in his or her monthly statement? Three, do any withdrawals appear in the check register that are not in his or her monthly statement? If this is the case, the reader should list and total these withdrawals or debits."

Joseph — "It is important to note, that if there are outstanding deposits and withdrawals missing from the check register, he or she should add deposits and deduct withdrawals to the check register. Lastly, to complete the reconciliation form, enter the account balance listed in the monthly checking account statement, add the deposits outstanding from step "two" and calculate the total. Subtract the total of withdrawals outstanding from step "three" and calculate the final total balance. Does this equal the total balance in the check register? If he or she finds errors in the bank statement, contact the bank immediately to have the error corrected. It is a good idea to visit the bank and speak to a customer service representative to report the error, and then follow up in writing stating the name of the account holder, account number, facts, and dollar amount in error, and the date the error recorded in the bank statement. It is important to include any conversations and outcomes with the bank's personnel regarding the reported error, and keep a copy of the correspondence for the record."

Maria — "I am learning that being financially competent also requires the reader to know what to do in the event of a checking account error. The reader should know how to proceed to correct the error, when to document the claim to protect his or her money. Managing a checking account and his or her finances wisely means taking responsibility for his or her money. Always, be sure to obtain all the information the reader needs from the financial institution before opening an account. In addition, he or she should not hesitate to shop around for a better account even after the reader opened an account. Record all transactions in the check register, including electronic ones—debit, automatic payments, ATM cash withdrawals, and debit card purchases. To keep good track of the money, reconcile the account as promptly as possible, so he or she always knows the available cash balance."

Module Summary

The reader has completed the "Earning and Saving," module of this personal banking and financial literacy teaching. He or she has learned about opening and maintaining an accurate checking account, benefits and types of checking accounts, using and reconciling a check register with the monthly bank statement. Equipped with this information the reader is ready to check once again how well he or she has traveled on road to financial competence.

Mastery Learning and Knowledge Check

Mastery learning and knowledge check is an alternative method of teaching, learning and validating the reader's reaching a level of predetermined mastery of personal banking and financial competence units of instruction, before being allowed to progress to the next unit, with a single focus, the reader is becoming financially competent for life. The review of the literature indicates positive effects of mastery learning on students, especially in the areas of achievement, attitudes toward learning, and the retention of content. Therefore, the reader will be focusing his or her attention on responding truthfully to the next fifteen questions, which will continue to enlighten him or her about what makes them act the way they do about money, and how beliefs, values, emotions and reactions affect financial conduct. As recommended before, the reader should write down his or her answers, fifteen correct answers, move on to the next module; seven responses correct, he or she should go back and review those they missed. When the reader masters all fifteen questions, he or she is moving successfully forward to the next level of financial competence.

Knowledge Check Questions

(1) Which of these is a benefit of having a checking account? (A) The reader can pay for things for things over time instead for all at once; (B) Better money management; (C) Lower taxes; or (D) He or she can save money-paying bills by check or online.

(2) When the reader writes a check and the check bounces, the bank charges you a fee what is it called. (A) an ATM fee; (B) a stop payment fee; (C) a minimum balance fee; or (D) an overdraft fee.

(3) Which of the lists below is MOST correct? To open a checking account the reader would need: (A) Photo ID, CIN and money to deposit; (B) Proof of residence, CIN and photo ID; (C) CIN a good credit history, and a deposit; or (D) Photo ID, proof of residence, and good credit history.

(4) Which of the following statements is false? (A)`The check register is a tool to keep track of the account balance. (B) If he or she makes a mistake in the check register and overdraws his or her account, the bank will not charge a fee. (C) The reader should enter all deposits and withdrawals in his or her check register. (D) Checks that the reader has written and not cashed will not show up in the monthly bank statement.

(5) Match the definition with the correct term. Balancing or Reconcile. (A) To determine the difference between the reader's checking account bank statement and its checkbook register. (B) Recording all transactions and maintaining totals so the reader always know how much money is in his or her account.

(6) Which of the following electronic banking activities allows the reader to conduct various transactions or services? (A) Cell phones; (B) Computers; (C) ATM or debit cards; or (D) all of the above.

(7) When using an ATM to withdraw money, which of the following might the reader needs to record in a check register? (A) Withdrawal amount; (B) Interest earned; (C) ATM fees if applicable; or (D) Monthly or annual account fees.

(8) The reader can use a debit card for which of the following: (A) Purchases (B) Cash withdrawals (C) Money transfers (D) Deposits, or (E) All of the above.

(9) Can the reader access electronic banking, and use certain devices to accomplish the following? (A) Use a computer to complete banking transactions (B) Use his or her cell phone to access or receive account information (C) Travel from bank-to-bank to complete transactions, or (D) Make purchases or payments with his or her cell phone.

(10) Overdraft programs are: (A) Free of charge at the bank. (B) These programs are available by banks in the event he or she overdraws the account. (C) Required by law for bank customers to purchase, or (D) An account feature that the reader must pay for only in months when he or she does not keep a minimum balance in the checking account.

(11) Are the following statements true or false? The reader does not need a checking account to have an ATM or debit card (A) True. Debit and ATM cards always work like gift cards at a store—they already have preloaded funds (B) True. Debit cards are like credit cards, and the reader can buy now and pay later (C) False. The reader buys with a debit card or withdraws from the bank with an ATM card is taken directly from his or her checking account (D) False. The reader must have a checking or savings account for funds withdrawal.

(12) Which of the following are ways to add money to the reader's checking account, select all that apply. (A) Direct deposit (B) In-person or ATM deposit (C) By mail, or (D) At any merchant/store.

(13) What is the first thing the reader should do before withdrawing money from his or her checking account? (A) Make sure he or she has enough money in its account (B) Complete or fill out the check correctly (C) Record the transaction in the reader's check register, or (D) Know its debit card PIN.

(14) Select all that apply. In comparing the check register with his or her monthly bank statement, the reader notices a discrepancy; he or she listed a deposit of €30,00 and the bank listed a deposit on the statement

as €35,00. Should the reader just make it €35,00 in its check register, or (A) Call the bank (B) Check the reader's deposit receipt, or (C) Add €5,00 somewhere in the check register.

(15) When using an ATM (A) The reader can deposit or withdraw money into or from his or her checking account (B) He or she can transfer money from its savings account (C) The reader must have a PIN to deposit or withdraw money, or (D) All of the above.

Financial Progress with a Sense of Success

The reader may be familiar with the psychological boosts that well groom produces. For example, a woman enters a beauty salon to be "made over," she leaves the salon with the impression that she is more beautiful and a better person. A man seeking a better job, for the initial interview, buys a new suit in the image of the better self he envisions upon securing the job. The same phenomenon is at work when the reader enhances a sense of financial well-being. These examples demonstrate that once the reader sees he or she can improve on his or her financial knowledge and discipline, and on earning and saving, the reader can no longer accept an old image of self. He or she knows how well it can do when the reader invests the time and effort to depart from the old financial habits and adopt the new. It is profitable and fun.

Financial progress is a constant practice in an atmosphere of success; the reader is going to practice that excessively. He or she will continue to learn to organize financial development in such a way that, at the end of each successive module, the reader will be successful at what he or she sets out to do. The reader will be subconsciously applying financial discipline, earning and saving to all financial decisions. There is no reason to be discouraged, because at this point the reader considers him or herself in a poor financial situation. The reader will notice that increments of improvement are invariably significant at the beginning of his or her effort. Financial discipline, earning and saving will become a conscious effort as the reader practices and applies these concepts to its every day financial transactions. The minute the reader stop believing he or she loses the motive to take action, and action is what transforms the reader into a financially competent person.

Not all the financial models and methods of the world to become financially competent are going to help if the reader cannot bring itself to begin. The reader might be familiar with the work avoidance phenomenon. It begins with he or she needs time to "get prepared" one tells oneself, and so wastes hours in the process. "Getting myself together" is a way of avoiding work. The reader may convince him or herself that he or she does not have enough money in the bank or immediately available access to cash, to solve the problem. Before he or she knows it, the reader has wasted the time it has set aside to work on the problem. The work avoidance phenomenon is a rational and understandable process. However, it becomes costly when adopted as a way of being.

This experience usually surfaces when the reader is about to pay some bills, or do something uncomfortable. Either he or she has never done it before, or the reader does not feel financially competent to succeed. So he or she concentrates on dreading, not doing. The solution is a simple one. Begin doing something that is relevant to the financial task, but does not involve any risk. For example checking the available cash balance.

To commit to an idea, for most people, is not easy thing to do. As Leonard Glass, tell his students in his writing courses: "Writing is easy. It is thinking that is hard. It is not what you write but what you think that is tough to come to term with."

Producing immediate order from chaos in the reader's financial situation at this point involves the exact same procedure as training for a championship. When he or she finds working under duress, it is usually because the reader has talked him or herself into trying to do several things at once. If the reader has a horrendous work load his or her blood pressure is up, his or her heart is pounding, he or she is tense and mentally confused, and the reader would like to run away, it is time for a financial coaching strategy session with his or herself.

First, stop everything and wait for a moment. Relax, sit down with his or her back straight and place feet flat on the ground to lower his or her blood pressure "I learn this tactic from, Hideo Mitarai, a Japanese master, my martial arts instructor, for over 25 years — who is today alive and well.—said Alvin Stevens" Then, determine the reader's top financial priority task. Turn to it and set the others aside. He or she is not going to be able to correct his or her financial situation all at once, but the main tasks are execute well—one at a time.

When the reader confronts a threatening financial situation, unemployment, medical emergency, auto accident, or mortgage past due, the tendency is to bring all his or her resources to bear. He or she feels the need to be as forceful as possible, try to marshal every possible ally—legal, financial, moral or spiritual—that can be effective against the foe. However, excessive response is not efficient. Whenever the reader is exasperated enough to respond, him or she grabs at every argument the reader has. However, after a good night's sleep, he or she can see the better effect of one argument simply stated.

Remember to separate thinking from doing. There is something sad to most of us in the spectacle of the super coach sending plays into the game. The athlete becomes the instrument of the coach's intelligence, nothing more. The truth is that those coaches who send in plays are right by eliminating the need of the player to think; they are simplifying the players' task and improving their performance prospects.

When it comes to financial performance, the preliminary mental factors — how much available cash does the reader has to resolve the first task, where is it, how fast can he or she accesses it — should be out of the way before an action begins. To be a maximal financial performer, the reader should refine his or her focus. Think when the reader has need to, and do when he or she needs to, nevertheless make it a financial rule to keep thinking and doing separate.

Earning and saving is about the intelligent use of money, weather the reader is selecting the type of account to best suit his or her needs, he or she can always save money, and this is the foundation of a financial future.

Chapter 10

Investing and Spending

Investing and spending what the reader has saved is the foundation of his or her financial future. The purpose of this CashMax³ module is not to render financial advice nor promote any particular financial product. It is a personal banking and financial education text that will show the reader and cast participants, how to lay the foundation to create his or her financial goals; and manage money by preparing a personal spending plan; identifying ways to decrease spending, increase income and realize savings. One of the first steps to financial security is planning and following through on a personal spending plan. Setting and meeting financial goals is about — choosing how to spend wisely, save and invest the reader's money.

Module objectives are to build upon financial discipline, earning and saving concepts. After completing this module, the reader will be able to understand how emotions influence the resulting financial decision-making. He or she should be able to identify and track his or her daily spending habits. In addition, to preparing a personal spending plan; estimate monthly income and expenses; identifying ways to decrease spending and increase income and savings. Further, the reader will easily recognize various tools that will help him or her manage money. By now, the reader should be in a position to determine truthfully what he or she knows about investing and spending, and his or her financial future, he or she will be prepared to learn how to set financial goals. The reader should consider moving forward with an open mind, because he or she could already know the answer to some of the question asked, he or she might be unsure about the exact application of some of the responses to these questions, or possibly unable to answer a question with a correct response.

Pre-learning

To help the reader in continuing self-evaluation he or she should be following the same interactive format applied to previous modules, using the question and answer format assigned to the cast to apply the correct responses to his or her particular financial condition. The format continues to build upon his or her accumulated knowledge to this point. In addition, this interactive method promotes a greater understanding and application of purposeful thinking about money. Further, it will bring the reader a step closer to a personal financial reality — to understand how his or her emotions trigger financial decision-making and resulting consequences.

Let it roll on again ... to action!

Alexander—"What is required to establish a viable financial goal: (a) **Realistic** (b) **Aligned with a timeline** and (c) **Organized by milestones**, or (d) Open ended?"

Margaret — "The answers are: "a" "b." and "c."

Carlos — "The main reason that is helpful to track daily spending habits is to: (a) Enter them on a computer spread sheet; (b) **Know exactly how your money is spent;** (c) Increase your income and savings, or (d) Decrease your spending."

Jacques — "The correct answer is: Know exactly how your money is spent or "b."

Benjamin — "Before the reader prepares a spending plan, the two most important things he or she must know are: (a) **Total income and**

expenses; (b) Its car payment; (c) How to plan for savings and food, or (d) What the reader spends on its phone bill."

Catalina — "Total income and expenses is my answer."

Albrecht — "Which of the following would the reader classifies as flexible expenses? (a) Car payment; (b) Auto insurance; (c) **Cell phone bill;** or (d) **Personal expenses.**"

Nicolaus — "My final answer is "c" and "d."

Joseph — "Which of the following would the reader consider examples of fixed expenses? Select all that apply: (a) **Car payment** (b) **Auto insurance** (c) Cell phone bill, or (d) Personal expenses."

Maria — "The correct answer is "a" and "b."

Louis — "Would the reader adopt a habit of paying him or herself first? On his or her work sheets, would the reader list savings as: (a) **A fixed expense** (b) Income (c) Entertainment, or (d) Flexible expense."

Juliet – "The reader should list this expense as a fixed expense."

Britani — "Increasing cash flow means: (a) The reader should find a part-time job to kill free time (b) Getting more money from an ATM (c) Borrowing money from a family member, or (d) **Lowering his or her expenses, so it will have more money at the end of the month."**

Larry – "The answer is lowering his or her expenses, so the reader will have extra money at the end of the month."

Laura — "From the following statement select the "pay-packet" deductions: (a) taxes (b) employee social security, (c) health and pension insurance, or (d) **All of the above."**

Alexander -- "The response is all of the above."

Margaret —"On a typical "pay-packet" counterfoil, net pay amount sometimes referred as take home pay, it is often less than: (a) Total Social Security deductions (b) **Gross pay** (c) Overtime hours, or (d) Bonus pay."

Carlos – "Net pay is always less than the amount of gross pay, or "b."

Sofia — "The following assigned example illustrates this concept. If the reader earns €12,00 an hour at a part-time job and he or she works 16 hours a week, his or her take-home "pay-packet" for that week will likely be: (a) Exactly €192. (b) Slightly more than €192,00 (c) **Less than €192,00, or** (d) automatically deposited."

Jacques – "The reader will take-home for that week, as pay less than €192,00 due to deductions."

Bejamin — "When the reader finds him or herself having trouble paying his or her bills he or she should first: (a) Increase the limit on one or more of his or her credit cards; (b) Talk to a payday lender to get some extra cash. Or (c) **Talk to his or her parents, or a friend (d) Call its creditors and explain the reader situation (e) Ask for an extension of time to pay** or perhaps (f) Stop all payments."

Catalina – "The appropriate responses are: "c," "d" and "e".

Albrecht — "My assignment is to remind the reader and the cast that if anyone has experience or knowledge on specific aspects of the material in progress that he or she sees it will benefit others, talk over his or her ideas with its peers and friends. One of the best ways to master learning is to learn from each other. The reader might be aware of some method that has worked well for him or her, as well as possible some pitfalls to avoid. For example, the reader might know of available software to reconcile a bank statement. The cast, reader, a peer, or a friend contribution to the reader knowledge base will enhance his or her learning experience. Therefore, if some of the content or questions are not clear, the reader should return to the subject in question and carefully read, and read again, until he or she can ascertain that the reader knows the subject. That is mastery learning."

Taking Control and Financial Condition

Nicolaus — "Taking control of a financial condition at any time, requires the reader to make a decision to implement and put to test the core concepts he or she is learning in this book, financial discipline, earning and saving and investing and spending. A good way to start is to develop a personal spending plan for immediate use and test. What is a personal spending plan?"

Joseph — "A personal spending plan is a step-by-step guide for meeting expenses in a given time period and is the key element to setting financial goals. The spending plan will help the reader to define what he or she wants to do with his or her money in terms of obtainable goals within a near future. In addition, this plan will give the reader a sense of financial security and peace of mind. He or she will benefit from preparing, and following a spending plan with using money wisely now and save where he or she can to meet defined goals."

Maria — "My assigned activity is to introduce the reader to the intelligent use of money by showing an application of this concept. First, consider his or her personal goals when creating a spending plan. For example, if the reader needs to buy a car, consider reducing the cellular phone bill and use the extra money to put in his or her savings account, until he or she has accumulated the price of the down payment he or she is willing to pay for the car him or her needs. If the reader wants to buy a new dress, consider working some overtime at his or her job to satisfy this desire or want."

Juliet — "No matter what goals the reader has for his or her money, a credible and sustainable spending plan must meet five key characteristics:

Be realistic. For example, if the reader is working part-time, it is not possible to afford a new car every two years.

Be specific. For example, the reader wants to save €5,000 for a down payment to buy a Fiat that the total cost will not exceed €13,000 including tax, license and first year full cover insurance.

Specify a period. For example, the reader wants to pay off his or her credit card balance within twelve months. The first action the reader should take is to determine the exact amount he or she needs to set aside for this purpose. Second, direct his or her bank that on the date the reader receives his or her direct deposit from the reader employer, to transfer the specified amount from the reader checking to a savings account. In addition, these savings are committed exclusively for paying off the credit card before spending any funds for other obligations.

Have milestones. For example, the reader establishes a goal to purchase a motorcycle that costs €1.800,00 by paying for it without borrowing money. To do so, he or she will ask his or her employer to direct deposit €50,00 from each of the reader "pay-packet", and direct deposit it into a savings account he or she sets up specifically to purchase this motorcycle.

Have a measure progress. The reader should measure his or her savings account progress to determine how much money he or she has saved to meet his or her spending plan of purchasing a motorcycle."

Britani — "My assignment is to communicate to the reader and members of the cast the elements of preparing a spending plan. A spending plan is about personal choices, it is also about financial discipline, saving and using his or her money wisely. Knowing what the reader income is and what expenses are every month should help him or her to take control of his or her current financial condition. In addition, knowing these facts are the key to specific financial goals the reader sets. There are four key steps to prepare a personal spending plan: (1) the reader should keep track of daily spending. (2) He or she should determine what his or her monthly income is and expenses are one month before they are due. (3) The reader should find ways to decrease spending; and (4) he or she find ways to increase income."

Laura — "My responsibility is showing the reader how to formulate and keep track of his or her daily spending. However, to place the subject in context, he or she should first consider the following questions: Does the reader know exactly where money goes each moth? What did he or she buy? Can the reader list everything exactly? Has he or she ever spent money however, it could not remember what he or she bought. What the difference between a "need" and a "want" is? In addition, can a want be a need?"

Alexander – "Needs are expenses that are absolutely necessary. For example, the reader needs food, housing, utilities and transportation."

Margaret—"Wants are optional purchases. For example, eating out, buying movie tickets, driving around with friends in a car without purpose; waiting in line at three in the morning in front of a store until noon when the store open – to buy the next Smartphone because all my friends already have it."

Carlos — "Sometimes a need can be both a need and a want. For example, the reader needs to eat. However, he or she could elect to pack lunch instead of eating out at a restaurant, bar or fast food place every day."

Sofia — "It is common for people to spend all the money they make and not have anything left over to save for their goals."

Laura — "The following is my story of a summer trip to Disneyland Paris. It will show to the reader the concept of distinguishing between needs and wants. The reader should abstain from taking any notes. Because at the end of the story there will be questions asked that would make a life- long difference to his or her perception of the distinction between these two key concepts. The following is the scenario. The reader assignment is to go with me to Disneyland Paris as a financial behavioral observer. He or she is to determine how it is possible to spend all the money, and not knowing exactly how it spent, nor having anything, left over."

This is what happened. My husband Larry and I took our daughters, the twins, Jenny and Joyce, to Disneyland Paris. Before we entered the gate, I checked my wallet. I had the entrance tickets and €400,00 cash. We bought the twins matching Mickey Mouse hats; then we ate pizza, sodas, and pretzels, watched old movies, and enjoyed most of the rides.

We stopped at the gift shop, and bought one "buy one – get one free" T-shirts; then we headed next to the music store for a "buy three – get one free" sale on compact discs (CDs). Jenny bought six CDs and Joyce bought a Disney sketchbook. Joyce asked Larry for money to surprise me with a Mickey Mouse wristwatch, which she gave to Larry to keep. Then Jenny and Joyce headed to the gift card store, to buy five post cards and stamps to send to my mother and father, and to Larry's brothers and sisters. I bought a pair of sneakers because my feet were killing me and I decided to wear these for comfort.

Soon, the park is about to close, it is midnight. All of us are tired from walking around since nine in the morning. The ride to the parking lot was free, but at the exit gate, an attendant extended his hand for €10,00 the cost of parking. I checked my wallet and had €5,00 left! Larry had given his only €50,00 to Joyce. How did that happen? Where did the €450,00 go?"

Alexander — "Without reading Laura's story over again, the reader should write down from memory an exact list of how Laura and her family spent €450,00. Then, compare his or her list with the facts. If the reader wants to be in control of his or her money, he or she should understand, and know exactly where the money goes at all times. One way to do this is to keep a personal spending diary, to record everything the reader spends. It is particularly important to track the money he or she spends on optional purchases or "wants," for example, eating out, stopping for coffee and conversation with friends at the local bar, and money spent on entertainment."

Activity 1: Tracking Daily Spending

Margaret—"My assigned activity is to show the reader and cast how to formulate a daily spending diary. By diligently following the plan, the reader will realize the enormous benefits to keep focus on gaining financial competence. This information is an important application of the central concept of this book, financial discipline. It will help the reader to determine what spending the reader can eliminate, or cut back in order to have money to meet monthly financial obligations. For example, pay his or her bills on time to save for personal goals. The reader may know some people who have a spending plan and without distress meet their monthly obligations. He or she might also know some people that constantly are distressed over monthly bills."

Carlos — "My assigned activity is to show the cast and communicate to the reader a way of living within means, and to have money to meet his or her financial goals, these may be to buy the things he or she needs, and to look forward to enjoying those things the reader might want. The reader should take a few minutes and write down everything him, or she spent money on yesterday, and today. What he or she anticipates spending money on tomorrow? With this detailed list, the reader has the baseline information to begin a daily spending diary. For seven days, he or she should keep a daily record of each purchase it makes. Because of this exercise, the reader can formulate a usual and habitual daily spending diary. At the same time, this information will serve him or her as a good indicator where he or she can eliminate or cut back on spending in order to experience saving for a financial future."

Activity 2: Monthly Income and Expenses

Sofia — "The reader next step is complete preparing a personal spending plan. He or she needs to determine a monthly income and expenses. Income is money that the reader receives from his or her job, gratuities, payment for services, allowance, spousal support, or government benefits, interest, dividends and any other source of cash. Expenses are the items the reader spends money on each month such as rent, food, utilities, cable, cell phone, gasoline, car payments, auto insurance, clothes, personal grooming, gym membership, entertainment, eating out and music down loads, to name a few."

Juliet — "After exchanging views with my peers on the cast, about preparing my personal spending plan, I took a lined sheet of paper and titled it "Juliet Monthly Income and Expenses Work Sheet." Then, I divided the sheet into two parts. On the left side, a detailed of my monthly income, hospital salary €1.900, child support and spousal support €1.120, and then added these up to determine my total monthly income €3.020. On the right side of the sheet, I wrote a detail of my monthly expenses: house mortgage payment €1.000; savings €200; utilities including cell phone €180; food €400; personal grooming for my two children and me €150; gasoline €120; clothing allocation $70; school supplies $40; and entertainment € $150. Then I wrote a subtotal of €2.310.

Next, I wrote down my yearly expenses. Property taxes per year €700; Home insurance €490; Auto insurance €600; Auto license €80; Allowance for car maintenance and repairs €$500. In addition, I added my charitable contributions €300. These yearly expenses added to a total €2.670.

To project my monthly expenses, all-inclusive, I added the monthly to yearly expenses (2.310+2.670=€4.980), and apportioned my yearly expenses into twelve months (4.980/12=€415). Then, added this total, as a monthly allocation setting it aside for those expenses payable once each year. To separate the two classes of expenses, I am depositing each month (€415) into a separate savings account to pay for those yearly expenses on the dates due. Therefore, my personal spending plan on a monthly basis is (2.310+415=€2.725).

The difference between my total net income and expenses is (3.020-2.725=€295). This is the amount I put in savings every month setting aside 50% to pay for a down payment of a new car in three years; and the other 50% is set aside for pre-retirement or available as a contingency to meet an emergency."

Expense Classification and Payment Scheduling

Laura — "My responsibility is to show the cast and communicate with the reader how he or she should distinguish and classify expenses. This classification is important to his or her financial decision-making process. It will give the reader the option to maximize earning and saving, by scheduling payments according to calendar dates that meets both his and her income deposit dates, and expense disbursements.

Therefore, there are two solid concepts the reader should master about expenses. One is to know that fixed expenses do not change from month to month. Two, flexible or variable expenses might change from time to time. For example, electricity may be higher in summer, due to a greater use of the air conditioner or the heating bill might be higher during the winter months due to colder temperatures."

Larry — "In the example given by Juliet, she listed some of her expenses as house payments, property taxes, home insurance, auto insurance, and "savings" as fixed expenses. This is because the reader should get into the habit of paying him or her first, by putting away first, the money the reader wants to set aside for his or her goals. The most effective way to achieve this objective is for the reader to authorize the bank to automatically withdrawn from his or her checking account and put into a savings or an investment account. He or she might consider joining a pre-retirement plan at work that deducts money from his or her "pay-packet". Alternatively, deposit his or her pre-retirement savings. This is the first thing the reader should do when he or she is paid. Therefore, the money the reader does not see he or she does not miss."

Juliet — "In my particular case I am setting aside specific amounts (200 + 415 =€615) each month from my "pay-packet" towards savings, meeting an emergency and to reach a personal goal to have the down payment and buy a new car in three years. This amount may not work for the reader, however, the core concept is to save, and save for a personal goal at a rate that is appropriate for him or her. In addition, I listed some expenses as flexible or variable expenses, which might change from time to time. For example, flexible expenses include entertainment (€150), utilities, including cell phone bill (€180) and gasoline (€120)."

Laura—"Now using this example, "Juliet Monthly Income and Expenses Work Sheet," the reader should add up fixed and flexible expense column. Compare his or her income and expense totals. Is there enough money to pay the bills each month? The reader should consider putting bonuses and raises towards savings and make savings a habit. It is not difficult, once he or she begins. Revisit its spending plan every three months to be sure the reader is on track. Income and expenses change over time."

Gross Income versus Net Income

Britani — "In light of my personal experience I have the responsibility to share with the cast and the reader, how important it is to distinguish between gross income and net income when preparing his or her personal spending plans. My experience is unique in this regard. When I first started working, I was 17 years of age. At that time, I had the notion I knew everything about all things. My first job was at a motorcycle parts retail store in Riga, Latvia. I was excited being there because I knew about motorcycles; I fixed my own and those of my friends.

The day I received my first "pay-packet," I expected to see €160,00 for my part-time work. When I opened the "pay-packet" envelope and saw my "pay-packet" for €121,00 I was mad, but did not say anything. When I arrived home, I wrote a letter to the owner of the store, telling him off and clearly, that if he was going to cheat me out of €39,00 on my first payday, I might have to reconsider working at the store, even though I liked the job very much. The following day, shortly after I delivered the letter to the main office, Mr. Ullmanis, the owner of the store, called me into his office and said, "Britani, as much as I appreciated your candid letter, I believe you may not know the difference between gross income and net income." What do you mean? I was already embarrassed.

Gross income, said Mr. Ullmanis, is what I offered you as pay, €160,00 per month and you accepted. Net income is the gross pay, minus deductions of €39,00 from you "pay-packet". These deductions include Member State income taxes, social security contributions, pension contributions and your partial contribution to your health insurance. The math looks like this: (160-39 = €121)."

I humbly replied, "Well Mr. Ullmanis, would you please excuse me and tear up my letter. I feel that I really do not know much about many things. This early in life experience taught me to ask my future employers about work place benefits. In particular, once you start working, it pays to find out if your employer offers a pre-retirement savings program. Many employers will match a portion of your pre-retirement savings contributions. In addition, the reader would most likely pay less taxes. Not participating in the pre-retirement savings program is like leaving free money on the table."

Understanding Net Income

Sofia — "My assigned activity is to bring to the cast and reader attention the importance of not counting on his or her gross income as the cash available to meet financial needs. This is good for me to talk about because until now, I did not have a good understanding of how significant it was to read my "pay-packet" counterfoil. I did not have a clear idea where deductions went until I became part of the think factory. This may sound like a poor excuse, because my employer pays me by direct deposit to my checking account. I receive in the mail, a non-negotiable copy of my "pay-packet" with a detailed listing of all deductions. Then, I know I have my money in the bank.

Therefore, why worry about reading the "pay-packet" counterfoil? Now that I am participating as a member of this cast, I am learning to become financially competent. I can clearly see that financial illiteracy has cost me a great deal of money. How that is, the reader may ask. I discovered last week, that my employer has since the company's inception, established a pre-retirement savings plan for all its permanent employees. The company matches 100% of whatever amount one saves up to €1.000,00 per month, how much did I lose due to financial illiteracy? Let me tell the cast and the reader, I have been saving €173,00 each month for my pre-retirement for the last seventeen months, since I started working at this company.

Therefore, had I asked my employer to enroll me in the pre-retirement savings plan after I became a permanent employee, I would have accumulated (173 X 17 = €2.941) of my own savings, plus €2.941

from my employer matching fund.

By now I would have saved to my own pre-retirement account the sum of (2.941,00 + 2.941,00 = €5.882). If I had the knowledge and application of personal banking and financial literacy, it would have helped me to earn €2.941,00 without any investment of my own."

Activity 3: Ways to Decrease Spending

Alexander — "There are simple ways to decrease spending, as there are myths and facts associated with this activity. I am learning that decreasing spending always increases the cash available to the reader checking account, or "increasing cash flow." What are some of the ways the reader can decrease its spending?"

The following are seven key suggestions the reader should consider for decreasing spending. (1) Carry only small amounts of cash in his wallet or her purse and limit spending to this amount (2) Avoid or limit the use of credit cards. (3) Avoid shopping without a purpose. (4) Take his or her written savings notes as a reminder when going shopping. (5) Determine whether the intended purchase is something, he or she needs or simply something it wants. (6) Limit what the reader plans to buy to what he or she needs. Lastly, (7) pay his or her bills on time to avoid late fees and extra finance charges."

Margaret—"I am assigned the activity to share with the cast and communicate to the reader some of the myths and facts on ways to decrease spending.

Myth, direct deposit is expensive.

Fact, most banks and credit institutions do not charge the reader to sign up for direct deposit. In truth, they may waive his or her checking account fees if the reader has a direct deposit.

Myth, people who do not have a bank account should not consider direct deposit.

Fact, if the reader has not yet signed up for a checking account, he or she may call the European Union Financial Services Directorate. Alternatively he or she may contact the country of residence Financial Services Scheme for help finding a financial institution in the reader country of residence that offers low or no cost checking accounts."

Activity 4: Ways to Increase Income

Carlos — "Other than finding a job or a job that pays more, the reader should consider increasing his or her income by selling some of his or her belongings or assets that the reader no longer uses or wants. For example, CDs, sporting equipment; use his or her talent or hobby to increase income, for example, writing, playing music or making things he or she can sell; explore what tax credits the reader may qualify for to increase income. In addition, investments are another source to increase the reader income."

Sofia—"I am to share with the cast and communicate with the reader, about some of the planning tools I am learning that will help him or her to keep spending and saving records. With these tools, the reader can easily put into action in a personal spending plan. The key tools are the monthly payment schedule and monthly payment calendar. The monthly payment schedule helps the reader plan in advance when he or she will pay bills. It allows the reader to record in advance specific dates when he or she will receive income to pay those bills. An integral part of financial discipline is to be able to formulate and create each document the reader needs, using simple tools, such as a note pad and pen. Once he or she has mastered this concept, the reader might want to use a computer program such as Microsoft Excel, Quicken books or other similar computer software."

Jacques—"I am learning to formulate and create a payment schedule. The reader should consider taking a note pad, turn it horizontally, and on top of the page write the title: "Payment Schedule – Month 1". Below the title from left to right divide the sheet into five columns and title each column from left to right; Income; Expenses/Bills; Date Income Received or Expense Due Date; Amount (€) Due; and Date Paid."

Catalina — "Now that the reader has formulated and created the skeleton of this document, he or she might proceed to fill in the pertinent information. For example, under the "Income" column he or she might write from top to bottom, net pay, tips, allowance, student loan allocation, child support, or alimony. Then, under the column "Date income received or expenses due date" enter the date his or her employer makes a direct deposit to the reader checking account, or when he or she receives a paper "pay-packet", tips, student loan allocation, child support or alimony; then move directly across to the column "Amount Due" and enter each corresponding amount. The reader should follow the same rationale to schedule payment of expenses. Under the column "Expenses/Bills; list savings, and then below it each bill due during Month 1. Extend the corresponding "Expense Due Date." Then, the "Amount Due" and "Date Paid."

Albrecht — "I noted that Catalina listed "Savings" first on the list of expense. Why should the reader savings due date be before other expenses? When able to save, the reader should always put its money in the savings account before he or she pays the bills and spends money for the month. Otherwise, he or she may not be able to accomplish savings goals."

Nicolaus — "The reader should assign early due dates to food, transportation, and other essential personal expenses, because he or she needs money for these survival necessities throughout the month. Therefore, it is important to set aside the money early, and spend it wisely, so it will last during the entire month. If he or she does this, he or she will live within means and avoid distress."

Joseph — "My assignment is to share with the cast and communicate to the reader regarding the use and application of the monthly payment calendar tool. However, it is most important to know that communicating and understanding information responds to three human characteristics. Some people understand more by reading, others by hearing, and others by seeing. Therefore, the monthly payment calendar tool is most valuable for people that need to see to understand and act on information. The reader needs to see the available cash balance in his or her check register, and seeing the due dates for payment of expenses or bills. With this information, all the reader needs to do is transfer the same data from its "Payment Schedule" to a visual calendar where he or she can see the entire month at a glance. This tool will facilitate acting on it, and meeting financial obligations due dates on time."

Laura — "Based on the information and knowledge accumulated from my participation as a member of the think factory, and cast, and personal experience over my married life, my assignment is to communicate with the reader about what payments he or she should consider to make first if the reader does not have enough money to pay all bills. I realize now that part of my interest in accepting the invitation to be a member of these focus groups was some distressful memories of seven years ago. Larry was unemployed for over nine months. As a result, we ran out of savings, available credit, and willing-to-help friends. Our financial situation was near desperation. One friend recommended we declare bankruptcy, another that we give up our house and rent an apartment, a third, that I have a talk with our parents. I would make these payments first, if I do not have enough money to pay my bills, food, mortgage or rent, utilities and transportation, other expenses or bills such as credit cards, telephone and cable would be secondary priorities."

Larry — "If the reader personal spending plan shows that it has more expenses than income, there are ways to get out of trouble. However, everyone has different priorities. There are at least three things he or she may want to consider doing; talk with a parent or an adult friend he or she trusts, let them know the truth about the reader financial situation; let them know that his or her bills exceed the money he or she is bringing in. Ask them for an independent view of the reader situation. He or she might be able to work together to identify ways to increase income, reduce expenses and accordingly adjust his or her spending plan."

Catalina—"I was in similar situation when began dentistry school, in addition of being financially illiterate my expenses exceeded my income. I arrived to San Diego, California from Coimbra, Portugal, with a master degree in dentistry. My first job in the U.S. was that of a dental assistant near the university, I bought a used car, invested most of my available cash, and four months into ownership the engine burned. The memories of this experience have increased my awareness and hope will contribute to the reader understanding in knowing what to do when facing a situation like mine. The reader should consider, first, pay the necessary expenses, for example, he or she might rely on its vehicle to get to and from your part-time job. Since this job is likely the biggest source of income, losing the car may result in also losing the job – worsening your situation. In this respect, staying current with your car payments would become a priority.

Second, the reader should pay off his or her credit cards with the lower balance first, thus clearing that debt, and eliminating monthly interest. This action may lead to reduce total credit card interest. In addition, may also give the reader a sense of accomplishment of paying off a debt. Third, contact creditors, as soon as the reader identifies the problem or he or she thinks it will have a problem making a payment. It is in the best financial interest of the creditor to accommodate the reader needs to reduce the risk of potentially losing a client and the money. The creditor may be willing to reduce his or her payments or change the terms of credit to accommodate the situation. Some creditors might offer extensions, accept smaller payments over a longer period, or accept partial payments."

Module Summary

The reader has completed the CashMax³ module on investing and spending of this personal banking and financial literacy teaching. The reader has learned about how to save for his or her future, how to track money each day, so he or she knows exactly where money is spent. In addition, the reader is equipped with the knowledge to prepare a personal spending plan, estimate income and expenses so the reader does not run out of money at the end of the month. He or she also learned ways to decrease spending and increase income to optimize the intelligent use of money. With this information the reader is ready to check once again how well he or she has traveled on the personal road to financial competence.

Knowledge Check Questions

(1) What are the elements the reader should consider when setting a financial goal, select all that apply: (A) Specific information (B) Milestones (C) Plan of action, (D) Items he or she wants to purchase, or (E) All of the above.

(2) What benefits the reader can experience by tracking daily spending habits, (A) Reducing deductions from your "pay-packet" (B) Working more hours (C) Purchasing a large number of items, or (D) Understanding how his or her money is spent.

(3) The reader cannot prepare a personal spending plan without first knowing these two things, (A) His or her income and expenses (B) Reader address and zip code (C) His or her overtime hours and vacation time, or (D) Savings account's interest rate and fees.

(4) Select all the flexible expense items from this list, (A) Personal expenses (B) Monthly car expenses (C) Cell phone bill; or (D) Savings.

(5) Select all of the fixed expense items from this list, (A) Monthly cable and cell phone bills (B) Savings (C) Personal expenses, or (D) Monthly car payment.

(6) The reader can pay him or her first by listing this item as flexible expense in its worksheet, (A) Clothing expenses (B) Entertainment costs (C) Savings, or (D) Tuition fees.

(7) To increase the reader cash flow him or her should, (A) Agree to work no fewer than four hours overtime each week (B) Lower expenses and increase the amount of money the reader has at the end of the month. Alternatively, the reader can, (C) Double the amount of cash he or she

is able to access from ATMs, or (D) Arrange for his or her employer to pay the reader twice a week instead of once a week.

(8) When the reader sees the word "Deductions" on its "pay-packet", it refers to payments made for, (A) Income taxes (B) Political contribution, (C) Social Security, or (D) European Union Income tax.

(9) Social Security benefits do not include, (A) Pre-retirement benefits (B) Employer funded-pension plans (C) Survivor benefits, or (D) Disability benefits.

(10) Gross pay on the reader "pay-packet" counterfoil is usually the larger amount when compared to what other items, select all that apply, (A) Year to-date earnings (B) Income tax deductions (C) Net pay, or (d) Deductions.

(11) If the reader works ten hours in one week at a part-time job, and earn €8 per hour his or her take home pay for that week will be (A) Slightly more than €80. (B) Withheld until the reader earns at least €100. (C) Less than €80 due to deductions, or (€) exactly $80.

(12) If the reader is having trouble paying bills he or she should consider, (A) Talking to a parent or trusted friend (B) Asking a close friend to loan him or her money (C) Stop paying until the reader has enough money to continue, or (D) Applying for at least one additional credit card.

Life Insurance Story

Catalina — "I have the opportunity to end this chapter with a life insurance story that will show the cast and the reader the benefits of considering buying his or her pre-retirement as early in life as possible. My story will be relevant to the knowledge questions. I spent three weeks in Sarno, Italy on vacation, visiting my brother Tomas who is excitingly waiting for his wife Lucia to give birth to twins. Tomas told me that he figured he had to buy some insurance when he learned that Lucia was having twins. He wants to insure his family security and ensure that his mortgage and payment for private college tuition would be paid should he died early. He understood that he had to jump on it. "I knew the longer I waited, the more expensive it would be," Tomas said.

I was happy for Tomas and the best decision he made was to call a reputable insurance agent to discuss his options and select the best insurance product for his situation. Tomas' visit with Gilbert Claure, the insurance agent, resulted on purchasing a life insurance policy. This policy cost less than he expected. "I was really surprised life insurance may be more affordable than I thought," Tomas told me. He also said that age is probably the most important factor in determining cost. Youth is generally an advantage, for example, "for you Tomas, the insurance agent said, at age 30 you would pay €400, per year. However, your brother Gino at 50 would be closer to €1.500."

Sofia—"Based on this information from Catalina, Lucia and the twins would be depending on Tomas income, for this reason he decided to buy his insurance policy early. Tomas is turning 27 next week. Therefore, as I understood, if the reader purchases an insurance policy when he or she is young and healthy, then the most important thing is to consider locking in the low rate for as long as possible. A comparable whole life or universal life insurance might go longer."

Laura — "As shared by Catalina, her brother Tomas is a diligent researcher. He found the correct information on time to discussed with Lucia, and give her a sense of peace. She also shared with me that "staying healthy is generally the second most important issue insurers consider when they set premiums." Most companies will charge smokers and the obese more. Rates also increase for those with other health conditions such as high blood pressure, heart disease, or diabetes. However, the way I understood if the reader can show that he or she take care of itself – by maintaining a healthy diet or exercise routine – most insures will keep the reader premium low. I see this life-story as a good example of an early investment in your financial future."

Chapter 11

Pre-retirement and Pensions

This CashMax[3] module will teach the reader more of what he or she already knows the reader knows it is smart to save money for those big-ticket items he or she really wants to buy a boat or a home. Yet the reader may not realize that probably the most expensive item he or she will ever buy in its lifetime is pre-retirement! Perhaps the reader has never thought of "buying" his or her pre-retirement, especially if the reader is a student, a Millennial or an adult who is not remotely near national pensionable age. Yet that is exactly what the reader does when he or she sets money aside into a pre-retirement savings account for future expenses or emergencies. He or she is paying today for the cost of his or her pre-retirement and enhanced pension tomorrow.

The information in this chapter is intended to help the reader understand the general concepts and issues on pre-retirement and pensions as applied to his or her personal banking and finances. This knowledge does not constitute tax or legal advice. Before considering any type of investment the reader should seek the qualify advice of a tax or investment advisor, licensed by the appropriate authorities in the reader's country of residence and the European Union.

The cost living on pre-retirement future years is becoming more expensive for most Europeans for three reasons. First, the reader lives longer after he or she becomes pensioner – with many spending 15, 20, even 25 years in pension – and he or she is more physically and mentally active by the wonders science and technology. Second, the reader may be paying a greater cost of his or her pre-retirement. Fewer employers are providing traditional pre-retirement pension plans. Employees continue to miss who pays for their pre-retirement pension plans. Employees pay for define contributions to his or her pre-retirement plan not the employer. Third, supplementary pensions are an important source of income for many Europeans, as the social security coordination does not apply to most supplementary systems.

The share of older people in Europe's population is raising fast. In addition, low levels of employment, pension systems will find it increasingly difficult to deliver adequate social protection at a reasonable cost. The reader may not have a pre-retirement plan available at work or he or she may be self-employed. This places the responsibility of choosing pre-retirement investments squarely on his or her shoulders. Many people mistakenly believe that pension systems will pay for all or most of their pension needs. The fact is, since its inception, the pension systems have provided a minimum foundation of protection, to ensure that Europeans have an adequate, safe and reliable pension. A comfortable standard of living for a new pensioner will require a combination of the following financial elements, pension system benefits; employer based pre-retirement plan, personal savings and investments.

Visualizing Retirement Costs

Retirement or living on a pension is a state of mind as well as a financial issue. The reader is not so much as retiring from work, as he or she is moving into another stage of life. Some people call it a "new career." What does the reader wants to do in that stage? Would the reader want to pursue a favorite hobby? Would he or she work part-time? Would the reader volunteer for charity?

Further, does the reader would consider going back to school? Does he or she want to travel? Does the reader want to enter this state of life earlier than normal pre-retirement age or later? His or her answers to these questions are crucial, when determining – how much money the reader will need to save and invest between now and then.

Embodying this teaching requires an assumption that is the reader plans to retire early, with no plans to work even part time. Therefore, he or she should consider building a larger reserve of money than if he or she plans to retire from work later, because the reader will have to depend on these reserves for a longer time. Now that the reader has a clear picture of its pension goal, it is time to estimate how large his or her pre-retirement reserves will need to be and how much he or she needs to save each month to reach that goal. This step is critical! The vast majority of people never take this step, yet it is difficult to save adequately for pre-retirement, if the reader does not at least have an idea of how much he or she needs to save every month. An easy rule is that the reader will need to replace 70 to 90 percent of its pre-retirement income to enjoy the same standard of living he or she had before retirement. Think of this as the reader annual "cost" of pre-retirement.

The lower the reader income, generally, the higher the portion he or she will need to replace. This annual cost is the equivalent of managing his or her money for a lifetime of growth. The reader probably will experience several major events in its life that can make it more difficult to start or keep saving towards pre-retirement and other goals. The key is to have a clear plan, to stay focused on his or her goals, and to manage money intelligently so that life events do not prevent the reader from keeping on target. Six major events the reader should consider in its plan for saving for pre-retirement, while financially managing some common life events:

Marriage, getting married creates new financial demands that compete for retirement euros, such as changing life insurance needs and savings to buy a home. However, it is usually less expensive for two working people to live together, thus freeing up euros.

Raising Children, in some cases a spouse may stay out of the work force to raise children, thereby cutting into the household income. In addition, this event will be reducing the opportunity to fund pre-retirement. Having a child may alter the reader major financial goals, however should never eliminate them, the reader should make the best effort he or she can.

Changing Jobs often puts the reader at risk of not investing in his or her pre-retirement with his or her current employer, or a new employer may not offer a pre-retirement plan. Consider asking a qualified investment advisor regarding rolling money over from an existing company pre-retirement plan to a new company plan.

Divorce, it is important that the reader knows the laws in his or her country of residence regarding spousal rights to social security, pre-retirement and pension benefits. Under specific country laws, spouses and dependents may have specific rights. Remember, retirement assets may well be the biggest financial asset in the marriage. Therefore, the reader in this situation should make sure to divide those assets carefully. It is also critical to review his or her overall financial situation before and after divorce. Income typically drops for partners in the wake of a divorce, particularly for women.

Disability, a severe or long-lasting disability can undermine efforts to save for pre-retirement. Although social security disability benefits can help sustain a family if, severe disability strikes. The reader may want to explore the availability and cost of other forms of disability insurance in his or her country of residence that are transferrable and made available in any other country in Europe.

Death, the premature death of a spouse can dent efforts for the partner to save for pre-retirement, particularly, if there are dependent children. That is why it is important for the reader to check the social security system of his or her country of residence to find out how much children will receive if a parent dies. Maintaining adequate life insurance is also important. The reader in all cases should have properly named the beneficiaries for any insurance policies, pre-retirement plans, and other pension vehicles he or she has purchased.

Core concept — Investing and Spending

This core concept is the third most important element of the reader financial future. The future is where he or she will be spending the rest of his or her life. Therefore, paying for the pre-retirement him or her truly desire is ultimately the reader responsibility. He or she should take charge. The reader is the architect of its financial future.

That sounds like an impossible task. Many people live from "pay-packet" to "pay-packet". Barely making ends meet. The reader may have more pressing financial needs and goals than "buying" a pre-retirement something so far in the future. Alternatively, perhaps he or she has waited until close to pension age before starting to save. Yet the reader still may be able to afford to buy the kind of pre-retirement he or she wants. Whether you are 19 year old like Sofia, of our think factory, or 41 like our divorcee Juliet, the reader can take steps toward a more secure future.

The reader financial competence has grown at the speed he or she has mastered the last three modules in this book. Now the reader understands that when setting his or her financial goals they will be seriously considering putting his or her pre-retirement high on the list of personal priorities to have peace of mind. The purpose of this module is to help the reader identify ways to save and invest money. It will also introduce saving options he or she can use to save towards pre-retirement and other goals.

The objective for this module is to demonstrate the reader is becoming financially competent. Explain why it is important to save and pinpoint saving goals; identify saving options; and determine which savings and investing options will help the reader reach his or her pre-retirement and other saving goals.

Pre-learning

By now, the reader is more relaxed with the concept and the purpose of self-evaluation, as to how much he or she knows about personal banking and financial discipline, earning and saving, investing and spending. Therefore, he or she can forward to cement these concepts and apply them to their current level of progress. The reader will learn the application of previous knowledge from this book to saving for pre-retirement by continuing with same format of questions and an answer dialog.

Let it roll on again... to action!

Alexander — "What is considered interest? (a) The percentage of money the reader has in its account (b) The amount of money he or she saved when he or she opened and account. Is it **(c) The amount of money banks pays the reader for keeping his or her money on deposit with them,** or (d) the amount of money the reader pays in order to keep his or her money in this bank or other financial institution?"

Margaret — "The answer is "c."

Carlos — "What is the Rule of 72? **(a) A formula that lets the reader know how long it will take his or her savings to double in value** (b) A rule his or her bank and other financial institutions use to determine interest rates. Is it (c) A formula to figure out how much money the reader can save; or (d) A rules he or she can apply to determine the annual percentage yield (APY)?"

Sofia — "My answer is "a."

Jacques — "The reader should consider before start on investing, the following? (a) Ask his or her employer how he or she can invest **(b) Talk to the reader's bank or a reputable financial planner** (c) Open a new savings account; or (d) Buy a house."

Benjamin — "The correct answer is "b."

Catalina — "In this account the reader leaves its money for a set term and cannot make withdrawals or deposits during the stated in advance term (a) Club account (b) Money market deposit account **(c) Certificate of Deposit (CD),** or (d) Statement savings account."

Albrecht "The answer is "c."

Maria — "What does paying the reader first mean? Select all that applies **(a) Putting some of your income into a savings account before paying bills** (b) Buying personal items before paying bills. Should it mean (c) Putting money into a savings account if there is any left after paying bills, or **(d) Putting tax refunds or gifts of money into a savings account before spending the money?"**

Juliet—"I would select "a" and "d" as my response.

Britani — "Savings is important so the reader can (a) Have money for emergencies (b) Achieve his or her financial goals (c) Manage its money better (d) Improve his or her standard of living, or **(e) All of the above."**

Larry—"The answer is all of the above."

Laura — "Which of the following are ways the reader can save for retirement? Select all that apply (a) Build home equity and then apply for an equity loan **(b) Invest in stocks, bonds and mutual funds** (c) Establish a 529 Plan **(d) Enroll in a pre-retirement plan."**

Alexander — "To save for retirement I would say "b" and "d."

Margret — "Which of the following strategies would the reader apply when selecting the best savings or investment option? Select all that apply (a) Select one product to save or invest all your money **(b) Choose savings and investment products that match his or her risk tolerance.** Should the answer be (c) Trust friends to give you good investment advice, or **(d) Re-evaluate the reader's savings and investments periodically."**

Carlos — "My answer is "b" and "d."

Sofia —"What should the reader consider when setting goals for saving money? Select all that apply (a) The amount of money he or she wants to save (b) Time frame of when the reader needs to access the money it saved (c) Ways he or she can cut spending and save (d) The APY of other saving products, or **(e) All of the above."**

Jacques — "The answer is "e" all of the above."

Laura — "Which of the following would the reader considers a need rather than a want? Select all that applies **(a) Paying rent or mortgage** (b) Buying new clothes because my friend is fashionable (c) Eating out regularly to impress other people, or (d) Getting a Smartphone because it is easy to text, send pictures and communicate with social media friends."

Larry — "The correct answer is "a."

Catalina — "Which of the following will help the reader to save money? Select all that apply **(a) Pay his or her bills on time to avoid late fees and extra charges (b) Consider opening a checking account rather than using a check-cashing service** (c) Make impulse purchases, or **(d) Save his or her pocket change and money the reader saved on discounts or purchases at the end of the day."**

Maria — "My response is "a" "b" and "d."

Britani—"The best definition of APY is (a) The amount of interest the reader pays on a loan **(b) The annual interest rate he or she earns on its savings and other deposit accounts.** Is it (c) The minimum percentage of his or her income the reader must save each year to keep his or her savings account open, or (d) to be aware of correct interest on the reader's savings account?"

Nicolaus—"The answer is "b."

Joseph — "Paying the reader first means that when he or she receives money from wages, salary, monetary gifts or other cash-value sources, the reader puts some of that money in his or her savings account before he or she buy things that the reader wants, or he or she pays its bills. The reader's spending plan is already established. Why the reader would want to pay his or herself before buying the things, he or she wants and waited so long for, or pay bills?"

Sofia — "Based on the material I am learning in this book, there are many benefits, and reasons to pay myself first. For example, I am learning to manage my money better. My goal is, within the next six months, to save money towards buying a new laptop computer. I think that the reader should consider paying him or her first, in order to improve its standard of living and have money readily available for emergencies."

Catalina —"This personal banking and financial literacy experience has inspired me to realize that being a university student, I need to start "buying" my retirement now, and I hope the reader, whatever his or her age does the same. Time is critical! I will start small, if necessary. Money may be tight, but even small amounts can make a big difference given enough time. The right kind of investments and tax-favored vehicles are good examples for the reader and I to consider. For example, use automatic deductions from the reader "pay-packet" and deposit to his or her checking account, for deposit in your mutual funds account, or other investment vehicle; save regularly, make savings a habit. I am making savings a monthly habit; I buy each month, and one pound of coffee and sweets, and these I really love!

The reader should be realistic about his or her investment returns. Never assume that a year or two of high market returns will continue forever. The same goes for market declines; roll over pre-retirement account money if the reader changes jobs. My final recommendation to the reader is do not dip into his or her pre-retirement savings! Saving for private college and continuing education at any age is a great investment. However, I am not all-out cold-hearted regarding VACATIONS; save for vacations and enjoy August vacations, experiencing the new in life; reading and learning. Use vacations to think about what makes you act the way you do about money."

Savings Tips

Alexander — "The more I read this book, and exchange views with the "think factory" cast, my family and friends, the easier I am realizing how my emotions drive my money decisions and as a result I am becoming aware of what makes me act the way I do about money. The foundation of these skills rests with accepting and believing that without financial discipline, earning and saving and investing in my future, and perhaps the reader, would be depressing at best. Many people spend all the money they make. However, saving money is important. The reader may believe he or she does not have enough money to start saving. Yet, what are some of the things he or she can do to start saving? Would the reader, consider needs vs. wants?"

Carlos — "Think of the items the reader buys regularly, these add up, where can he or she save? Does the reader eat out often, I do. I like food my parents like food, and my family likes food; thus, they own a small chain of family restaurants. However, as I am becoming financially competent, I realized that eating out to escape from my family's well-established menu is where I can save the most. Can the reader cut back on daily expenses, such as drinking coffee at the luxury price of €3 a cup? Pay his or her bills on time to save on late charges, for example, utilities disconnection fees, and fees to reestablish connections if the reader home services are disconnected, avoid the cost of eviction from its apartment or home; avoid repossession of his or her vehicle. To protect you from these terrible mistakes, the reader should be proactive by using electronic bill pay."

Sofia — "When the reader receives his or her "pay-packet" from his or her employer he or she should place a portion of his or her pay in savings through direct deposit or automatic transfer from his or her checking account. Money the reader does not see you do not miss. The reader may consider purchasing his or her country of residence savings bonds through "pay-packet" deductions if available. Another good source of saving would be for the reader to consider saving the money he, she receives from bonuses, or salary increases."

Margaret — "The reader would want to avoid debt that does not help build his or her long-term financial security. For example, avoid borrowing money for vacations, clothing and meals at restaurants. Alternatively, the reader should consider these examples of debt that contributes to long-term financial future may include paying for private college or continuing education; buying or remodeling a house; buying a car to get to work. The reader should keep making monthly payments to itself once he or she makes a final payment on a loan, also should consider placing this money in his or her savings account. In this manner, the reader can save or invest that monthly payment to reach its future goals."

Juliet — "The reader should consider how I save when shopping. I save the money saved on the price of items I had budgeted for my daily purchases, I save the money on discounts when I did not know about these until the time I am ready to pay at the cash register. In addition, I save my change at the end of each day, and deposit it in a separate savings account, once every two weeks. The reader should consider saving its tax refunds, join his or her employer pre-retirement program or plans that deduct employee contributions from his or her "pay-packet", many employers will matchup to €0,50 for each €1,00 the reader commits to contribute from his or her "pay-packet". This matched amount is free money! In addition, the reader's contributions can lower the income tax bill, so he or she may hardly even notice the money he or she has invested. Therefore, even if the reader retirement is 45 years away this is an excellent way to save for the future."

Nicolaus — "By starting now, the reader should be able to save more money than if he or she waited until he or she older to start saving. This is because of the power of compound interest that allows money the reader may have saved early in life to grow significantly with the passage of time. To put it in context, the reader should exam his or her current financial resources, this is important, because as he or she will learn later in this book, his or her financial resources affect not only his or her ability to reach his or her goals, but also the reader skill to protect those goals from financial crises. The reader needs these resources to draw on to meet life events. Calculate the reader's net worth – this is not as difficult as it might sound. His or her net worth is simply the total value of what is own (assets) minus what he or she owes (liabilities). It is a snapshot of the reader financial health at a moment in time."

Benjamin — "My assigned activity is to share with the cast and communicate how to calculate his or her net worth. First, add up the approximate value of all his or her assets. These include personal possessions such as stamp collections, home, vehicle, checking and savings accounts and cash value (not the death benefits) of any life insurance policies the reader may have. Include the current value of investments such as stocks, other real estate, certificates of deposit, pre-retirement accounts, and the current value of any pension the reader may have. Second, add up the reader liabilities. These include remaining unpaid mortgage on his or her home, credit card debt, auto loans, student loans, income taxes due on the profits or his or her investments, if the reader cash them in, and any other outstanding bills. Subtract your liabilities from the reader assets.

Does the reader have more assets than liabilities? This means he or she has a positive net worth. Alternatively, is it the other way around? This means the reader has a negative net worth.

The reader aim is to create a positive net worth, and he or she want it to grow each year. His or her net worth is part of what the reader will draw on to pay for his or her financial goals, and pre-retirement. A strong net worth also will help the reader through financial crises. Review the net worth annually – recalculate the net worth once a year. It is a way to monitor his or her financial health."

Joseph — "My assigned activity is to call the attention of the cast and the reader to identify other financial resources. He or she may have other financial resources that are not included in his or her net worth. However, these can help you through tough times, and might include the death benefits of the reader life insurance policy, social security survivor's benefits, health care coverage, disability insurance, auto and home insurance policies. Although the reader may have to pay for some of these resources, they offer financial protection in case of illness, accidents or other catastrophes."

How Can Money Grow?

Albrecht — "How can money grow? Here is where financial discipline would bring enormous benefits. The reader should consider scheduling monthly payments by making regular payments to itself first. Even small amounts can add up over time. The amount of his or her money growth depends on the interest earned and the length of time he or she leaves it in the account. As the reader already knows, simple interest is the amount of money banks and other financial institutions will pay for keeping money in savings with them. However, there are other options for the reader to benefit from its financial knowledge."

Activity 1: Compound Interest

Catalina — "My assigned activity is to communicate about compound interest. Compounding interest is how the reader money can grow when he or she keeps it in a financial institution that pays interest. The bank compounds the interest on the reader account balance; he or she earns money on the previously paid interest. In addition, to the paid interest the reader earns on the money already in the account, this interest can be compound daily, monthly or annually. The following examples would illustrate this compounding concept.

The first example considers compounding annually. If the reader puts €1.000, in a savings account that pays one percent (1%) annually, at the end of the year, the interest is calculated. He or she would have earned €10. This is more than if the reader has stashed the money under a mattress.

Now, the reader may want to evaluate compounding. Put the same €1.000, in a savings account that pays one percent (1%) annually and has daily compounding, at the end of the first day you would have €1.000,03.

The next day, the interest will calculate because of the reader original deposit of €1.000, plus the previous earned interest of €0,03. By the end of the year, the reader will have €1.010,05. The extra €10,05 does not seem like much.

The next example will give the reader a clearer picture of the power of compounding as it adds up over time. He or she does not need €1.000, to see the power of compounding. The following common example should bring to heart the power of this compounding concept.

Do you like chocolates?

If the reader buys a chocolate bar that costs €2, once a week for the next year he or she would spend (2 X 52 = €104.) Now, if the reader continues to buy a chocolate bar for 50 years he or she would spend (104 X 50 = €5.200,) on chocolates and no investment. However, if the reader has given up that chocolate bar and invested the money in an account earning eight percent (8%) compound interest, for example, he or she could have earned €64.578,87 after 50 years. Which would the reader rather have with that money – chocolates that cost €5.200, or more than €64.500 in his or her savings account?"

Annual Percent Yield

Maria — "My assignment is to communicate with the cast and the reader on the concept and application of annual percent yield. As I am becoming financially competent, there is another important concept I am learning that the reader needs to know about. It is annual percent yield (APY). It reflects the amount of interest the reader will earn on a yearly basis. The APY includes the effect of compounding. The more often his or her money compounds, the higher the APY and the more interest the reader will earn. This is most important when comparing different accounts. The reader should compare the APYs of the savings products, not the interest rates.

This is the formula to calculate APY:

APY = 100 [(1 + Interest/Principal) (365/Days in term) – 1]

Principal is the amount of funds on posit at the beginning of the account.

Interest is the total dollar amount of interest earned on the Principal for the term of the account.

Days in term means the number of days in term of the account.

This example will use the days in term to be 365.

Expressing the APY by using the following formula:

APY = 100 (Interest/Principal).

The following example will illustrate this point. The reader will be placing €1.000 on deposit for 365 days. His or her banker will access the calculation chart and says, "You will earn €61,68" Using the general APY formula, the reader interest rate is 6.17 percent. The following is the mathematical formula:

APY = 100 [(1 + 61,68/1.000) (365/365) – 1] = APY = 6.17

Alternatively, using the simple formula with a term of 365 days:

APY + 100 (61.68/1.000) APY = 6.17 percent."

Getting More out of your Money

Carlos — "My assignment is to ask the reader, is he or she planning to open a savings account, or want to get more out of the one the reader already has? Ask your bank's customer service representative for the "Truth in Savings Disclosures." These disclosures must list the APY and other important information that the reader should know about the accounts of his or her interest. This knowledge represents experiencing the meaning of financial progress and competence in action."

Rule of 72

Sofia — "Another important concept I am assigned to communicate is the Rule of 72, it is a formula that lets the reader estimate how long it will take for his or her savings to double in value. This calculation assumes that the interest rate remains the same over time and interest compounds once a year. This is how you calculate the Rule of 72: Divide 72 by the current interest rate to determine the number of years that it will take to double your initial savings amount. The math is:

72 / interest rate = Number of years.

The following example will show how this works. If the reader invests €50, in a savings account, at a 4 percent interest rate, it will take 18 years for his or her initial savings of €50 to double. The math again is 72/4 = 18.

The reader can also find out, how much compound interest he or she needs to have when it knows how many years the reader needs for its initial savings amount to double.

The following example will show how this works. If the reader puts €500, in an account that he or she wants to double in 12 years, the reader will need an interest rate of 6 percent.

Formula, 72/12 = 6 percent.

Now, the reader should take his or her own personal savings goal, and see if he or she can figure out the rate of interest it needs to double his or her money. For illustration purposes, if the reader wants its savings account to double in 20 years, what interest rate would his or her account need to have? Answer: 72/20 = 3.6 percent."

Jacques — "It is important for the reader to know that the Rule of 72 was determined based on series of mathematical equations that involved basic calculus. There are many other related terms to savings and interest in the glossary of "Personal Banking and Finance Terms." I am encouraged and the reader should consider reading the "Resources" for the meaning and application of these terms, repeatedly, so he or she can memorize these terms. This is as true as with the sports example in a soccer game. As you may remember; the referee monitors the written rules, while the coach keeps an eye on how each player is measuring up to his or her responsibilities to the team. Every team player has to do his or her job, to make the offence and defense solid, few of these guidelines exist on paper; they are just in memory, drilled into habit by repeated practice. Therefore, the reader financial discipline brings the benefits of his or her optimum use of money."

Activity 2: Saving and Investing

Bejamin — "My assignment is to share with the cast and the reader about different types of savings and investment options he or she may want to consider when consulting with his or her bank or licensed investment professional. He or she already learned that with a savings account, he or she make money by earning interest. The bank, or other financial institution pays you interest for the opportunity to use the reader money. A savings account also ensures that money is safe, and he or she has easy access to it. Two other common savings products include money Market Deposit Accounts (MMDAs), and Certificates of Deposit (CDs)."

Nicolaus — "I am assigned the continuation of this dialog regarding the aspects the reader should consider before putting his or her money in a MMDA account. Money market Accounts tend to offer higher interests rates than regular savings accounts, and often give the reader check-writing privileges. MMDAs require a minimum balance, for example €1.000. A word of caution, the reader should not confuse MMDA(s) that are insure by the Deposit Guarantee Scheme with money market mutual funds these are not insured."

Louis — " I am to continue this assignment and communicate the subject of Certificate of Deposit (CDs,) these are accounts in which the reader leaves its money for a set period, for example six months or two years. This time is the "term." The reader will earn a higher rate of interest, than with a regular savings account. The longer he or she promises to keep the money in the account, the higher the interest rate. Usually, these accounts require a minimum deposit of €500,00 or €1.000. In the event the reader wants to take the money early, he or she will have to pay a fee called an early withdrawal penalty. That is if the reader withdraws money before the term has ended."

Britani—"I am to communicate with the reader about some of the most important considerations he or she would think through about checking, savings and deposit accounts, as discussed the Deposit Guarantee Scheme insurance covers all deposit accounts including checking and savings accounts, money market deposit accounts and certificates of deposit up to the maximum amount allowed by law. It is my understanding that this amount is €100.000, per depositor per bank. In the event the financial institution where the reader has a deposit account goes out of business and cannot pay his or her money, the Deposit Guarantee Scheme will pay it. A word of caution, the Deposit Guarantee Scheme does not cover stocks, bonds, mutual funds, life insurance, annuities or securities."

Activity 3: Savings Products

Joseph — "My assignment is to show scenario to illustrate the application of an appropriate saving product. The reader has €500, he or she wants to set aside, and does not need to withdraw this money for at least one year. The reader wants to place it in an account that earns a higher interest rate of interest than in a regular savings account. Which is the best product for this situation?"

Louis — "The best product for this scenario is a Certificate of Deposit (CD)."

Nicolaus — "The reader receives €1.000 for your graduation present, and he or she wants to start saving money. What is the best place for your money?"

Benjamin — "My response is to open a regular savings account, because there is no saving goal associated with this transaction."

Margaret—"The reader has €3.000 that he or she would like to deposit to open an account that provides you higher interest rates than a regular savings account. In addition, he or she wants to be able to write checks from this account. Which product should the reader consider?"

Maria -- "Given the facts, my answer is to open an deposit this money in a Money Market Account (MMA)."

Laura — "It is important to know that with savings products, the reader will receive a statement from the bank or other financial institution. Therefore, he or she should always check the statement to be sure it is accurate. As we have mastered personal banking and financial discipline, earning and saving, investing and spending, we should be feeling more confident about our level of financial competence. Therefore, it is time to look at investment options to understand the formulation and application of long-term savings goals."

Non-deposit Investment Products

Albrecht — "My assignment is to communicate to the cast and the reader the essence of an investment, it is a long-term savings option that he or she purchases for future income or financial benefit. In fact, the reader might lose the entire amount if the investment fails to perform. On the other hand, his or her investment may earn and grow more than a regular savings account, because of the risk the reader takes when he or she invests its money. In general, the higher the risk, the higher the expected rate of return on the investment. The reader makes money on investments, by selling them for more than he sells or she paid for them, or by earning dividends and interest. The profit the reader earns because of its investments becomes taxable income. Therefore, early tax planning is another smart investment!"

Think about this, the U.S. Billionaire, Warren Buffet, announced publicly in 2010 that he paid less tax than his secretary, who earns just €62.000 per year. Buffet regards tax money as a great investment.

Obviously, Buffet knows how to best invest tax money, better than the U.S. government does."

Types of Investment Products

The more popular types of investment products the reader can buy include stocks, bonds, mutual funds, government securities and retirement investments.

Stocks

When the reader buys a stock, he or she owns part of the company, called a share. The reader may receive dividends or a portion of the company's profits periodically if the company does well financially. The value of the investment changes as the company's stock price changes. When the reader sells the stock, he or she may either earn additional money or lose money.

Stocks have historically had the greatest risks and highest returns among the three major asset categories. As an asset category, stocks are a portfolio's "heavy hitter," offering the greatest potential for growth. Stocks hit home runs, but also strike out. The unpredictability of stocks makes them a very risky investment in the short run. Large company stocks as a group, for example, have lost money on the average one out of every three years. Sometimes these losses have been quite dramatic. Investors willing to ride out the instability return of stocks over long periods, generally enjoy the rewards with strong positive returns.

Bonds

When the reader buys a bond, he or she is lending money to a corporation or government entity for a certain period of time, called term. The corporation or government entity promises to repay the amount of money the reader is lending it on a specified date in the future, or by making regular interests payments to the reader. He or she might lose money if the corporation fails to honor its promises.

Bonds are generally less unpredictable than stocks, but offer more modest returns. As a result, any investor approaching a financial goal might increase his or her bond holdings relative to stock holdings, because the reduced risk of holding more bonds would be attractive to the investor despite their lower potential for growth. The investor should keep in mind that certain categories of bonds offer high returns similar to stocks. However, these bonds, known as high-yield or junk bond, also carry higher risk. The reader should consult with a licensed financial advisor and discuss this example to determine what investment products will be suitable for his or her financial situation within the European market that can help the reader achieve same results as this example.

Cash

Cash and cash equivalents – such as savings deposits, certificates of deposit, money market deposit accounts, and money market funds, these are the safest investments, however offer the lowest return of the three major asset categories. The chances of losing money on an investment in this asset category are generally low. In this example of the United States context, the federal government guarantees many investments in cash equivalents. Investment losses in non-guaranteed cash equivalents do occur, but infrequently. The principal concern for investors, investing in cash equivalents is inflation risk. This is the risk that inflation will outpace and erode investment returns over time.

Mutual Funds

Mutual funds raise money from shareholders and invest it in stocks, bonds, options, futures, currencies or money market securities. These funds offer investors the advantages of diversifications and professional management by a licensed fund manager. Therefore, by combining the reader's money with the money of other investors, he or she can diversify even a small investment. Diversification is a popular colloquial concept known as – "do not put all your eggs in one basket." Diversification reduces the risk that the reader will lose money, because he or she spreads the risk of loss across many savings and investment options, investors hope that if one investment loses others may gain and the other investments will more than make up for those losses.

Pre-retirement Investments—New in Europe

Pre-retirement investment products are a new concept in Europe. These investment vehicles are under consideration to help the reader to save towards his or her retirement, for example, Individual Pre-retirement Account (IPRA) Plans and Variable Annuities. A note of caution, the reader should seek the expert advice of a licensed investment advisor and a tax expert to verify the types of pre-retirement investment options suitable to the reader.

IPRAs

An IPRA, commonly known as an Individual Pre-retirement account, is the most basic sort of pre-retirement arrangement. With an IPRA, the reader deposits the money into an account that may include a combination of stocks, bonds, mutual funds or treasury securities. These types of accounts might be tax-exempt and generally designed to ensure adequate income to pensioners. Though an IPRA generally grows over time, due to interest earned and the reader's contributions, it may lose value, depending on the stock market and his or her investment choices. The reader should talk with an experienced, licensed, investment professional and tax expert for help in making the best investment for the reader.

Variable Annuities

A variable annuity is an investment towards pre-retirement. It is an insurance contract that invests the reader premium in various mutual fund investments. He or she can buy this product from a licensed securities broker or an insurance agent. Brokers and agents earn a commission on the annuity sold, and may be motivated to sell the reader a product that may not be ideal for his or her specific financial situation. Variable annuities can be extremely costly in fees in the event the reader does not keep the annuities for at least than ten years. The reader should hold the annuity for at least 10 to 20 years to justify the fees. Therefore, it is most important that the reader continue to educate him or herself on this subject, and learn as much as he or she can, about the type of investment, in order to make intelligent decisions and best use of his or her money.

Why Asset Allocation is Key

The reader should consider including asset categories with investment returns that move up and down under different market conditions within his or her portfolio, he or she as an investor can protect against significant loses. Historically, the returns of the three major investment categories have not moved up and down at the same time. Market conditions that cause one asset category to do well often cause another asset category to have average or poor returns. By investing in more than one asset category, the reader will reduce the risk that he or she will lose money and his or her portfolio's overall investment returns will have a smoother ride. If one asset category's investment return falls, the reader will be in a position to counteract its losses in that asset category with better investment returns in another asset category.

Portfolio Diversification

The reader should consider portfolio diversification a key element of the investment plan. In essence, diversification is the practice of spreading money among different investments to reduce risk. By selecting the right group of investments, the reader may be able to limit loses and reduce the fluctuations of investment returns without sacrificing potential gain. Portfolio diversification takes place when considering two levels:

between asset categories and within asset categories. So, in addition to allocating his or her investments among stocks, bonds, cash equivalents, and possible other asset categories, the reader will need to spread out the investments in segments of each asset category that may perform differently under different market conditions. One way of diversifying his or her investments within an asset category is to identify companies and invest in a wide range of companies and industry sectors. This means that a typical portfolio diversification should contain at least twelve (12) individual stocks.

The reader should give especial attention to the fact that a mutual fund investment does not necessarily provide instant diversification, especially if the fund focuses on only one particular industry sector. If the reader invests in narrowly established mutual funds, he or she may need to invest in more than one mutual fund to get the diversification it seeks. Asset categories means considering, for instance, large company stock funds as well as some small company and international stock funds. In addition, asset means considering stock funds, bond funds, and money market funds. Of course, as the reader adds more investments to his or her portfolio, he or she will likely have additional fees and expenses, which will, in turn, lower its investment returns, therefore, the reader will need to consider these costs when deciding the best way to diversify his or her investment portfolio.

Activity 4: Matching Investment Products

Alexander — "My assigned activity is to ask the cast and the reader what is the product that he or she can purchase at any financial institution for as little as €25,00. Earns monthly interest; and payment is made at end of the term?"

Carlos — "The product is a Bond."

Maria — "The reader may purchase this product when he or she buys a share of a corporation. The reader may periodically receive dividends or a portion of the corporation's profits."

Sofia—"This product is a Stock."

Jacques — "This product is available for purchase from companies that combine money from many investors to purchase numerous separate investments."

Louis – "Those are Mutual funds."

How to Choose the Best Investment

The reader can benefit financially from investments; however, he or she needs to be well prepared and ready to take on the investment responsibility. The reader should not rush into any investment; he or she needs to get all the facts and information to consider when choosing an investment. Before the reader invests hard-earned money, it is best to consult with his or her bank, a reputable financial advisor or a professional investment firm. In addition, the reader should have a savings cushion that will cover all usual and customary monthly expenses for a period of at least six months before considering becoming an investor. These reserves, or cushion funds, should be in an account that one can access easily, for example, a separate checking or savings account open for this specific purpose. Because of this, the reader may want to wait until he or she is financially stable before investing. While the reader might find this reserve funds hard to attain, even a small rainy day cushion fund is important.

Therefore, the reader should save all he or she can now because it will all pay off when him or her start their investment portfolio. Before investing, the reader should read and understand the investment prospectus; learn about the investment product from the plan administrator. The reader has learned in this book that past financial performance of an investment is not an indication or guarantee of future performance. He or she should consider how long they plan to keep their money in the investment. Investments can help the reader protect money form the difficulties of the stock market by following a consistent pattern of adding new money to his or her investments over a long period. The reader should diversify its investment portfolio. He or she should consider having a mix of investment products that reflect his or her needs for return, safety and long-term saving goals.

Therefore, the reader should periodically re-evaluate its investments as his or her life situation changes or priorities shift. Determine how much risk of losing its investment the reader is willing to tolerate. He or she should always keep this in mind there is a tradeoff between risk and return.

Avoid circumstances that can lead to fraud. Fraud artists often use highly publicized news items or deceptive claims to lure the reader in and make their investment opportunity sound legitimate. Ask questions and check the answers with an unbiased source, for example, a family member who the reader knows is an investor, a friend who has experience in investing or an independent financial planner. Check with these sources before investing. Do not invest in anything the reader does not fully understand. If the reader is interested in learning about investing, he or she should consider joining an investment club. Investment clubs are groups of people who work together to understand the process and value of investing even small (€10. to €20.) amounts of money.

Before investing for pre-retirement, ask your employer about any pre-retirement programs offered through his or her job. If its employer matches his or her pre-retirement savings contributions, be sure to save as much as you can to maximize the employer's match. In addition, as in the poker game, cash is king, planning is queen and diversification is royal flush.

Other Investments

Sofia — "The reader should consider owing a home or business as a vehicle to invest money. My assignment is to communicate to the cast and the reader why owing a home can be a good investment, because the house market value may increase or appreciate. This is the case in my family. 20 years ago, my father bought the house we live in now for

€97.000 he has made several improvements and there is a mortgage of €52.000, today this house is on the market for sale. The house market value is €560.000 our home has increase in value, and as debt decreases by payment of the mortgage resulting in equity increase."

Laura — "Based on the progress I am making toward becoming financially competent, and using Sofia's example, my assignment is to communicate what equity is and show how to calculate it. Equity is the difference between the market value of this house and the outstanding mortgage. Therefore, the appraised value of this house is €560,000 minus the mortgage of €52.000, then the equity in this home is

(560.000 - 52.000 = €507.500).

Larry — "My assignment is to communicate why considering owning a business can be a good investment. Starting a new business can be risky, especially when the reader has no prior experience. In the event the reader is considering owning a business, the first element to focus on is the preparation of a written business plan. This plan should contain the integration of several elements or sub-plans, for example, product or service that the reader has knowledge or capability to produce and supervise, definition of needs of buyers or market for the product or service, financial and risk management, business management, and public communications sub-plans. The reader should consider a three-year start up face before reaching a break-even point. In other words, the reader should have savings that meets its personal needs and obligations for at least one year before considering starting a business that will increase his or her future financial security."

Activity 5: First to Be Paid Action Plan

First, to be paid action plan is the mid-point on the roadmap of financial literacy. Therefore, the reader would be establishing the truth and benefits of this personal banking and finance model, using the mastery-learning tool, and incorporating the three core concepts in this book financial discipline, earning and saving, investing and spending.

Juliet -- "Now, I am to show in action, the concept "first to be paid." What action steps the reader needs to consider saving towards his or her goals. The reader should consider applying the principles in this book on what makes him or her act the way it does about money and the money survival skills they will be using for the rest of their lives. I would say that without financial discipline, there is no way to earn and save, and save invest, to pay myself first or, for that matter to have a financial future.

Preparing this plan is easy. Take a note pad and divide a page in two. At the top the title: "Pay (YOUR NAME) First Action Plan." The top half of the page the reader will use to write down the answers to the decisions he or she needs to make before deciding on the steps they will take. The bottom half of the plan gives the reader space to record the steps it can start taking now, a month from now, and a year from now to achieve his or her specific goal."

Britani – "There are three factors for the reader to consider when selecting the best savings and investment options. How much money wants to accumulate over a certain period. How long can he or she leave its money invested? In addition, how does he or she feels about risking their money?"

Maria – "Regarding how much the reader wants to save over a period he or she can figure this out by using the Rule of 72. This Rule show how long it will take savings to double in value. It also indicates to the reader what interest rate he or she will need when he or she knows in how many years wants its money to double."

Albrecht — "On the subject of how long the reader should consider leaving money invested if he or she has some money it will not need for several years. He or she might consider investment options such as stocks, bonds or mutual funds. On the other hand, if the reader thinks he or she might need access to his or her money right away or in the short-term it might be best to keep it in a savings account, where the reader not only has an immediate access to it, but without penalty of early withdrawal. How the reader does feels about risking money? If he or she is not comfortable with some level of risk and cannot afford to lose money, the reader might consider depositing in a checking or savings account that best meets his or her needs."

Financial Goals Action Plan

Joseph — "I am to respond to how to ensure the goals action plan will work. The reader can make this plan work by considering each financial goal, and purposefully decide how he or she can save to reach each goal. For example, the reader financial goal might be saving for the down payment on a new car in three years. To accomplish this goal, easily he or she might be able to cut back on the number of specialty cups of coffee each day. Saving €5 a day, 365 days a year, adds up to €1,825 by the end of the year.

What can one do by the end of the month to save? He or she might be able to cut back on eating out twice a month, saving €50; a month represents €600 by year-end. What can the reader do by the end of the year to save? He or she may save your year-end bonus of €500 and its tax refund of €720. Therefore, by the end of the first year the financial goals action plan, will show the following results:

(1.825 + 600 + 500 + 720 = €3.645).

The reader application of the core principles in this book, financial discipline, earning and saving, investing and spending will afford to experience and understand what makes him or her act the way it does about money. These examples make it easy to apply the money survival skills the reader needs for life. In addition, it will establish the truth of his or her financial competence by the evidence based on meeting their financial goal of buying his or her new car in three years. This is the mathematical proof:

(3.645 X 3) = €10.935) New Car, Down Payment!"

Module Summary

The reader has completed the pre-retirement and pension's module. The members of the think factory cast covered a lot of information to this mid-point including how to earn and save how to save for pre-retirement and invest for the future. The evidence-based exercise includes how to accomplish a specific goal. The reader learned to make its pre-retirement a priority. In addition, he or she is to start buying it now. The most important lesson learned is that retirement is the most valuable investment of his or her lifetime. This teaching is one of the most valuable financial benefits of this book.

The reader has learned the concept paying itself first, also learned how he or she can benefit by implementing financial discipline. He or she has participated along with the cast of peers in a dialog, and learned a number of saving options. He or she learned how to decide what savings and investment options are best. The reader has gained knowledge of how their money can grow with compound interest and guidelines to save more. With this information it should be able to begin saving and sharing with its family and friends as well as inspire others to seek a brighter financial future.

Mastery Learning and Knowledge Check

Mastery learning is a lifelong process, and continues to grow as the reader moves purposefully to meet his or her needs for personal banking and financial competence, at the closing of this module, and mid-point of this financial education work. He and she will be experiencing financial competence in a completely new way, looking forward to participating in the continuation and discovery of how emotions drive his or her financial decision-making to determine what makes him or her act the way they do about money. The evidence based on your progress and self-discovery consists of twelve questions.

Knowledge Check Questions

(1) What is compound interest? (A) The percentage of money the reader has in his or her account (B) The amount of money save when you open an account (C) The amount of money banks pay the reader for keeping money on deposit with them, or (D) The money you earn on previous paid interest and the money already in your account.

(2) Which of the following does the Rule of 72 allow the reader to estimate? (A) The number of years it will take to double savings (B) The amount of money he or she can save with a specific interest rate (C) The amount of money the reader can save in a specific number of years or (D) The compound interest rate needed to double savings within a specific number of years.

(3) The following products have no guarantee from the Deposit Guarantee Scheme: (A) Certificate of Deposit (CD) (B) Stocks or (C) Mutual Funds.

(4) The reader can save money at a higher interest than a savings account and write checks from this account: (A) Club account (B) Money market deposit account (C) Certificate of Deposit, or (D) Statement savings account.

(5) This is a product that allows the reader to diversify its investments to reduce the risk of losing money (A) Bonds (B) Stocks (c) Mutual funds or (D) Pre-retirement Plans.

(6) What benefits the readers realize by paying his or herself first? (A) Improve standard of living (B) learn to manage money better (C) have money for emergencies or (D) All of the above.

(7) What is the major difference between saving and investment products? (A) Saving products are guaranteed by the Deposit Guarantee Scheme, investment products are not (B) Saving products are at risk of loss, investment products are not (C) Investment products do not have as high a potential for growth as savings products do or (D) Savings and investment products are the same.

(8) The reader receives a tax refund, what can him or she do to make sure saves some of the refund? Select all that apply (A) Direct deposit of some or all of the refund straight into a checking account (B) Deposit some or all of it into a savings account with a higher interest rate, for example, a CD or MMDA, or (C) Use the money to invest in a savings bond.

(9) Which are non-deposit investment products? Select all that applies (A) CDs (B) Money Market Deposit Accounts, or (C) Bonds.

(10) You can save money by paying your bills on time because you would avoid paying: (a) Late fees; (b) Extra finance charges; (c) Disconnection and reconnection fees; (d) Cost of eviction repossession, and collection fees; or (e) All of the above.

(11) Which of the following strategies can help the reader choose the best investment? Select all that apply (A) Make choices based on a friend or family member's recommendations (B) Limit the number of savings and investment options chosen to reduce the risk of loss (C) Select savings and investment options according to risk tolerance, or (D) Consider how long he or she plans to keep their money in the investment.

(12) Which of the following are ways readers can save for private college? Select all that apply (A) Build home equity then applies for a home equity loan (B) Invest in stocks, bonds and mutual funds, or (C) Enroll in a pre-retirement Plan.

Money Survival Skills Application

The following CashMax^3 modules are to help readers in their life-long money survival skills and application of strategic thinking. These modules will also help him or her to reinforce its financial discipline, earning and saving, as well as investing and spedning. CashMax^3 uses the materials the reader has mastered to this mid-point as guidance in the real-life application of sustainable financial competence. The best way to define the application of sustainable financial competence is to determine what it is not. Financial competence application is not just accumulation of knowledge. It helps the reader to discover facts and concepts, but it does not stop there. History is rich with examples of people, who read the Bible, and cannot find the connection between the timeless principles of Scripture and the present problems of day-to-day living.

In the same way, history is rich with facts about banks profiting from nonsufficient funds (NSF) fees proves that tens for millions of the Europeans know the basics of personal banking, but cannot connect or apply it to the day-to-day financial transactions. Hence, they fail to apply this truth to their daily personal banking lives. These truths keep them both from believing and changing, and from becoming free from financial worries. The reader, and the think factory cast may think that understanding these subjects is the end goal of this book of study on personal banking and financial education. However, it is only the beginning.

Financial competence application is not an illustration; illustration only tells one how someone else handled a similar situation, while the reader and the cast may identify with that particular person in the real-life scenarios, he or she still has little direction for its personal situation. Financial competence application is not just making a CashMax^3 module "relevant," making personal banking and financial literacy relevant only helps the reader see that the same principles are as true today as they were around 2.500 years ago, when ancient Israel had no lending institutions or banks in the modern sense. Commercial transactions and lending of credit were entirely in the hands of private individuals, landowners and merchants. To help readers understand better the roots of money, banking, credit and borrowing, it is necessary to review these fundamentals. Contemporary cultures in Mesopotamia lent or produced an interest, in some cases as much as 33 ½ percent per annum. The widespread introduction of coined money after 500 B.C. and the expansion of travel and commerce in the Roman Empire aided the establishment of banking institutions. In the Hebrew culture, borrowing indicated economic hardship, not a strategy for expanding business or households.

Chapter 12

Credit Scores and Home Ownership

This CashMax[3] module on credit scores and home ownership will teach the reader the long-term money survival skills he or she needs for life. It will show how to manage credit and credit scores as key components of building a solid financial future. This module will educate the reader on borrowing money from banks and other financial institutions. In addition, the reader will learn how loans work, and how financial institutions make lending decisions. The objective for this module is to define credit, explain why he or she must guard its credit. Identify key types of loans and costs associated with securing these loans, and protecting the reader rights against discrimination in the lending process. He or she will also learn to categorize key components lenders use to make home loan decisions, and explain why it is important to be prudent regarding rent-to-own and refund expectation services.

Pre-learning

The reader should be comfortable with the purpose of self-evaluation, and his or her knowledge regarding personal banking and finances. In addition, he or she has mastered the foundational CashMax[3] modules and most importantly, they are this book – financial discipline, earning and saving, investing and spending. The reader has successfully completed pre-retirement and pensions CashMax[3] module. Therefore, this chapter will be exclude the "Knowledge Check Correct Answers." From this point forward, the reader and the cast will be engaged in a fast-paced dialog to emphasize the facts the reader should know and remember, and at the same time, consolidate his or her personal banking and financial competence.

Let it roll on again… to action!

Alexander — "My assignment is to ask two fundamental questions to set the pace of this teaching, what is credit? In addition, what is a loan?"

Margaret -- "Credit is a predetermined amount the reader can borrow when needed. A loan is money he or she can borrow but must also repay."

Carlos — "Which type of loan will the reader use to pay for personal expenses? What type of loans is most likely to be unsecured?"

Sofia – "Based on what I am learning in this book my response is unsecured loans are consumer installment loans and credit cards. Furniture and student loans are also unsecured loans."

Jacques—"What type of loan replaces a home loan in order to get a better interest rate? What type of interest rate stays the same during the entire contract time?"

Catalina – "My answer is a home refinance loan. The interest rate that stays same is a fixed rate"

Albrecht — "What documents should the reader review before buying a home? What should he or she compare when shopping for a home loan? In addition, what factors do lenders generally use in their loan making decision?"

Catalina – "The most important documents to review are the annual percentage rate, fees, and Truth and Lending Disclosures. In addition, the key factors that the lender will consider are capacity, capital, collateral, and character. Therefore maintaining a good credit is most important."

Britani – "I would illustrate this concept with a powerful life story. It cost my mother's health, my father's business and my separation from my family. I am 58 years old and single. When I graduated from high school, I was 17, my parents, Robert and Eunice, asked me what I wanted for a graduation present. I said, "A party for my friends and a trip to Europe. My father owned "Center Stage," a film and stage equipment rental business for 23 years when I left for Europe. As his only daughter, he wanted to impress and reward me for graduating fifth in my class.

As a first present, they gave me a graduation party at his membership club, "Baja Mar Vista Golf and Country Club." The party was fantastic, good food, drinks, live music and fun; 143 people attended it. I do not remember how many gifts I got, but there were gifts all over the "18 Hole Room," that overlooked the Pacific Ocean. To make me feel secure and in control during my trip to Europe, my father ordered a company credit card with my name on it. It was my first real credit card. It was an American Express Platinum, with no spending limit. "So," my dad said, "I could enjoy my trip and use it as needed.

This was the beginning of my troubles with money handling and by default, credit mismanagement. Simply put, it ended up as a tragic consequence of my financial illiteracy. My best friend Gloria, whom I have known since first grade, wanted to go with me but her parents were poor. I pleaded with my mother to intercede on my behalf with my father and let me take her with me. "Just to be and feel safe—I said." My father, a goody-goody type of person, however, was not too excited with the idea. Mother and I began to work on him by touching his key button; it was golf.

My mom began her attack, by recounting how many trips he took to Saint Andrews in Scotland to play in the Pro-Am and watch the Masters Tournament with "Club privileges, to the Royal and Ancient Club of St. Andrews." In turn, I began my soft attack by claiming how many times he neglected to call on my birthdays that fell on April 13. During the week of my birthday is the time of the year when Saint Andrews Golf turns onto King George's heaven. On a Saturday afternoon, two weeks after my graduation party, my father texted me and wrote, "Would you and Gloria like to go tonight to eat sushi with mom and me? I jumped at the invite and texted back "yes," for Gloria and I, even without calling her. We love sushi! We arrived at the beautiful Kyoto Sushi, the heart of angler's wharf in San Francisco.

My father proceeded to order hot sake while placing the order of sushi. After three little bottles, my mom asked my dad, "Would you tell me a secret?" A teasing game she sometimes played with him. He ignored her repeatedly, until she reminded him of a loving promise he signed on a champagne cork during their memorable trip to Beijing, China. He became quite "simpatico" and laughed loudly. However, Gloria and I were excited to hear his answer, about the tell-me-a-secret question, which never came. As always, he was tight lipped.

Never before had Gloria or I drank in front of, nor with my parents, much less this smooth and most exquisite liquid. I thought it was heavenly but Gloria was not too sure. After an hour, we all were acting a feeling happy, enjoying this gorgeous, large, round, beautifully decorated and appealing to the eye plate of sushi. Suddenly, my father reaches for his pocket and hands me an envelope. "What is it?" I asked. "Open and see," he said.

I opened it as fast as I could, and wow! Inside the envelope, two business class airfare tickets for Gloria and me on Alitalia. It was a direct flight to Rome departing at 7 pm the following Friday night. Gloria almost passed out. She cried, hugged, and kissed my parents, like there was no end. She graduated with me as second in our class and turned 18 that night. I turned 18 years old during the second week of the trip.

My father said, "You girls go and have a good time, all on me, "how could I ever imagine what this free and wonderful trip would do to my life, my father's business and my parents' marriage? Gloria immediately called her parents, Eduardo and Beatriz to secure their okay. She placed the call on her Smartphone loud speaker so we all could hear their reaction. "Hello, answered Eduardo. Beatriz was in the background and shouted: "Who is that making such a racket?" Gloria responded, "Mom, it is me, Gloria. I have great, great news for you."

Gloria — "Mom and dad, May I have your blessings? I am going overseas with Britani. "When are you leaving?" asked Eduardo. Gloria responded, "next Friday!" "Have a great time... and thank you Robert." Then Beatriz said, "Be safe and keep your eyes and pockets in check." Immediately, they hung up!"

Britani — "Look Dad, I am going to tell you "a secret." I love you so much that no matter what I will always be there for you and mom, I ecstatically stated. On hearing this, mom jumped in and asked Dad, "Are you going to tell me a secret?" Dad was tight-lipped again. She laughingly recalled the memory of having a great time together and free champagne again on their flight to Japan. That night Gloria stayed with me. We simply could not sleep, talking about and planning all the places and things we were to see and do."

Fast forward... It is Friday at 7:00 p.m. We are to board the Alitalia flight, feeling as beautiful as movie queens do, Gloria, a petite brown-haired woman 5 foot 4" tall, and I 5 foot 10" with a giraffe like neck. We walked as on a catwalk, causing heads to turn as we passed the security check and walked to Gate 3. All was dreamy, the onboard attention, food, drinks, and comfortable sleeping seats. We talked, for maybe an hour and slept. The flight attendant softly calling my name and offering a hot face towel before breakfast, an hour before arrival at *Fumicino* International Airport in Rome.

It was 8:30 am on Saturday. We planned all kinds of activities for the day including some night clubbing that evening. We got to our hotel, unpacked, showered and took a little snooze. Before long, it was Sunday, 4:34 p.m.!

Gloria — "We walked outside the hotel, streets looked ghostly. We passed by the U.S. Embassy located next to our hotel on *Via Vittorio Veneto* with no one in sight except the U.S. Marines, standing like statues on every corner of this ornate building. Finally, we asked a woman coming out of the embassy side gate, what was happening and why there was no one around. She told us that "today" is Saint Michael Fest in Rome, and people were celebrating... Hum, are they celebrating? Where can you tell us? "Every house eats a special meal at 4:00 p.m. and I am already late..." the nice lady waved us good bye."

Britani — "Gloria and I exchanged glances, a little disconcerted, and agreed to be adventurous, we pulled out our city map, and walked to "*Termini*" the Rome train station. There was life, people speaking many different languages, talking loudly, coming and going, people everywhere. We liked it, we felt alive again. There was life and handsome men. We noticed what appeared to be a group of students looking at the arrival and departure boards. We observed them for a little while, noting their eyes on us. One of them commented loudly in English: "Let us go to Lyon and from there to Monaco.

I looked at Gloria and said, "Well it's time to sign my first American Express purchase, let us go to Lyon and follow those guys and see what takes place." Gloria, much more conservative and money conscious, commented that it might be too expensive. She asks; "What are we going to do with the hotel room and personal belongings?" Do not worry my dad is paying for all of this. Besides, at this hour of the evening we were not sleepy – but hungry.

We ate "*Panini*," beer and chocolates for dessert. After that, we went downstairs to the ticket counter and purchased two reserved train tickets to Lyon, France. The trip was great; however, no people were in sight. When the train conductor came by to collect our tickets, we asked him about the group of people we saw earlier. "Oh yes," the conductor responded, "they are traveling in unreserved seats, three wagons to the rear." "Would you take us there?" I asked.

"It is my pleasure, please follow me." Therefore, we did. Three hours later we were engaged in a great time and inviting the seven of them, three girls and four handsome men, to beer and food. Gloria noted that our reserved cabin was empty and we were almost in Lyon, France. "Do not worry. Dad is taking care of this too," I responded. Upon arrival in Lyon, each of us was secretly choosing whom we wanted to spend time with and how we could get rid of the rest.

I invited all to a farewell dinner. By now, Gloria and I knew we are going to Monaco, the intriguing place we all talked and fantasized about from Rome to Lyon. Dinner was just right. The girls were a little tense towards us, especially when I asked the waiter, "How do we get to Monaco?" Giorgio responded for the waiter, "I will be taking the bus, because the scenery is breath taking, especially at night – it is beautiful." I felt as if I had butterflies in my stomach when I heard this little man approximately 5 foot 7 inches tall describe the trip to Monaco. It sounded romantic.

I feel special attraction to men that are shorter than I am. Soon after dessert, the girls got up, thanked us for the food, and asked the people "Are you staying or going to Monaco?" Giorgio and Pietro responded in unison, "We are going to Monaco with Gloria and Britani!" When I heard that, Gloria glanced at me and we knew we would be experiencing Europe and romance!"

Britani — "Gloria was holding Pietro's hand, near to his almost 6 foot tall nice and trimmed body. I was playing a little conservative and walking abreast with Giorgio, we arrived at the bus station and I purchased four one-way tickets to Monaco, departing at 9 pm that evening. The bus ride was smooth and the scenery almost inviting to silence. Because the night was so clear and lit up, I felt something extraordinary was taking place. Suddenly, I pointed ahead and asked Giorgio, "What is that bright light in front of us?"

With a gorgeous smile, he said, "It is the Northern Star, the brightest and most beautiful of all. It was the star that guided the shepherds to the birth place of Jesus." I was spellbound, and my heart, ever grateful that I met someone who knew that life was beautiful, and could see and communicate so eloquently. For the remaining two hours, I could not take my eyes of the Northern Star. I forgot how handsome Giorgio was. I forgot where I was going. I forgot all about me, and let my heart feel how fortunate I was to believe in the Bright Morning Star.

Gloria was whispering with Pietro, and soon I noticed both were asleep. We arrived at Casino Royale, where the driver announced, "It is time to play and this is the place." By now, we looked tired and less than elegant for this place. Where can we go to buy some clothes? Our driver smiling responded: I will arrange it for you, and states: "All you need in Monaco is energy and money." Our driver called on a driver of a Rolls Royce parked a few feet away. A man walked up to us and greeted us, saying to be at our service as he proceeded to open the rear door.

We all got in and I asked if he could take us somewhere to buy some clothes and then to refresh. "Yes, Madam," he obliged, as he drove to a small boutique. Upon arrival, a valet attendant opened the door and we exited this fantastic car. The driver stood by his door and said, "I will leave you here, and take the gentlemen to a men's place." I simply responded okay. Gloria just waved to Pietro. This was the exact point in my life where financial literacy could have saved me from negative consequences affecting the rest of my life, saved Center Stage, and most importantly, saved my parents' marriage.

Paying for all expenses and gambling incurred by Giorgio, Pietro, Gloria and me cost €97.523. My father paid the first American Express bill, which was €42,437. He called me several times at the hotel in Rome, where we were still registered, and where all our belongings were. However, we were in Monaco for the entire week.

Upon arriving back in Rome, I had a message from the U.S. Embassy, to call the U.S. Consulate immediately. Now Eduardo, Beatriz and my parents had filed a missing persons report, causing havoc at home and at the "*Prefecture Di Roma*" police, which showed up at the hotel, within three minutes of our arrival. The police were going to arrest Giorgio and Pietro, and asked Gloria and me to accompany them to the police station for questioning. After nearly three hours of exhausting interrogation, the police brought all of us back to the hotel and notified my parents that there was no foul play, just an expensive fun loving foursome.

Center Stage is now paying Cash on Delivery (COD) from all supplies; my father's credit score is below 500, and all as a direct result of my financial illiteracy. After a short time, my dad could not sustain the cash outflow, and it ended in him having to file bankruptcy. The distress and blame landed square on my mother, who, on the day of our return to Rome, suffered an aneurism and is now in a convalescent home. My father divorced her and became an alcoholic because he could not deal with Mom being paralyzed and not able to talk or feel from her waist down. Also traumatizing, I am not welcome by Gloria's family. I can only see Gloria in secret. All I have now is my life and trust in the Bright Morning Star, I hope for forgiveness by my father and mother before she dies, so I can start anew.

Now, as I am becoming financially competent, I want to help others to prevent the misfortune of being financially illiterate and never to forget how important it is to protect your good name, family and credit."

Laura — "This is a tragic story and I am sure I can speak for everyone when I say we are sorry to hear of Britani's circumstances. At the same time, I am delighted you are a part of the think factory cast and now on a new path that will lead you to the hope filled and responsible goals you are setting for yourself now, and for your future."

Larry — "With this dramatic life changing financial illiteracy lesson, I am to talk with my peers form the cast and communicate to the reader why is it important to build and keep a good credit score and pay attention to the credit report? The credit report shows information about how the reader has used credit, how much credit it has, how much of the available credit he or she are using, whether they have made payments on time, and whether anyone has sent a loan the reader owes to a debt collector. What is a credit score? A credit score is a mathematical developed number used to predict how likely he or she are to pay back a loan. The credit score starts with the information about the reader from its credit report. This report uses a mathematical prediction formula from a scoring model that creates a FICO. This acronym stands for Fair Isaac and Company, and it is the reader credit score number.

Unfortunately, the fact is that an identical pattern of credit reporting protocol does not exist within Europe, since different types of Credit Bureaus and Public Credit Register exists in different Member States. In some cases, there is Credit Bureau that only reports negative credit data "black list." In some others, there is Credit Bureau registers both negative and positive data. Moreover, in some countries, there is no Credit Bureau. Further, in some Member States it is possible to access different information from the Credit Bureaus, which the banks use in order to verify the trustworthiness of the consumer with reference to payments.

For example, in Germany where Laura and I just to live it is not possible to obtain a loan without giving the permission to the lender to store private data in a Credit Bureau. Legally this permission is voluntary. However, without it, many banks will reject lending. Though, a borrower can obtain credit when he or she can provide evidence that proves their income sources, expenditures, and existing credit obligations."

Laura — "The interesting fact is that when I worked in the bank, I was one of the assistants to the head of the Business Loans Unit, my job was to compile the necessary documentation to validate due diligence. Therefore, I know that all banks and major companies that make credit-granting decisions over €25.000 use FICO credit scores. For example, a home loan finance company will use FICO to pre-approve a mortgage at a certain interest rate. Banks use FICO to consider granting large loan and to issue a credit card that has no spending limit. Different lenders use different scoring formulas so the reader credit score can vary from lender to lender. A higher FICO score makes it easier to qualify for a major loan and it means a better rate of interest. Most scores range from 300 to 850, although there is one scoring method that uses a range from 501 to 900.

Alexander—"The reader might not be thinking or in the process of applying for a large amount loan, is there any proactive action the reader should consider to secure and keep a good credit score?" He or she should pay its loans and credit cards on time, make sure information related to income, expenses, and current debt obligations is current and accurate. Therefore, when he or she needs a loan, its information matches exactly what the lender Credit Bureau has in its database. In addition, he or she should not use too much of the credit available."

Sofia—"One way to make sure payments are on time is to set up automatic payments from the reader's checking account. However, he or she should watch bank balances to ensure there is enough money in the account to cover payments on specific dates. In addition, do not just pay the minimum amount; pay more because it will take the reader much longer to pay off its debt. My father, for example has kept the best credit score paying off its credit cards in full every month."

Carlos — "What happens when the reader uses its available credit to the credit limit? Credit scoring models look at how close you are to being "maxed-out," because the formulas predict that people who are using too much of their available credit, may have future difficulties with repayment. If the reader use too much of its total credit lines, it can hurt his or her credit score. Therefore, keeping and using credit at no more than 30% of established credit limits is a good financial competence rule."

Jacques — "I am to share with the cast and communicate with the reader what happens when the reader receives offers to open new accounts and pay off other credit cards. Closing some credit card accounts and putting most or all credit card balances onto one card, will hurt his or her credit score, because it will indicate to the creditors that they are using a high percentage of total credit limit, and therefore signaling a potential credit risk. In addition, the reader should not apply for new credit in a short time, especially if he or she is in the process of applying for a mortgage or a car loan. Opening new credit card accounts frequently to take advantage of the promotional rates or store discounts will show up on the credit report as many new credit accounts, which will hurt the final credit score. The basis of credit scores is experience over time, the longer the credit history the better the FICO. The more experience the reader has with getting and paying for credit, the more information there is to determine whether the he or she is a good credit risk. The reader should seek and obtain a copy of his or her credit report every year."

Benjamin — "The reader should read its credit report and dispute any errors. If he or she finds something wrong with the credit report, write to both the Credit Bureau and the creditor that provided the information. If applicable, tell them what he or she believes is wrong and why. Include copies of any documents that support his or her position. When the reader as a consumer, disputes credit report information the Credit Bureau and the creditor has to investigate the dispute and correct inaccurate information.

Avoid paying to "repair" negative credit history. Many places promise to "repair" or "fix" credit for a fee. However, the fact is no one can remove negative information, such as late payments, from a credit report if it is accurate. The reader can only get its credit report fixed if it contains errors and the reader can do this on his or her own."

Joseph — "Should the reader experience having trouble paying creditors on time, the sooner he or she contacts the creditors the more likely it is to work something out with them, such as a temporary payment plan, especially if needed help to deal with his or her mortgage payments. The mortgage lender is not in the business of buying or selling homes, its business is to lending money and selling mortgages. Therefore, it is in his or her best interest to make suitable arrangements to avoid foreclosure on the loan. Telephone calls or mail collection letters must pass these two questions: Does the reader have or had an account with the creditor? Alternatively, is the call from someone he or she has never heard from before? Answers to these questions will indicate the appropriate response. Either way the reader should not ignore the problem, act on it and act timely.

A study on means to protect European consumers in financial difficulty prepared by London Economics in part states: “The objective of this study is to identify debt reduction solutions which allow consumers to return to a financially sustainable path by eliminating some or all of their debts or reduce their debts significantly…” In essence, these are the consequences of decisions made during the 1970s. Europe had developed an economic model where credit became widely available to the vast majority of consumers. Whether in the form of mortgages, personal loans, checking accounts overdrafts, or credit cards, mass consumer credit became common ad remains so to this day. European governments have attempted to deal with this problem, which causes a multitude of social problems, by creating debt adjustment processes for consumers, often springing out of the pre-existing and long-lived corporate insolvency legislation they already had in place. The recession following the credit crunch of 2007-2008, however, brought this issue once again into focus.”

The reader as he or she becomes financially competent should consider debt cancellation not as an automatic right but as his or her responsibility. The consequences of its financial decision-making today will affect its future and that of his or her families. Financial discipline, earning and saving, investing and spending intelligently should be the guides to all money decisions.

Home Ownership

Home ownership is the third most important financial investment of the reader’s life, after paying for its continuing education and buying his or her pre-retirement. A home is a financial asset and more, it is a place to live and raise children; it is a plan for the future and it is an investment in the reader’s community. Home ownership is a comprehensive subject requiring a book solely dedicated to this topic and thus beyond the scope of this personal banking and finance reference book. However, the personal banking and financial discipline, earning and saving, investing and spending the fundamentals discussed throughout a book all apply to home ownership. Therefore, key information and practical application will lead the reader to make a well-informed home ownership decision. This real property investment carries a careful degree of consideration, for in most cases, it is a 30-year financial commitment, and therefore, diligent research is paramount. The more knowledge the reader has about the process of home ownership, the house him or her is interested in the community it is located in, and the seller of the property, the better off he or she will be in the negotiation process.

Alexander — "My assignment is to talk with the cast and communicate with the reader about how does one know if it is ready to buy a home? The first thing anyone needs to realize is that the buyer should have a steady source of income that means a job! Be employed for at least three years; pay its bills on time, have money saved for the down payment, closing costs and moving costs. Most importantly, have the ability to pay the monthly mortgage and mortgage related costs. A mortgage is a loan obtained to purchase real estate. "The mortgage" itself is a lien or a legal claim on the property the reader is planning to purchase. That mortgage secures the promise to pay the debt. All mortgages have two features in common: principal and interest.

Mortgage related costs are mortgage insurance, homeowners insurance and property taxes. These taxes are the annual city and province assessed on the property, divided by the number of mortgage payments the reader will make in a year. If the reader answers NO to any of these statements, I am sorry but he or she is not ready to buy a home. Please, do not feel bad about this; I am not yet ready to buy a home because I am still in secondary school. However, now I know my long-term plan will be to buy a home. I will accomplish buying my dream home by starting now. I will put into action what I am learning in this book, financial discipline, while earning and saving some money and spending some now."

Margaret — "I am to convey to the reader the types of mortgages. There are many types of mortgages, and the more the reader does know about these before starting the consideration process the better.

However, most people use a fix-rate mortgage, in a fix rate mortgage, interest rate stays the same for the term of the mortgage, which normally is thirty years. The advantage of a fixed-rate mortgage is that the reader always knows exactly how much its mortgage payment will be, and he or she can plan for it. Another type of mortgage is an Adjustable Rate Mortgage, with this kind of mortgage, interest rate and monthly payments usually start lower than a fixed-rate mortgage. However, interest rate and payment can change either up or down, as often as once or twice a year. The adjustment rate ties to a financial index, such as the European Union Treasury Securities index.

The advantage of an adjustable rate mortgage is that the reader may be able to afford a more expensive home because its initial interest rate will be lower. Notice that lenders now offer affordable mortgage options, which can help first-time homebuyers overcome obstacles that made purchasing a home difficult in the past. Lenders may now be able to help first-time homebuyers who do not have a lot of money saved for the down payment and closing costs, have no or poor credit history, have more than 41% long-term debt or have experienced income irregularities. To learn the programs available in the reader's country of residence he or she should consult with a licensed home lender or mortgage company."

Carlos — "My assignment is to communicate about how one begins the process of home ownership. The lender will take an application and consider the reader's debt-to-income ratio, which is a comparison of his or her gross (pre-tax) income to housing and non-housing expenses. Housing expense is the rent. Non-housing expenses include long-term debts such as car payments, student loans, alimony, or child support. Based on what I am learning in this book and as member of the think factory cast the reader's monthly mortgage payments should not exceed 29% of its gross income and the combined non-housing expenses should not be more than 41% of net income."

Sofia—"I am assigned the responsibility to communicate to the reader about how he or she can determine its housing needs before the search for a home. The home should fit the way the reader lives, with spaces and features that appeal to the whole family. Before he or she starts looking for a home, make a list of priorities. For example, I will look for the house location close to work, schools, or public transportation. What kinds of amenities are required? I would make "a wish list" for the things I would like, such as a garage and a view. In addition, I will get all the members of the family who live with me to incorporate their wishes and negotiate the best option for all."

Britani — "The agenda shows my assignment to talk with the reader about what one needs to consider when deciding on a community where its prospective home is located. The reader as the prospective homebuyer should select a community that will allow the best in living its daily life. How close the prospective house will be to public and private schools? Does he or she want access to shopping and public transportation? Does the reader need access to public libraries? I do. Does he or she have an active life?

Once the reader finds the community he or she likes, introduce him or herself, talk to people that live there, they know the most about the area and will be the future neighbors. Visit the police department and ask to see the city's quality of life statistics that means find out in advance the city's crime rates. This is most important for everyone but specially for families with young children."

Joseph — "My activity is to inform the reader on the key elements to home ownership. Good representation is paramount. A real estate agent has the knowledge and experience to guide the reader through the home identification and negotiation process, giving access to pricing and sales trends in the neighborhood he or she has identified as the area where the family would like to live. However, if the reader wants someone who can help to come up with the best offer, steer away from a dual agency agreement. What is a dual agency agreement? Dual agency is where the real estate agent represents both the buyer and the seller. The best choice as a homebuyer is to hire an exclusive buyer agent."

Nicolaus — "My assigned topic is comparable sales. The reader should ask the agent to show comparable sales in the area. His or her agent should educate the reader on the area's pricing trends, what other homes of similar age, build, and comparable size have sold in the most recent past, the seller motivation, ask the agent for information as to why the seller is moving? While the seller's agent does not have to reveal this information, many times, they do and it can help the reader to create a win-win offer for both him or her and the seller. While the reader may not be able to determine immediately how much the seller owes on the property under consideration, the agent can find out from the seller's agent or the title company. The reader can also find out by looking up the province tax records for the property that are public information and free of charge. All the reader needs is a little time and determination to make the best deal."

Maria—"My responsibility is to discuss the issue of why is the property time on the market important information The property under consideration time on the market gives the buyer an indication of his or her purchasing power. The longer the property has been on the market, the more negotiating power it has. Therefore, the reader should decide in advance the maximum amount of money is willing to pay for the property and negotiate to reach an agreement not to exceed that price."

Catalina — "I am assigned the task to show the importance of establishing negotiation priorities, minimize the list of things the reader as a buyer would like the seller to consider when negotiating the best price, such as leaving certain appliances, or paying some of the closing costs. The reader should remember it is buying a used home not a brand new one where he or she should expect all things to be in optimum condition. In addition, the buyer should make the moving process easy. Sellers are more receptive to negotiate with those buyers that are flexible and understanding to the moving needs of the seller, such as time to remain in the property for a short time after the close of escrow."

Louis—"What can I communicate to the reader about what a prospective home buyer should look for when walking through a potential home? In addition to comparing the potential home to the buyer minimum requirements and wish lists, consider the following: Is there enough room for the present and the future? Are there adequate number of bedrooms and bathrooms for his or her family size? Is the construction of the house structurally sound? Do the mechanical systems and appliances work properly?

Is the yard big enough to accommodate the reader family life style? Is the floor plan appealing to the buyer? Will the buyer furniture fit in the space? Is there enough storage space? It is wise to bring a tape measure to answer these questions In addition; does anything need repairs or replacement? Imagine the new house in good and bad weather. Would he or she be happy year-round?"

Maria — "My assignment is to communicate with the reader as a potential buyer about the functions of the home inspector, and how does the inspector figure in the purchase of a home? A home inspector is a professional licensed by the country of residence of the buyer; the reader should make sure the inspector is experienced in the area where the reader plans to purchase. The inspector checks the safety of the potential new home. He focuses his attention especially on the structure, construction, and mechanical systems of the house. He must make the reader aware of only repairs needed. The inspector does not evaluate whether he or she is getting a good value for the money. Generally, an inspector checks and gives prices for repairs on the electrical system, plumbing and waste disposal, the water heater and insulation, ventilation and air conditioning systems, water source and quality, the foundation, doors, windows, ceilings, walls, floors and roof."

Britani—"My task is to communicate with the cast and the reader that is a good idea to have an inspection clause included in the offer to purchase. Since, once the deal is close, he or she as buyers have bought the house as is, or the reader may want to include an inspection clause in the offer when negotiating the purchase price of the house. An inspection clause gives him or her an "out" on buying the property if serious problems are present, or gives the ability to renegotiate the price if repairs needed. An inspection clause can also specify that the seller must fix the problem(s) before concluding the purchase."

Larry — "I am to communicate whether or not the reader as buyer needs to be present for the inspection it is not required, but it is a good idea. Immediately following the inspection, the home inspector will be able to answer questions about the report and any problem areas. It is also an opportunity to hear an objective opinion on the home the reader would like to purchase. Moreover, it is a good time to ask general, maintenance questions."

Laura — "The reader should consider other important issues when purchasing his or her own home. Ask the real estate agent if the home is located in a flood plain area. If it is so, the lender will require that the reader as the buyer purchase flood insurance before lending him or her any money. Always check to see if the house under consideration is located in a low-lying area, in a high-risk area for natural disasters such as floods, earthquakes, fires, hurricanes, sand storms, tornados, or in a hazardous materials area such as landfills. The reader should verify that the house and any additions made by the previous owner meets local building codes and local zoning laws, which could affect future remodeling or making an addition to the house. The reader also should make an effort to go to city hall and request to see all building permits issued for the address of the house he or she is contemplating to purchase. Now that the reader has found the house, he or she is ready to buy, leave emotions out of the purchase negotiation."

Home Purchase Documentation

Alexander — "My assignment is to communicate with the cast and the reader regarding the basic documents to start the process of applying for a home loan, and why these documents are necessary. He or she should be ready to submit a copy of the European Country issued identification (ID), driver's license and health insurance card. These documents are required for the same reason as when opening a bank account; to show that the reader is who he or she says it is. In addition, the mortgage lenders will ask for copies of the last thirty days of "pay-packets" and counterfoil copies of the last two years preceding the year when the reader is applying for the home loan. These documents are necessary to demonstrate the source of income stream and ability to repay the loan. Moreover, the mortgage lender will ask for the last two years of properly signed income tax returns. In addition, the mortgage lender wants to examine all pages of the last two months of your bank statements, this is a method lenders use to determine the source of funds, where the reader's money is coming from and how it matches with his or her income stream."

Margaret — "My task is to inform why would the reader needs to provide a copy of its most recent pre-retirement account statement. This documentation will give the mortgage lender the information it needs to formulate the reader's cash liquidity and use it as part of its calculation to identify the applicant asset to debt ratios. In the event that an applicant for a home loan is divorced, why should the lender want a certified copy of the Divorce Decree, signed by the judge? This document determines many financial issues, for example, is the applicant for a home loan to pay child and spousal support, or is the applicant to receive the stipulated amounts? The lender will use this information to increase or decrease the reader's monthly income. In turn, this result will affect its debt to income ratios. The Divorce Decree will stipulate what real property is now own by the home loan applicant, these facts contribute to determine the applicant encumbrances and ability to make the mortgage payments and other financial obligations."

Carlos — "Why would a mortgage lender ask for a copy of pre-retirement account statement and social security pension benefits award letter, for a retired person who is applying for a home loan and it for any child living in the same household that is receiving Social Security benefits? The award letter is an evidence of the monthly amount the government will pay the applicant. This amount will be part of the income stream calculations. When income from a child receiving benefits is part of this equation, the lender will ask for a copy of the child's birth certificate."

Sofia — "What happens if the applicant has in the past-declared bankruptcy? Can the applicant get a loan? The mortgage lender would want a full and complete copy of the Bankruptcy Discharge Order, to determine the level of risk in processing the application. This information will also affect the rate of interest. What other documents does the reader needs to provide to the lender? He or she will submit the name of the insurance agent chosen by the applicant to provide the homeowners insurance. What is earnest money, and what is the reader to expect from the lender?"

Jacques — "Earnest money is the amount the buyer provides the seller as a showing of good faith, to proceed with the purchase of property. Most of the time earnest money is subject to home loan approval. Why would the lender require copies of the front and back of the earnest money checks that have cleared the bank, and copy of the statement showing that the exact check has been paid to the bank? The reader country of residence Treasury Department is empowered to determine, if funds used for the purchase of real property in the Europe are part of any terrorist organization finance fund or money-laundering scheme."

Louis — "If the applicant for a home loan, owns a home, and will not be selling prior to the closing on the purchase of the new home the lender is considering financing, what documents should be ready and available? The reader or buyer would need to provide a copy of the mortgage invoice, copy of the tax assessor's statement and copy of the homeowner's insurance declaration page. What should the reader submit to the lender if he or she is selling its present home? It will need to provide the lender with a copy of the Settlement Statement."

Nicolaus—"There are other aspects of applying for a home loan; it requires an open mind and new mentality. It is a way to determine the reader financial competence."

Benjamin — "The loan documentation process is a matter of fact and for best results; it must be approached and responded with a positive attitude. Other aspects of timely disclosure affect the loan process. For example, if the reader has any deposit for €1.000, or more deposited to his or her account during the loan application process, the reader should make sure to provide the lender with a copy of the front and back of the check, as shown in the corresponding bank statement. Thus, he or she should make sure to check all bank statements before submitting these to the lender. A word of caution, do not deposit cash in his or her bank account while undergoing the loan process. When a family member is providing a "gift" of money to pay as part of the down payment, make sure to notify the lender for proper documentation of the origin of all monies, and must be verified by bank statements dated no longer than ten days before the closing of escrow. Credit report inquiries or disputes must be resolved, or removed and properly documented; the loan underwriter will give special attention to credit reports that do not have the reader's current address, or within the prior twenty-four months, in this case, the reader should explain the situation with the truth."

Catalina — "My assignment is to communicate to the cast and the reader that every time the lender makes a loan change such as locking the interest rate or if the loan amount or sales price changes, these activities generate a new set of disclosures. Therefore, in order to close the transaction on time, the applicant must have provided all the requested documents at least five business days prior to closing of escrow. Since each applicant is unique and circumstances are equally private, the reader should be prepared to respond to the underwriter's request on time with the truth and a good disposition. The process of home ownership is one that can demonstrate the buyer financial competence. His or her willingness to grow and learn will enrich his or her life. Therefore, when the reader is ready to sell the home he has just purchased with so much emotion, the next home purchase will become simply another profitable financial transaction and nothing more. What are a real estate property title and a clear title?"

Laura – "My response to the question is that these documents provide evidence of ownership of a piece of land or property. A clear title is a title in which the ownership is clearly identifiable, while a "cloudy" title indicates that there may be more than one claim to a particular property. A cloud on the title can also mean that there are unresolved issues regarding the property, similar to a mechanic or contractor's lien."

Larry – "Before completing a real estate transaction, the reader should consider a title search as a must activity to ensure that the property he or she are purchasing or selling has a clear title. The title document will show a chain of titles that documents each transfer of the property ownership. The investigation of transfer of ownership should be for at least twenty-four months, while the title search may be expensive; it is one of the most important steps in the purchase process. Without knowing that the reader has clear ownership of the property, he or she should never complete a purchase transaction. Often, cloudy or defective title issues are easy to resolve. Many times, the mortgage company has simply failed to report the payoff of the lien. However, without a complete title search done by a competent and experienced real estate lawyer, the reader's investment in the property may be at risk."

The reader's selected exclusive real estate agent will assist in making an offer, which follows a legal format outlined by his or her country of residence Department of Real Estate. It should include: complete legal description of the property; amount of earnest money; down payment and financing details; proposed move-in date; price the reader is offering; proposed closing date; length of time the offer is valid and details of the transaction. Remember, the best purchase is the one made by the buyer, who makes an offer with the thought that the property is for sale upon closing of escrow. In addition, the reader should remember the last thing a seller wants is to take their home off the market and have the transaction fall through. A house that is back on the market could be even difficult to sell if the potential buyer perceives something is wrong with it.

All real estate transactions, from initial offer to the last signature on the closing date, are subject to Member State regulations and subject to accurate and time-sensitive documentation. All of these activities obligate both the buyer and the seller to adhere to country laws. Failure to perform by either party carries significant monetary penalties and losses.

Financing Your Home

Home ownership becomes a reality when financing and paying for it are completed. These activities are also Member State regulated processes, requiring specific time-sensitive documentation and strict adherence to norms of due diligence. Therefore, in March 2011, the Financial Stability Board published a thematic review of residential mortgage underwriting and origination practices. Lenders are to consider buyer's ability to repay home loans before extending them credit. The main reason for this ruling was the failed home loans made during 2006 and 2007. Another reason for these phenomena was loose underwriting practices by some creditors—including failure to verify the buyer's income or debts and qualifying buyers for home loans based on "teaser" interest rates that would cause monthly mortgage payments to jump to unaffordable levels after the first few years. These underwriting practices and failures contributed to the mortgage crisis of 2008 that led to Europe's most serious recession since the Great Depression of the 1930s.

In response to this crisis, the European Union Consumer Protection Directorate mandates that residential mortgages, creditors must make a reasonable and good faith determination based on verified and documented information, that the home loan buyer has a reasonable ability to repay the home loan according to the terms and conditions. However, this does not dictate that underwrites follow particular underwriting models. The following are the minimum requirements for creditors making buyer's ability-to-repay determinations. The buyer most show current or reasonably expected income or assets, present employment status, monthly payment on the covered transaction and monthly payment on any simultaneous loan. In addition, monthly payment for mortgage-related obligations these include mortgage insurance, fire and casualty insurance, home owners insurance and property taxes. Moreover, present debt obligations including alimony and child support, monthly debt-to-income ratio or residual income, and credit history. In addition, creditors should use reliable third-party records to verify information underwriters use to approve home loans.

Financial Emergency Preparedness

Being financially ready for a man created or natural disaster is more than storing water and supplies. The reader needs to be financially prepared. Starting early and having a plan to pay bills and access his or her important records and accounts help the reader get back on its feet faster and avoid problems with its credit when need it most. Pre-disaster financial planning is essential for individuals and families to complete, because disasters leave many European residents without access to finances or with expensive damages. Thousands of European residents just like the reader – its neighbors and friends – have a plan and keep their important documents in their home disaster kit.

To be financially prepared means more than planning for natural or man created disasters. Help ensure a strong financial future for the reader and its family by taking simple steps now to make the intelligent use of money work for the reader in the end. Safeguarding its finances and important records is easy if you start now. These steps can get you started:

- Identify personal and important documents and place them in a safe space. The reader can use the Safeguarding Your Valuables Activity and Emergency Financial First Aid Kit to help him or her get started available from the country of residence emergency preparedness Unit;
- Download Smartphone applications that can help him or her during emergencies and access disaster preparedness response and recovery resources including disaster assistance;

- Plan ahead of time to recover; and
- To be financially prepared consider saving money in an emergency savings account or keep a reasonable amount of cash at home. Emergency preparedness is a pro-active decision not a reactive consequence. Financial emergency preparedness is the ultimate test of financial competence in action.

Conclusion

To complete the purpose of this work of empowering secondary school, university and vocational training students, members of the Millennial Generation, and adults' residents of Europe is to set the stage for a new generation of financial competent men and women capable of experiencing peace of mind today and tomorrow by applying the intelligent use of money. Understanding the far-reaching consequences of financial illiteracy, explained why Europeans are in financial trouble, recognizing that the gap between the rich and the poor has widened. Income inequality is just one of several dimensions of widening inequality across the European Union. The interaction of all these dimensions—the income gap, skills gap, an age gap, a gender gap, the digital divide, the polarizing effects of new technologies, and the heightened vulnerability of financial illiteracy within household compositions. Women financial education is essential. It will provide females and youth with the foundation to take advantage of economic opportunities in their own country and within Europe, moreover, educating the reader to build lifelong financial survival skills by learning truthful, practical, and easy-to-understand information to enabling readers to apply lessons learned to their unique financial condition immediately. In addition, learning and experiencing with real-life scenarios how emotional reactions and financial literacy drive financial decision-making.

The comprehensive research-based practical application mastery leaning to a proprietary financial model has turned this work onto the most powerful financial transformation teaching to the readers who will embrace the fundamentals in this book. These are financial discipline, earning and saving, investing and spending, while building the pre-retirement fund as early as possible. These reachable goals are the most important investment in the reader's life after investing in education, keeping a good credit and name to purchase a home using the lessons learned in this book to last a lifetime. Finally, the reader financial emergency preparedness is the ultimate test of financial competence in action.

Resources

Millions of secondary, university and vocational students, and adults of all ages residents of Europe use financial products that include savings, credit cards, mortgage loans, private school student loans and other investment vehicles to lay the foundation for a better tomorrow for themselves and their families. Financial competence is one of the most valuables keys to that better tomorrow. The reader has invested the most valuable resource known to man—his or her time. The result of this effort will be seeing in a tangible way with each financial decision made from this point onward.

The reader that has mastered each CashMax^3 module can safely claim becoming financially competent, and to be in a position to implement the intelligent use of money with each financial-decision-making in action. This personal banking and finance terms used in this book are focus points of reference to the fundamentals in this book, and the "answers" resources to validate the path of a profitable and peaceful financial future.

PERSONAL BANKING AND FINANCE TERMS

Account, a banking service allowing a bank to handle and track a customer's money whether in a checking account, savings account, or certificate of deposit.

Account Balance, net of debits and credits at the end of the reporting credits at the end of the reporting period.

Account Reconciliation, the process of verifying an adjusting the balance of a checkbook to march the bank statement.

Account Statement, summary of all checks paid, deposits recoded, and resulting balances during a defined period.

Annual Percentage Yield (APY), an annual percentage of interest a bank will pay to an account holder of a savings account.

Appreciation, the amount of value an item gains over time from the original purchase price, for example, a home, a bank certificate of time (90 days, 360 days) deposit that an account holder has placed in a bank for a specified period of time. In addition an investment, which is an instrument that signifies ownership position in a corporation (shares of stock) a creditor relationship with a corporation. These financial instruments are blue chip common stocks, bank certificates of time deposit, or public traded shares of stock, or known as register securities.

Automated Teller Machine (ATM), a kiosk or electronic terminal where a bank account holder can deposit, withdrawal, or transfer money immediately. The balance shown by the bank appears in real-time, when the balance inquiry takes place, and may not reflect all deposits and checks issued.

Average Daily Balance, is a method of computing interest or finance charges on bank deposit accounts, credit cards, lines of credit and revolving charge accounts.

Bad or Bounced Check, is a check that the bank will not pay because the account holder does not have sufficient money in the account to cover payment. It is a return check. All banks charge will charge an "Insufficient Funds" service fee for each bad check. Writing bad checks can seriously harm the account holder credit score, and present and future relationships with banks.

Balance, the exact amount of money the account holder has in its account according to the bank. This figure may be different from the amount shown in the account holder's own records because of checks written or deposits made not yet been processed by the bank.

Bank, a business that offers the reader a safe place to keep its money, uses this money whether in checking, savings or time deposits to make investments, loans to business or other bank customers, and charges these interests and service fees.

Bank Statement, a monthly record of the deposits and withdrawals an account holder made to its account. It also records direct deposits made by employers, payments made directly by the bank on behalf of the account holder. The bank statement will show all service charges incurred, for example the use of an ATM at a different financial institution.

Bond, is any interest-bearing or discounted corporate or government security that obligates the issuer to pay the account holder (bondholder) a specific sum of money, at specific intervals, and to repay the principal amount of the loan at maturity. The bondholder has an "I owe you" from the issuer, but not corporate ownership privileges as common stockholders do.

Check, a written order instructing the bank to pay a specific amount from the account holder's account to specific person or entity. The check must contain the following legal elements: date, payee (name of a person, organization, or entity to be paid) amount, and signature. In addition, it should contain a memo note specifying the purpose of the payment.

Checking Account, is a type of bank account that allows the account holder to deposit and withdraw money to write checks, pay bills, or to buy goods and services. Using a checking account is a safe and convenient way to manage cash.

Clear, when the banks pay a check that the account holder has written and immediately subtracts the amount from the holder's available balance. Technically, the check has cleared the bank.

Compound interest, is interest earned on principal plus interest that earned earlier.

Debit Card, a special card issued by the bank that looks similar and treated like a credit card. However, when used the total amount of the purchase, or cash withdrawal deducted immediately from the account holder's checking account, rather than drawing on available credit. Normally debit cards have a daily draw limit.

Deposit, cash, checks, or drafts placed with a bank for credit to the account holder's account. Banks broadly differentiate between demand deposits (checking) and time deposits.

Deposit Slip, a document that tells the bank how much money the account holder is adding to its checking or savings account.

Direct Deposit, a deposit made directly into the checking, or savings account holder by the employer or payer without the use of a paper deposit, or deposit slip. It is becoming the common method of deposit a pay packet from employers and benefits payments from governments.

Fees, the amount a bank charges for an account activity or services.

Fee Schedule, a bank disclosure listing the fees an account holder will be charge for account activities.

Fixed Expenses, are expenditures with specific amount that do not change from month to month.

Flexible Expenses, are costs with amounts that often change from month to month.

Financial Institution, banks and other Financial Services Scheme regulated business that provide a wide range of money management products and services to consumers. These institutions collect funds from the public and place them, or invest these funds in financial assets such as time deposits, loans and bond.

Global Remittance, is a form of Electronic Funds Transfer (EFT) that allows the account holder at a bank to send money outside Europe from its checking or savings account.

Gross Income, is the total income from employment or investments without deductions.

Interest, is the amount of money paid by the bank to a lender in exchange for the use of its money for a period, for example, an account holder can earn interest from its bank when it has a savings or a deposit account.

Individual Pre-retirement Account (IPRA), an individual account established by the account holder with a mutual fund manager that may include a combination of stocks, bonds and mutual funds. This type of arrangement is relatively new in Europe. The reader should consult with a licensed tax professional, or a licensed financial planner to determine if this option is suitable for his or her situation.

Line of Credit, an arrangement by which a lender bank extends a specific amount of credit to an account holder, or borrower for a limited time. As long as the principal and interest are paid on time, the account holder may continue to borrow against its line of credit during an agreed upon period. A line of credit can be secured or unsecured.

Liabilities, the amount owed to a bank or a person.

Loan money, borrowed from a bank or a person with a written promise to pay it back later. a loan carries an agreed rate of interest.

Minimum Balance, a certain balance that a bank might require the account holder to open an account that earns interest, or avoid service charges and other bank fees.

Mobile Banking, allows the account holder to access checking or savings accounts through a secure web browser from a mobile device such as smart phone or computer tablet.

Money Order, a document issued by a Post Office or an authorized financial intermediary ordering payment of a specific amount of money to an individual, or a business. It is similar in value to a paper check.

Mortgage, a debit instrument by which the borrower gives the lender a lien on a real property as security for repayment of a loan. The borrower has the unrestricted use of the property. The lien is cancel when the obligation is pay in full.

Mutual Fund, a fund operated by a licensed Investment Company that raises money from shareholders and invests it in stocks, bonds, options, futures, currencies, or money market securities. The fund offers investors the advantage of diversification and professional management.

Net Income, is the gross income from employment minus deductions including Social Security, union dues and taxes.

Non-sufficient funds (NSF), the lack of enough money in the account holder checking account to pay for a check or scheduled payment, a NSF check be returned by the bank to the account holder marked "unpaid" and will carry a service charge. This activity has a negative impact on future applications for loans and may prevent the opening of new accounts at other banks. If the account holder persists in overdrawing its account, the bank may close the account and report it to the Credit Bureau.

Overdraft, a term used by the bank to indicate an item such as a check, ATM purchase or other transaction presented to the bank is paid by the bank even though the available cash balance in the checking account is less than the amount of the item. This creates an overdraft, or negative balance. Banks will charge the account holder and overdraft service fee.

Payee, is a person, company or organization to whom the account holder wrote a check, and who is to receive the money.

Personal Identification Number (PIN), a secrete combination of letters and numbers the account holder uses to access its checking, savings, or investment accounts through a computer or another electronic device.

Phishing, is a two-part fraud involving an e-mail and spoof website. Fraudsters or phishers, send e-mail to a wide audience that appears to come from a bank, or a reputable company requesting personal information and account numbers. This practice is phish e-mail.

Portfolio, combined holdings of more than one stock, bond, commodity, real estate investment, cash equivalents, or other assets by an individual or institution.

Privacy Notice, is a written explanation of how the bank handles and shares the account holder personal financial information.

Reconcile, the process an account holder uses to determine if the balance in the account register matches the balance reported by the bank on checking or savings account statements.

Remittance, is a money transfer from the account holder's checking or savings account that goes to a bank of another person outside Europe.

Return Item, also known as NSF, and carries same bank fee charges.

Rule of 72, formula for approximating the time it will take for a given amount of money to double a given compound interest rate. The formula is simply 72 divided by the rate of interest.

Savings Account, a bank account that allows the account holder to deposit and withdraw money and earn interest.

Signature Card, a form all would be new account holders complete and sign when opening a checking, or savings account verifying the authenticity of the name and the person opening the account.

Simple Interest, is a calculation based only on the original principal amount. Simple interest contrasts with compound interest, which applies to principal plus accumulated interest.

Spending Plan, is a systematic written plan for meeting expenses in a given period. Its purpose is to keep track of an individual's daily spending habits, determine income and expenses are the month before they are due; find ways to decrease spending, and create new sources of income.

Statement, a monthly accounting document sent to the account holder by the bank that chronologically lists the account balance at the end of the accounting period, normally a month. The statement must list all deposits, checks paid, and service charge fees.

Stocks, are ownership position represented by shares that claim rights on the corporation's earnings and assets. There are two distinct types of stock common stock entitles the stockholder to vote in the election of directors and other matters taken up by the stockholders meeting, or by proxy. Preferred stock generally does not conferred voting rights, but it has a prior claim on the assets and earnings. Dividends on preferred stock paid before any paid on common stock.

Substitute Check, is an electronic image of a check that has same legal standing as the actual check.

Term, is refer to the time in which loan payments are paid, or the time when interest payments be paid on a certificate of deposit. Another example, a car loan may have a three-year term, while a home mortgage may have a 30-year term.

Transaction, is an agreement between buyer and seller to exchange an asset for payment.

Transaction Register, is a register that allows the keeping of accurate records of deposits and withdrawals on a checking or savings account.

Withdrawal, is money taken out of a checking or savings account.

Wire Transfer, is a form of transferring money from one bank to another.

ANSWERS TO QUESTIONS—CHAPTER 8

1 Correct Answer, (C) 2. Correct Answer, (B) 3. Correct Answer, (A) 4. Correct Answer, (D) 5. Correct Answer, (A) 6. Correct Answer, (A) 7. Correct Answers (B) and (C) 8. Correct Answer, (A) 9. Correct Answer, (C) 10. Correct Answer, (D) 11. Correct Answer, (A) 12. Correct Answer (A) 13. Correct Answers (B) and (C).

ANSWERS TO QUESTIONS—CHAPTER 9

1 Correct Answer, (B) 2 Correct Answer, (D) 3. Correct Answer, (A) 4. Correct Answer, (B) 5 Correct Answer, (A) 6. Correct Answer, (D) 7. Correct Answer, (A) 8. Correct Answer, (E) 9. Correct Answer, (A) (B) (C) and (D) 10. Correct Answer, (B) 11. Correct Answers (A) False; (B) False; (C) False; (D) True.

ANSWERS TO QUESTIONS—CHAPTER 10

1 Correct Answer, (E) 2. Correct Answer, (D) 3. Correct Answer, (A) 4. Correct Answer, (A), and (C) 5. Correct Answer, (B), and (D) 6. Correct Answer, (D) 7. Correct Answer, (B) 8. Correct Answers (A) and (C) 9. Correct Answers (A) and (B) 10. Correct Answers (B), (C) and (D) 11. Correct Answer, (C) and 12. Correct Answer (A).

References

Agarwalla, S. K., S. Barua, J. Jacob, and J. R. Varma, (2012), A Survey of Financial Literacy among Students, Young Employees and the Retired in India, Indian Institute of Management Ahmedabad.

Alderfer, Clayton P., An Empirical Test of a New Theory of Human Needs; Organizational Behavior and Human Performance, volume 4, issue 2, pp. 142-175, 1969.

Alderfer, C.P., Existence, Relatedness, and Growth Human Needs in Organizational Settings, New York: Free Press, 1972.

Alessie, Rob, Maarten Van Rooij and Annamaria Lusardi (2011). "Financial literacy and retirement preparation in the Netherlands." Journal of Pension Economics and Finance, 10, pp 527-545.

Almenberg, Johan and Jenny Säve-Söderbergh (2011). "Financial literacy and retirement planning in Sweden." Journal of Pension Economics and Finance, 10, pp 585-598.

Alpha Research (2010) Financial Literacy Survey, Report on the Key Findings of the Survey Prepared for the World Bank, Alpha Research, June 2010, Sofia, Bulgaria.

Andura, Albert 176. Social Learning Theory Englewood Cliffs: Prentice-Hall Publications.

ANZ (Australia and New Zealand Banking Group) (2011) Adult Financial Literacy in Australia. Full Report of the results from the 2011 ANZ Survey. December 2011.

ANZ–Retirement Commission, (2009), 2009 ANZ–Retirement Commission Financial Knowledge Survey.

ANZ– Commission for Financial Literacy and Retirement Income, (2013), 2013 Financial Knowledge and Behaviour Survey.

Atkinson, A, S. McKay, E. Kempson, and S. Collard (2006), "Levels of Financial Capability in the UK: Results of a Baseline Survey", Consumer Research 47, Prepared for the Financial Services Authority by Personal Finance Research Centre University of Bristol, Financial Services Authority.

Atkinson, A., and Messy, F-A. (2012), "Measuring Financial Literacy: Results of the OECD / International Network on Financial Education (INFE) Pilot Study", OECD Working Papers on Finance, Insurance and Private Pensions, No. 15, OECD Publishing.

Australian Government and Financial Literacy Foundation (2008), Financial Literacy – Women Understanding Money, Australian Government, Financial Literacy Foundation.

Azerbaijan Micro-finance Association, (2009) Final Report - Results of the Financial Literacy Survey, Baku, Azerbaijan Micro-finance Association, Azerbaijan: December 30, 2009.

Banco de Portugal, (2011), Survey on the financial literacy of the Portuguese population.

How Do Emotions Drive Money Decisions?

Barber, Brad M. and Terrance Odean (2011), "Boys will be Boys: Gender, Overconfidence, and Common Stock Investment", Quarterly Journal of Economics, 116 (1): 261-292.

Bucher-Koenen, Tabea and Annamaria Lusardi (2011). "Financial literacy and retirement planning in Germany." Journal of Pension Economics and Finance, 10, pp 565-584.

Bucher-Koenen, Tabea, Annamaria Lusardi, Rob Alessie, and Maarten van Rooij (2012) "How financially literate are women? Some new perspectives on the gender gap". Netspar Panel Paper 31.

Capital One (2009). "Capital One Survey of High School Seniors Reveals Gender Gaps in Financial Literacy."

CCFSI (Central Council for Financial Services Information), (2011), Financial Literacy Survey of Japan.

Central Council for Financial Services Information, Bank of Japan.

Clark, Mary 1989. Ariadne's Thread: The Search for New Modes of Thought. London: Palgrave.

Clark, Mary. Meaningful Social Bonding as a Universal Human Need" in Burton (1190b), pp. 34-59.

Coate, Roger A., and Rosati, Jerel A.1988 The Power of Human Needs in World Society. Boulder: Lynne Rienner Publishers.

Freud Sigmund 1989a (Reissue ed. Edited by James Strachey and Peter Gay) The Future of an Illusion

New York: N.W. Norton.

Maslow, Abraham 1954. Motivation and Personality. Reading: Adison Wesley Publishing Company.

McLellan, David, ed. 1977. Karl Marx: Selected Writings. Oxford; Oxford University Press.

Schiller, Claire. Instinctive Behavior. 1957. Hall Press, New York.

Siegfried, J., and R. Felds. 1979. Research on teaching college economics: A Survey. Journal of Economics Literature, 17 (3); pp. 923-969.

Skinner, B.F. 1965 Science and Human Behavior. New York: Free Press.

Skinner, B.F. 1976 Walden Two Boston: Allyn and Bacon, Sites, Paul 1973. Control: The Basics of Social Order. New York: Associated Faculty Press.

Sites, Paul. Needs as Analogies of Emotions," in Burton (1190b) pp.7-33.

Walstad, W.B. 2001 Economic Education in the U.S. high schools "Journal of Economic Perspectives, 15 (3): 195-210.

---and Rebeck, K. 2001a Test of Economics Literacy: examiner's Manual (3rd edition) New York: National Council of Economics.

---and Rebeck, K. 2002 Assessing the economic knowledge and opinions of adults Quarterly Review of Economics and Finance, 42 (5): 921-935.

---and Robson, D. 1997 Differential item functioning and male female differences on multiple choice tests in economics. Journal of Economics Education, 29 (2): 155-71.

About the Author

Jorge Rivera, Ph.D., is an economist and behavioral science specialist; adjunct professor of transnational economics, personal banking and finance strategy, U.S. Department of Defense; and a member of the U.S. Council of Economics and Financial Literacy. He holds senior consultancy status with the United Nations, The World Bank Group, International Monetary Fund, and the International Finance Corporation. Rivera is Chief Executive Officer, American Hope Charities.

Index

A

Accounts 92, 96, 131, 134, 196-7, 199-200, 204
Action, corrective 66-7
Action plan 179, 209
Amount 144, 163, 170-1, 173-4, 195, 236-7, 246-9
Amount due 176
Amount of money 22, 74, 134, 179, 188-9, 213, 248-50
Annual percentage yield, see APY
Answers 86-9, 92-3, 95, 137, 162-3, 189-90, 252
Applicant 236-8
Application 77, 79, 85, 113-14, 200-1, 214, 230-1
APY (annual percentage yield) 96, 188, 190, 196-7, 246
Assessments 10-11, 88
Asset categories 202-3, 205-6
Assets 20, 85, 175, 186, 194, 240, 250-1
ATM (Automated Teller Machines) 99-105, 115-16, 122-4, 127, 140-2, 154-6, 246-7
ATM, bank's 134-5
ATM cards 102, 105, 122, 124, 132, 135, 155
  bank's 134, 143
ATM cash withdrawals 116, 148, 150-2
ATM fees 122, 143, 154
ATM withdrawals 90, 100, 136, 142, 144
Automated Teller Machines, see ATM

B

Balance 100-2, 123-4, 135-6, 140-2, 151-2, 246, 249-51
  daily 135-6
  new 151
Balance match 151
Bank 87-107, 111-16, 122-3, 130-40, 142-5, 147-8, 245-51
  insured 94, 130
  prospective 96
  reader's 151, 188
Bank accounts 74, 78, 100
Bank certificates 246
Bank charges 89, 127, 143, 148, 154, 248
Bank customers 140, 155, 246
Bank deposit 97
Bank deposit accounts 246
Bank employees 81, 114
Bank fee schedule 134-5
Bank fees 124, 134, 249
Bank loan 41, 104
Bank online 101, 147
Bank products 113, 129
Bank service fees 133
Bank services 81, 113
Bank statements 57, 109, 121, 123, 149-52, 238, 246-7
Bank teller 113, 138
Bank withdrawals 98, 124
Banker 57, 197
Banking 19, 36, 51, 60, 84, 95, 99
Banking relationship 95, 99, 105, 129, 136, 138, 143
  personal 127, 133

Banking services 79, 81, 103, 113-14, 133, 245
Banking system crises 60
Banking systems 60
Banking transactions
limited personal 140
personal 129
Banknotes 7
Bankruptcy 42, 52, 74, 177
Banks and Credit Institutions 94
Behaviors 1, 12, 21, 37-8, 52, 58, 115
Benefits 27-31, 81-2, 139-40, 164-5, 179-80, 195, 212-13
Bills 22-3, 89-94, 104, 109, 146-7, 174-7, 190-2
money-paying 154
Bondholder 247
Bonds 90, 200, 202-4, 206, 210, 213-14, 247-50
Borrower 226, 248-9
Branch manager 100, 113, 116
Bucher-Koenen 16, 254
Budget 22, 24
Business 93-4, 98, 107, 133, 208-9, 228, 246
Buyer 209, 230, 232-5, 237-40, 251

C

Car payment 163
Card 97, 102-5, 107, 115, 126-8, 132, 227
gift 103, 116, 124, 155, 168
Carl Gustav Jung 48, 50
Cash 89, 91-4, 122-6, 139-40, 173-4, 203, 247
Cash equivalents 203, 206, 250
Cash on Delivery (COD) 225
CashMax³ 34, 79
CashMax³ module 215, 217
CashMax³ module 79, 81, 121, 161, 178, 183, 245
CD (Certificate of Deposit) 189, 199-200, 213-14
Central Council for Financial Services Information 254
Certificate of Deposit, see CD
Channels 66, 68
Character 36, 38-9, 46, 106, 218
Charges 57, 96-7, 122-3, 134, 142-5, 154-5, 246
Checking accounts 115, 121, 125, 130-1, 136, 140, 149
Child support 132, 169, 176, 231, 241
Chocolates 196, 222
CIN (Country Identification Number) 111, 122, 154
Closing 15, 40-1, 98, 212, 227, 237-9
COD (Cash on Delivery) 225
Company 111-12, 141-2, 173, 181, 186, 202, 206-7
Compound interest 8, 193, 195-6, 198, 212-13, 247, 250
Consequences 38-9, 58-9, 85, 87, 162, 229
Consumers 6, 11, 26, 35, 226, 228-9, 248
Correct Answer 87, 93, 104, 162, 252
Correct answers 34, 115, 117, 122, 153, 252
Correct responses 89, 115, 122, 162
Costs 29-30, 94-5, 125, 127-8, 183-6, 196, 230
closing 230-1, 233
Countries 7-11, 13-17, 21-2, 24-6, 28-9, 32-3, 60-1
Country Identification Number, see CIN
Creator 40, 70, 77
Credit 25-6, 105-6, 143-4, 215, 217-18, 225-9, 245-9
available 177, 225, 227, 247
Credit Bureau 142, 226, 228, 249
Credit card balances 165, 227
Credit card bills 76, 109
Credit card number 91, 106, 110
Credit cards 75-7, 106-7, 111-12, 144-6, 177-8, 226-7, 245-7
Credit department 145
Credit history, good 122, 154
Credit Institutions 94, 174
Credit report 109, 112, 225-6, 228
Credit scores 81, 143, 146, 217, 225-8

Creditors 110, 164, 178, 227-8, 240-1
Currency 7, 75, 77, 87, 125, 203, 249
Customer service 96, 99, 111, 113, 116, 133-6, 138
bank's 91, 111, 148, 197

D

Daily spending diary 168-9
Daily spending habits 161-2, 179, 251
Date 88, 124, 141, 143-4, 147-9, 152, 176
Days 138, 140, 149, 197, 236, 238, 246
Death benefits 194
Death grants 27-8, 30
Debit card numbers 107
Debit card purchases 90, 106, 143, 148, 150-2
Debit card transactions 142
Debit cards 96, 101-5, 115-16, 124-5, 127, 131-3, 154-5
Debt 58, 178, 192-3, 227, 229-30, 236, 240
Deductions 70, 164, 172-3, 180, 248
Deposit accounts 90, 101, 103, 115, 190, 200
money Market 199
Deposit cash 123, 238
Deposit-guarantee scheme 89, 93-5, 102, 115, 130
Deposit Guarantee Scheme 199-200, 213
Depositing 139, 170, 211
Deposits 89-90, 96-8, 122-3, 138-41, 150-2, 154-6, 246-8
certificates of 194, 200, 203
direct 127-8, 131-3, 137-8, 140, 165-6, 173-4, 247-8
money market 189, 213
savings accounts 101
Differences, gender 13-17, 20
Distress, financial 35, 66, 73-5, 77, 118, 149
Diversification 203-6, 208, 249
Diversify 203, 206, 208, 213
Divorce 42, 186
DNA 40, 44-5, 47
Documentation, time-sensitive 240
Documents 92, 108, 136, 175-6, 235-9, 247, 249
important 218, 241

E

Earning 34, 76-9, 121, 128-30, 137, 156, 229-30
Earning and saving 121, 129, 153
Economics 1, 19-20, 48, 83, 254-5
Education 5, 8, 11-14, 17, 58-9, 191, 193
Electronic banking 132, 144, 155
safe 147
Emergency preparedness, financial 241-2, 244
Emotional intelligence 4, 73-6, 79-80, 85-6, 118
Emotional Intelligence and Money 73
Emotions 1, 21, 37, 39, 43-4, 66, 143
Employees 27, 95, 110-11, 113, 133, 163, 184
Employer 103-4, 125-6, 132, 172-3, 184, 192-3, 247-8
Employment 15, 27-9, 31, 67, 184, 248
Entertainment 163, 168-71
Entitlement 31-2
Errors 19, 142, 148, 152, 228
Escrow 233, 238-9
Euro 6-7, 60, 82, 84, 87, 125, 185
Euro Card 102-3, 105-6, 144
EURO Friendly Bank 135
Europe 6-11, 13-15, 59-61, 81-3, 86-7, 219, 248
residents of 1-2, 5, 243
European Commission 2, 8, 11, 40-1, 60
European residents 5, 12, 22-3, 63, 69, 241
European Union 5-8, 10-13, 28-9, 36, 60-1, 97, 105
Europeans 8, 10, 22, 37-8, 79, 82, 183-4
Evidence 10, 15-16, 18-19, 86, 89-91, 211-12, 236
Exact amount of money 148, 246

Expenses 161, 163, 166-7, 169-71, 175-9, 224, 227
fixed 163, 171, 248
flexible 163, 171, 179, 248
yearly 170
Extroversion 48-50, 53
Extroverts 49-50, 53-4

F

Factors, emotional 45, 73
Family benefits 27-8, 31-2
Fees 96-7, 122-3, 127, 134-5, 143-4, 154, 205-6
monthly 100-1, 127-30
Fees bank charges 134
Fees4Cash 126
FICO 226, 228
Finance model 33, 77-8, 84, 209
Finance terms 36, 84-5, 114, 198, 245
Finances 8-9, 16, 19-20, 22-3, 87, 141, 253-4
Financial 146, 253
Financial affairs 2, 23
Financial behavior 11, 15, 18, 21-6, 33, 45-6, 52
Financial behavior statements 22-3
Financial competence 79, 114-15, 128-9, 153, 211-12, 237-8, 244-5
sustainable 214
Financial competence application 214-15
Financial condition 3, 29, 80, 86, 162, 164, 166
Financial conduct 2, 5, 21, 54, 64, 84, 86
Financial decisions 5, 14, 19, 41, 55, 58, 60
Financial difficulties 52, 75-6
Financial discipline 77-81, 84-6, 114-15, 128-9, 137-8, 146, 229-30
Financial education 3, 8-9, 11, 13-15, 20-1, 38, 80
Financial goals 161-2, 165-6, 169, 187, 189, 194, 211
long-term 24
Financial goals action plan 211
Financial illiteracy 1, 5, 63, 66, 173, 219, 243
Financial illiteracy problem 5-7, 37
Financial information 111-12, 142, 147
personal 105-6, 116, 250
Financial institutions 93-5, 105-6, 109, 115-16, 130-1, 146-7, 199-201
Financial issues 18, 184, 236
Financial knowledge 12, 14-15, 17-18, 34, 36, 115, 118
Financial literacy 1-3, 9-19, 35-8, 78, 86-8, 117-18, 253-5
level of 17, 31, 37, 78
low 10-11
Financial Literacy and Retirement Planning 16
Financial literacy education 8, 10, 15, 82-3, 85
Financial literacy survey 25-6, 253
Financial personality 38-40, 45-6
Financial products 9, 11, 15, 22-3, 25-6, 161, 245
Financial progress 69, 117, 156, 197
Financial services 11, 13-14, 77, 94
Financial Services Authority 253
Financial situation 32, 56, 156-8, 177, 186, 203, 205
Financial terms 34, 36, 51, 55, 78
Financial wellbeing 21, 74
Financing 240
FINRA 8
Foundation 146, 150, 159, 161, 234, 243, 245
Funds 89-90, 93, 124, 142, 145, 236-7, 248-9
money market 203, 206
Funds fees 122, 138

G

Gap, gender 6, 15-17, 243, 254
Goals 24, 165-7, 185, 187, 189, 193, 210-12
personal 165, 168, 171
Great Depression 60, 240

Great Recession 59-60

H

Holguin 76-7
Home 65-6, 149, 183, 194, 208-9, 229-35, 237-40
  potential 234
Home inspector 234-5
Home insurance 170-1
Home loan 218, 235-7, 240-1
Home ownership 217, 229-30, 232, 240
  process of 230-1, 238
Homebuyers, first-time 231
Hours, overtime 163, 179
House 188, 193, 208-9, 222, 230, 234-5, 239
Human behavior 1, 5, 12, 34, 39, 42-6, 65

I

Identity theft 91, 106-8, 114, 116, 137, 147
  victim of 110, 112
Income 69-70, 73-7, 161-3, 169-72, 175, 177-9, 184-6
  fixed 31
  gross 172-3, 231, 248-9
  household 17, 24, 186
  monthly 161, 166, 169, 236
  total 162-3, 248
Income inequality 5-6, 243
Income stream 74, 236
Incomes, higher 73, 75
Individual Pre-retirement Account, see IPRA
INFE (International Network on Financial Education) 8-9, 13, 253
Information 24-8, 105-6, 108-9, 112-14, 177, 225-8, 236-7
Initial savings amount 198
Inspection clause 234-5
Institutions 30-1, 95, 248, 250
  competent 30-1
Insurance 28, 30-1, 165, 180
  auto 163, 169-71
Insurance and Private Pensions 9, 14, 16, 253
Intellectual quotient, see IQ
Intelligence 73, 75-6
Interest 19, 130-1, 148, 195-201, 213, 215, 246-50
Interest rate 196-8, 200, 210, 218, 231, 237-8, 249-50
  higher 200-1, 214
International Network on Financial Education, see INFE
Interpersonal affinity 54-5
Introversion 48-9
Introversion-extroversion 54-5
Introverts 48-50, 53-4
Invalidity 27-8, 30
Investment clubs 208
Investment options 189, 199, 201, 204, 210, 212, 214
Investment portfolio 206-8
Investment products 61, 102, 189, 202-3, 207-8, 213
  non-deposit 201, 214
Investments 19, 52-3, 191, 194, 201-8, 212-14, 246
  best 204, 207, 214
  good 208-9
  mutual fund 204, 206
Investors 19, 202-5, 207-8, 249
IPRA (Individual Pre-retirement Account) 204, 248
IQ (intellectual quotient) 58, 73-5, 77
IQ scores 73, 75-7

J

Job, part-time 163-4, 178, 180
Journal of Pension Economics and Finance 16, 253-4

K

Killers, silent 63-4, 66

L

Learning 17, 78, 112, 149-50, 152-3, 173-5, 191
Legislation 28-31
Lender 106, 218, 226, 231, 235-8, 240, 248-9
Level, lower financial literacy 17-18
Liabilities 74, 194, 249
Life 1, 37-8, 43-5, 78-9, 180-1, 184-5, 222-5
Life insurance policies 181, 194
Life insurance story 180
Lifelong learning 6, 11
List 99, 163, 166, 168-9, 176, 179, 232-3
Loans 92-5, 101, 103, 217-18, 225-8, 236-7, 246-9
Losses 89, 93, 202, 204-5, 240
Lusardi 16-18

M

Mail 108-9, 111-12, 138, 140-1, 143, 149, 151
Market 106, 191, 209, 233, 239
Market conditions 205-6
Mastery learning 78, 80, 83, 86-7, 103, 110, 114
MBTI (Myers-Briggs Type Indicator) 48
Member State, competent 30, 32
Member State of residence 31
Messy 9, 16, 253
Mid-point 209, 212, 214
Millennial Generation 1, 3, 9-10, 32, 34-5, 243
Minimum balance 131, 133, 155, 199, 249
Minimum opening balance 96
MMA (Money Market Account) 199, 201
MMDAs (Money Market Deposit Account) 131, 199-200, 203, 214
Module 80, 117, 161-2, 187, 212, 214, 217
Money 63-70, 85-91, 165-9, 187-93, 195-205, 210-15, 245-51
  borrowing 41-2, 163, 166, 217
  deposit 125, 144
  earnest 237, 239
  extra 163, 165
  free 53, 173, 193
  keeping 130, 195, 213
  lending 202, 228
  losing 203, 213
  reader's 161, 203, 236
  saving 25, 133, 137, 189, 192, 242
  tax 201-2
  transfer 104, 156, 246
  transferring 92, 103, 116, 251
  withdrawing 146, 155
Money and Stress Silent Killers 63
Money decisions 84, 192, 229
Money management 66, 68
Money management skills 14
Money Market Account (MMA) 199, 201
Money Market Deposit Account, see MMDAs
Money markets 115, 199
Money orders 92-3, 103-4, 125, 137, 249
Money problems, time-sensitive 68
Money skills 37, 88
Money survival skills 138, 210-11
Money transfers 92, 103, 116, 155, 250
Monthly balance 96
Monthly bank statement 123, 143, 148, 150, 153-5
Monthly expenses 170
Mortgage 11, 177, 181, 190, 209, 226-7, 229-31
Mortgage lender 228, 236-7
Mortgage payments 228, 230-1, 236
Mutual funds 115, 199-200, 202-4, 206, 210, 213-14, 248-9
Myers-Briggs 54-5
Myers-Briggs Type Indicator (MBTI) 48

N

Net 19, 74, 77, 163, 176, 180, 193-4
Net income 172, 231, 249
Non-deposit accounts 100, 102, 114, 116
Non-housing expenses 231
Non-Sufficient Funds, see NSF
NSF (Non-Sufficient Funds) 134, 141, 215, 249-50
NSF fees 122, 135, 141-3, 148

O

Occupational diseases 27-8, 30
OECD (Organization for Economic Co-operation and Development) 2, 8-9, 13-17, 21, 253
OECD Working Papers on Finance 9, 14, 16, 253
Online banking 92, 96, 115, 147
Organization for Economic Co-operation and Development, see OECD
Overconfidence 19, 254
Overdraft 67, 96, 122, 124, 135, 142-3, 249
Overdraft fees 96, 134, 143, 154
Overdraws 123, 142, 144, 154-5

P

Password 110, 147
Pay-packet 125-6, 132-3, 138-40, 171-3, 179-80, 187, 191-3
Pay-packet cards 103, 126
Pay-packet counterfoil 163, 173, 180
Payee 92, 247, 250
Paying 78-9, 163-4, 166, 183-4, 189-91, 212-14, 227-9
Paying bills 74, 92, 94, 180, 189
Payment schedule, monthly 175
Payments 145-6, 163-4, 169, 177-81, 225-7, 231, 246-7
  down 165, 170-1, 211, 230-1, 238-9
  monthly 132, 193, 195, 231, 240
Pensions 11, 14, 29, 183-4, 194
Perception 21, 54, 56-8, 63, 167
Periods of insurance 28, 30-1
Person
  insured 28-30
  unemployed 31
Personal banking 1-5, 22-3, 32-4, 36, 76-80, 82, 84-7
  application of 36, 78, 174
  fundamentals of 44, 81, 114, 117
  glossary of 34, 84
  regarding 34, 150, 217
  sustainable 1, 12
  systematic 77
Personal Banking and Finance Model 77
Personal Banking and Finance Terms 85, 198
Personal Banking and Financial Discipline 81, 114
Personal Banking and Financial Illiteracy Reality 7
Personal banking knowledge 128
Personal expenses 163, 179, 218
Personal Identification Number, see PIN
Personal information 93, 105-8, 112, 147, 250
Personal spending plan 161, 165-6, 169-70, 172, 175, 177-9
Personality 34, 45, 48-50, 53, 67, 80, 254
  outgoing 53
Personality-Financial Behavior and Money 58
Personality traits 40, 48, 51, 55
PIN (Personal Identification Number) 102, 107, 116, 140, 156, 250
Plan 130-1, 163, 165, 174-5, 185, 209-10, 241-2
Portfolio 202, 205-6, 250
Portfolio diversification 205-6
Pre-retirement plan 171, 184, 186-7, 189, 213-14
Pre-retirement savings contributions 173, 208
Pre-retirement savings plan 173
Privacy 87, 93, 105-6, 114
Private Pensions 9, 14, 16, 253

Problem 5-6, 65, 67, 157, 178, 228-9, 234-5
Process 36, 55-6, 78, 86, 97, 150-1, 157
new thinking 3, 33, 35
Products 25-6, 101-2, 106, 130, 133, 204-7, 209
Programs, pre-retirement savings 173
Property 119, 230, 233-4, 237, 239, 249
Purchases 102-3, 116, 124-7, 132-4, 206-7, 234-5, 237

R

Reader's bank statement 148, 151
Real estate agent 232, 235
Real estate transactions 239
Reason 89, 94, 131, 134, 136, 235, 240
Reconcile 121, 148-51, 153-4, 164, 250
Reconciling 123-4, 143, 149-50, 153
Register 56, 89-90, 120-1, 123-4, 141-3, 146, 150-6
Regulation 28, 31-2, 34, 94, 148
Rejection 39, 41-3
Repairs 170, 228, 234-5
Research 2-3, 8, 32, 34, 74, 254
Residence 28, 30-1, 46, 73, 112, 154
country of 28-9, 82, 175, 186, 234
Resources 2, 4, 34, 69-70, 193-4, 198, 245
financial 70, 193-4
Respondents 11, 21-6, 49
Responses 22-3, 25, 106, 108, 130-1, 162-4, 238
Responsibilities 23-4, 81, 84, 170, 172, 229, 231
Retailers 92, 102-3, 116
Retirement 24, 28, 30-1, 184-5, 189, 191, 193
Retirement planning 16, 253-4
Risk 18, 20, 137, 201, 203-5, 208, 213
financial 20
Rorschach's EB 54-5
Rule 188, 198, 210, 213, 250
Rules 29, 31-2, 68, 84, 188, 199

S

Saving goals 187, 201
Saving products 190, 200, 213
Savings 23-5, 77-9, 128-30, 170-1, 187-93, 198-201, 209-14
best 143, 189, 210
double 213
pre-retirement 171, 191
start 192-3
Savings accounts 25, 90, 101, 104, 115, 194, 200
Savings deposits 203
Savings on Bank Fees 134
Savings products 196, 200-1, 213
Scenario, real life 99, 111, 126, 130, 135
School 38, 51, 85-6, 88, 95, 99, 107
Secondary school 1, 3, 6, 12, 83, 230, 243
Security, money market 203, 249
Seller 230, 232-3, 235, 237, 239-40, 251
Service charges 247, 249
Service fees, monthly 124, 131-5, 137
Services 34-5, 93-6, 101-3, 125, 134-5, 146, 247-8
cashing 94, 101, 126
check-cashing 101, 114, 121, 190
Sign 98, 100, 102, 109, 114, 136, 139
Skills 1-2, 10-11, 14-15, 23, 78-9, 192-3
Small Plaza Bank 99-100, 106
Spending 76-9, 161-2, 165-6, 168-9, 174-5, 187-90, 229-30
daily 166
decreasing 174
Spending plan 78, 162, 165-6, 168, 171, 177, 251
Start saving money 200
Statement 24, 101-2, 123-4, 148-52, 201, 236-7, 250-1
monthly 92, 143, 151-2
Statement balance 150-1
Statement savings 189, 213
States 28-30, 65, 67, 117, 121, 126, 184-5

Stocks 115-16, 200, 202-4, 206-7, 213-14, 246, 248-51
common 246, 251
preferred 251
Stop payment 134-5
Stress 63-8
chronic 64-5, 67
Survey 8, 14, 17, 19, 21-6, 253-4
Systems, financial 36, 81, 84

T

Take-home 164
Tax refunds 189, 193, 211, 214
Taxes 35, 163, 165, 172-3, 183, 201, 230
Teller 92, 113, 122-3, 138-9
bank's 98, 139
Terms 27-8, 85-6, 104, 197-200, 202, 249, 251
Time 22-3, 34-7, 89-94, 144-8, 156-8, 171-2, 190-6
Time deposits 246-8
Title 34, 117, 175, 210, 239
clear 238-9
Tools 119, 123, 151, 154, 161, 175, 177
monthly payment calendar 176-7
Track 101, 103, 136-8, 143, 161-2, 166, 168
Transactions 89-90, 142, 146-8, 150, 152, 154-5, 238-9
corresponding 150-1
debit 102, 124
Truth 68, 86, 117, 209, 211, 215, 238
Type Indicator 54-5
Types 94-6, 114-16, 125-6, 129-32, 204-5, 218, 230-1

U

Unauthorized charges 140, 144-5
Unemployment 26, 31, 59-60, 74, 103, 158
Unemployment benefits 27-8, 31, 104
United Kingdom 7, 11, 13, 15, 17, 22, 24
Unsecured loans 218
Utilities 26, 132, 167, 169-71, 177

V

Value cards 103, 115, 122, 125-7
Variable annuities 204-5
VISA logo 102, 105-6, 127

W

Wealth 20, 68, 73-6
Withdrawals 97-8, 100-2, 140, 142, 152, 246-7, 251
Women 10-11, 13-20, 36, 61, 66, 68, 243
married 17
single 17, 20
young 19
Women Understanding Money 18, 253
Women Understanding Money research campaign 18
Work part-time 99, 184
Workers 11, 29-30
World 46, 49, 53, 55, 68, 70, 81-2
financial 56-7
World Bank 2, 8, 13, 253

Y

Youth 10-11, 13, 181, 243

Z

Zagorsky 73-7

CPSIA information can be obtained at www.ICGtesting.com
Printed in the USA
LVOW10s1318030115

421352LV00001B/9/P

9 780986 347887